GW00502836

Parents and Teachers
2   From Policy to Practice

Parents and Teachers
2   From Policy to Practice

Edited by John Bastiani

NFER-NELSON

Published by The NFER-NELSON Publishing Company Ltd.,
Darville House, 2 Oxford Road East,
Windsor, Berkshire SL4 1DF, England.

First published 1988

© 1988, John Bastiani
© For individual chapters remains with the copyright holders

All rights reserved, including translation. No part of this
publication may be reproduced or transmitted in any form or
by any means, electronic or mechanical, including
photocopying, recording or duplication in any information
storage and retrieval system, without permission in writing
from the publishers.

Photoset by Illustrated Arts Limited, Sutton, Surrey.

Printed in Great Britain by Billing & Sons Ltd, Worcester

ISBN 0 7005 1181 4
Code 8301 02 1

Contents

Acknowledgements   vii

Introduction   ix

Part One   The Formulation of Policy: A Wider View
Aspects of Accountability (from *Accountability and
   *the Middle Years of Schooling: an analysis of policy
   options*)   *Sussex University/East Sussex LEA*   3
Parents and Politics: Choice and Education
   Andy Stillman   15
Parental Partnership in Education – a case for
   Policy (from *Parental Participation in Children's
   Development and Education*)   *Sheila Wolfendale*   35

Part Two   Policy and Practice in Different Settings
Parents and Pre-school (from *Parents and Pre-school*)
   Teresa Smith   49
Family and School – the Relationship Re-assessed (from
   Family and School)   *Daphne Johnson and
   Joyce Ransom*   59
Involving Parents from Minority Groups (from
   Involving Parents in Nursery and Infant Schools)
   Barbara Tizard, Jo Mortimore and Bebb Burchell   72
Partnership Between Home and School (from *Partnership
   with Parents*)   *Peter and Helle Mittler*   84

**Part Three   The Development of Practice
               i) At the LEA Level**
Supporting Work with Parents (from *Raising
   Standards: Parental Involvement Programmes and
   the Language Performance of Children*)   *Paul Widlake
   and Flora Macleod*   104
Clwyd Community Education Pilot Project: Some
   Lessons Learned   *Alwyn Morgan*   113
Improving Home/School Relations in London's Schools
   (from *Improving Secondary Schools (The Hargreaves
   Report)*)   *ILEA*   129

Part Three   The Development of Practice
            ii) At the School Level
Partnership in Education   *Gulzar Kanji*   147
Home/School Liaison: A Community Teacher's First
    Report   *Fiona Roy*   153
Involving Parents and the Wider Community   *John*
    Bird and Bob Croson   160
Teacher Attitudes and the Involvement of Parents
    (from *Partners in School. A Primary School Parent-*
    Teacher Initiative in an Inner City Environment)
    Sheila Bainbridge   171
Staffroom Mythology and Teacher Ignorance –
    concerning parents and family life (from *Your Home-*
    School Links)   *John Bastiani*   177

Part Four   The Evaluation of Home/School Practice
Evaluating an LEA Approach: the Liverpool Parent
    Support Programme   *John Davis*   189
'How Many Parents Did You See Last Night?' A critical
    look at some of the problems of evaluating home/
    school practice   *John Bastiani*   206

Part Five   Training and Teacher Development
The Missing Links Between Home and School: a
    consumer view (from *Summary and Recommendations*)
    National Consumer Council   223
Parenting, School and Mutual Learning (from *The*
    School and the Family in the European Community)
    Michael Marland   232
Training Teachers to Work with Parents   *Janet*
    Atkin and John Bastiani   243
The Future: Proposals for a School and Family
    Concordat (from *The Child Between: a report of*
    school-family relations in the countries of the
    European Community)   *Alistair Macbeth*   254

References   260

Acknowledgements

Acknowledgements are due to the following for permission to publish extracts in this volume.

Basil Blackwell Limited
T. Smith (1980). Extracts from *Parents and Pre-School*, 39–40, 150–155, 163–164, 165–169
B. Tizard, J. Mortimore and B. Burchell (1981). 'Involving Parents from Minority Groups'. In: *Involving Parents in Nursery and Infant Schools*, 221–229, 233–238

Commission of the European Communities
A. Macbeth *et al.* (1984). Extract from, *The Child Between: a report on school-family relations in the countries of the European Community*, 195–199. Commission of the European Communities, Brussels and Luxembourg. (Available through HMSO).
M. Marland (1983). 'Parenting, schooling and mutual learning: a teacher's viewpoint'; contribution to the EEC conference on the School and the Family. Printed for the Commission of the European Communities, Luxembourg.

Coventry Community Education Development Centre
P. Widlake and F. Macleod (1984). 'Supporting Work with Parents'. In: *Raising Standards: Part 1*. The Coventry Community Education Project.

Croom Helm Limited
D. Johnson and J. Ransom (1983). 'Family and School – The Relationship Re-assessed'. In: *Family and School*, 117–128.

Gordon and Breach Science Publishers Inc.
S. Wolfendale (1983). 'Parental Partnership in Education – A Case for Policy'. In: *Parental Participation in Children's Development and Education*, 171–181, 185, 188, 189.

Inner London Education Authority
ILEA (1984–5). Extract from, *Improving London's Secondary Schools* (The Hargreaves Report).

National Consumer Council
The National Consumer Council. Extract from, *The Missing Links Between Home and School*, 75–83.

National Council for Special Education
P. Mittler and H. Mittler (1982). 'Partnership Between Home and School'. In: *Partnership with Parents – Developing Horizons in Special Education Series No. 2*, 24–33.

New Education Press.
Extract from J. Bastiani (1986). 'Your Home/School Links', pp. 23–27.

School Organisation
G. Kanji. 'Partnership in Education'. In: *School Organisation* Volume 4.2.

University of Sussex Continuing Education Area
R. A. Becher, J. Barton, A. Canning, J. Knight and M. R. Eraut (1979). 'Aspects of Accountability'. In: *Accountability in the Middle Years of Schooling: An Analysis of Policy Options*, 96–107.

Introduction

The current scene

For some time now, relationships between parents and their children's schools have been an object of concern for governments, schools and families alike. This book, the second in a series which attempts to bring together the study and the practice of home/ school relations in a more constructive relationship, explores some of the themes relevant to these concerns. For, since the publication of the first collection of accounts less than a year ago, issues concerning the role of parents in their children's schooling have moved even higher up the respective agendas of politicians, professionals and parents, often in strident and contradictory ways.

In the first place, the 'politicization' of education has reached new and unprecedented levels. Politicians continue to see parents as a crucial constituency and have been quick to seize upon educational concerns as a source of electoral support, to use parents as a sounding board for proposals for far-reaching changes in the organization and funding of schools. Not that politicians get it all their own way. Attempts to exploit public concern about educational 'standards', for example, have tended to backfire recently, focusing parental anxiety and attention on standards of provision and levels of resourcing in the education service.

Professionals, for their part, are still shell-shocked from a long and extremely damaging conflict with the government, which has probably caused as much damage to the development of more effective home/school relations as any other single previous event and has certainly changed the way many teachers think and feel about their work, in deep and permanent ways. Paradoxically, the dispute and the continuing discussion about the nature of a teacher's contract and responsibilities, came at a time when there was a steadily spreading willingness to consider the cooperation of the parents of the children they teach, not as an optional extra but as the necessary basis of an essential partnership. It remains to be seen how far such changes will survive shorter term conflicts to re-establish themselves as part of the long-term evolution of the educational service.

Parents, too, have been dragged, often rather reluctantly, into the arena of educational politics. Whilst events of recent years have had widely differing effects upon individual schools and their families, they have shattered the apparent consensus of established parent pressure groups and organizations. Some have been deeply divided and fragmented; in other cases, new groups have formed, with very different goals and styles of operating. What has certainly happened is that many parents, as a result of their recent experience, have been able to see for themselves in a clear and heightened way, both the problematic nature of family/school relations and the intractability of some of its major concerns.

But this is only one part of the overall picture. In spite of such tensions and obstacles, there remain grounds for qualified optimism for those committed to the development of more effective thinking and practice in the field of home/school relations. This can be illustrated by examples drawn from different levels of the service:

(a)   *Government legislation.* Whatever the merits or otherwise, of particular Acts and proposals (for example, those deriving from 'parental choice' or the increased representation of parents on school governing bodies), it is clear that governments now see an important role for legislation in the management of relations between schools and families. In the last few years, no less than four new Acts have provided important new areas of legislation (GB. DES, 1980; 1981; 1986; 1987) each of which has important implications for policy and practice, although these are not usually recognized at the level of resourcing. However, government legislation can now be seen as an instrument in the shaping of home/school policy and practice.

(b)   *LEA initiatives.* In recent years there has been a steady increase in the number and type of LEAs declaring policies and supporting developments in the home/school field. Such initiatives differ enormously in purpose and character, ranging from a whole authority review, the dissemination of good practice, the introduction of home/school liaison schemes as a way of combatting educational disadvantage and the involvement of parents as part of a broader community education strategy. As with central government, a focus upon the formulation of policy reveals an important role, and responsibilities for LEAs (which are outlined and illustrated here).

(c)   *At the institutional level.* Increasingly the improvement of home/school relations is coming to be seen as a task for the education service as a whole. Having said that, it is still the case that much of the interesting pioneering and development work grows out of the work of individual schools, through their growth and development and the productive ways in which they involve their parents.

Relations between families and schools are located in the shadowy areas between contractual obligation, 'custom and practice', voluntary commitment and the development of extended professionalism. In spite of this, or perhaps *because* of it, there is still a great deal of scope and room to manoeuvre, opportunities for 'grass roots' development, for positive thinking and an improving practice, all of which are illustrated in the present collection of accounts.

Theory, research, policy and practice

In the home/school field (as elsewhere in education) it has generally been the case that the study of its key concerns and the development of practice in schools, have remained as separate enterprises, run by different people and located in separate institutions. Indeed the situation could be readily caricatured. Academics write books exploring their largely unsupported pet theories; researchers, whose experience of schools is often very limited, write unreadable reports based upon inpenetrable investigations; policy-makers issue neatly worded declarations of intent from large offices, which are smooth statements of how they would like the world to be, without any idea of how to get there; practitioners, for their part, have improved their work on the hoof and by following intuitions, which then spread contagiously throughout the system.

Whatever the merits of such a parody, it serves as a foil against which recent changes can be seen more clearly. For there has been a considerable reformulation of the relationships between academic study and research and the development of policy and practice. Much of the impetus for this has come from developments in two areas:

(i) the emergence of new forms of research and inquiry and their links with in-service work (INSET) and professional development; and

(ii) the growth in the status and significance attached to 'policy-relatedness'.

Each is briefly illustrated below.

(i)   Action inquiry and professional development
The politicians' drive towards improving the quality of the teaching profession, made possible by the contraction of the education service, has served as a catalyst to a number of changes that are already taking place. For a long time now, teachers have shown an increasing willingness to:

- examine their own work critically, both individually and with colleagues;
- work within agreed policies and planned programmes;
- look for evidence of their effectiveness;
- see the need for engaging in continuing development and change, through the adoption of appropriate strategies and techniques.

As a consequence, considerable emphasis has been given to in-service activity that can be partly located on-site, is school-focused and grows readily out of the basic, everyday work of teachers. More recently, this has been accelerated by the funding arrangements for INSET and teacher release (GRIST – Grant

Related In-Service Training) which has given a considerable boost to action-inquiry approaches, whose overall aim is the development of more effective practice.

Such approaches seem to have much to offer to the thoughtful practitioner in the home/school field. For they provide a framework and a process through which the concerns of hard-pressed teachers and the anxieties and frustrations of parents can be examined in a critical, but constructive way. For action-inquiry is built upon an underlying sympathy for the problems that teachers and parents face in their everyday lives. It requires access to the sharply observed realities of the school gate, the corridor and the classroom, to the voices of parents and the experiences that they express.

Above all, action research and inquiry requires an investigative spirit, a willingness to examine existing policy and practice, and to think it through in ways that suggest and pinpoint areas of growth and further development. Such approaches, which are substantially represented in both the organization and contents of this collection, have a valuable contribution to make to both the study and practice of family and school relations.

(ii) The growth of 'policy-relatedness'

The last decade or so has witnessed, for a wide range of different reasons, increasing demands for institutions and services in the public sector, to convince the rest of the world that they are doing an effective job. More and more, the development of clear policies has come to be seen as the basis for the planning and evaluation of educational activity and a cornerstone in the processes through which the education service gives an account of itself.

An interesting window on these processes has been provided by a series of major accountability studies set-up at the end of the 1970s and located in each of the major phases of schooling (described in more detail elsewhere, Bastiani, 1983). Although established independently, these influential studies, carried out in Cambridge, Oxford and Sussex, showed a common interest in the role and influence of 'policy-relatedness' in the home/school field. This might be defined as follows.

- The clarification of *means*, rather than ends – which were largely regarded as given and non-problematic.
- The formulation of policy and practice congruent with 'official'

definitions of current issues and problems (the funding or sponsoring body, the government or the DES); so many of the rules of the game were established *before* the projects really got down to work (as they often are for teachers planning new developments in schools).

- Incorporating some kind of empirical base. In the home/school field this usually means some 'market research' which seeks the views of 'consumers' (i.e. parents) about a range of salient issues. Here, theory takes a back seat to 'evidence', or gets re-hashed as a kind of practical reasoning.
- Seeing policy as strongly related to action. So 'policy-related' work operates in the context of a need to develop feasible policies that pay due regard to existing practice and incorporate a realistic notion of what changes are possible. Increasingly this takes place in the context of making more effective use of existing, or even declining, resources.
- Policy-relatedness, in addition to informing decision-makers and identifying strategies for action, also tends to be concerned to uncover ideas for practitioners, to identify and promote existing examples of 'good' practice, and to endorse professional development generally.
- Such projects and studies are often located close to the arena of educational politics, in ways that shape their definition, form and style. Whilst acknowledging the possible claims of political expediency, they do have a pragmatic flavour, a combination which might extend their influence upon professionals, who often see them as 'official guidance' in all but name.

'From Policy to Practice': key themes and processes

This book is the second in a series which attempts to bring together a wide range of material, much of it specially written, on the theme of relations between parents and teachers. Its main purpose is to contribute both to the better understanding of complex home/school issues and, as a consequence, to the development of more effective practice. Indeed, the development of thinking and practice are seen as inextricably linked.

In the first volume, 'Perspectives on Home–School Relations', considerable emphasis was given to the problems of studying home/school relations, through the exploration of a number of academic perspectives which are currently thought to be useful and their application to a number of central professional issues and concerns. In these accounts, an attempt was made to provide a broad view of the field, through challenging material which explores its essentially problematic nature and illustrates some of the more salient features of issue, perspective and method. It drew upon distinct modes of inquiry and analysis, whilst giving a special emphasis to those which are based upon the exploration of parental perspectives and experience themselves.

'From Policy to Practice', carries on where the previous volume leaves off. Here, emphasis is given to both the substantive concerns of policy makers and practitioners and, especially, to the processes through which we attempt to translate ideas into effective action.

The process of development and change

'From Policy to Practice' attempts to reflect something of the logic and the dynamic of the complex processes of development and change, as they are frequently conceptualized. Curriculum development, for example (with which there are a number of strong parallels) is often depicted in the simplest form as consisting of three linked stages; there is a world of plans and intentions, processes through which ideas are realized and the consequences or outcomes in the form of the learning that takes place.

In a similar way, this book, in exploring a number of applied issues and problems, incorporates a process which could be characterized as a series of linked stages:

(i) the formulation of ideas, intentions and policies (at different locations in the education system, from the government to individual schools);

(ii) their operationalization and implementation in the form of wide-ranging programmes and practices;

(iii) the evaluation of their effectiveness in relation to declared aims or other criteria.

Whilst open to the charge of over simplification, such a framework does open up the possibility of drawing striking parallels with other areas of planned educational development. It also draws attention to a key problem – that of turning good ideas into effective action – and to the complex interplay of attitudes, structures and resources that characterize home/school relations. It also enables the field to be depicted as one which presents on the one hand the challenges of change and the opportunities that are created, with, on the other hand, an awareness of the obstacles and problems that will almost certainly be encountered.

Home/school relations and the education service

There is also a widespread view that the development of more effective home/school relations is a task that, either formally or by implication, is a task solely for individual schools and families.

The present collection of material, by contrast, is built around the deliberate recognition that such a huge and complex task is the joint responsibility of the education service as a whole, calling for:

- genuine political leadership and professional support, rather than lip-service and empty rhetoric;
- the development of clear policies, accompanied by adequate and appropriate resources of finance, staffing and teacher release etc.;
- the support of the inspectorate and advisory services (at both national and LEA levels) in:
  - monitoring standards and provision (for example, by giving greater emphasis to home, school and community matters in school inspections)
  - in identifying training needs and taking relevant initiatives
  - in setting up, and becoming involved in, the evaluation of important areas of policy-making and practical development in the field.
- the effective use of educational support services in:
  - communicating information about policies, areas of innovation and development

- in providing resources, of different kinds, for projects and development work
- the facilitation and provision of training opportunities and INSET experience.

The relationships between training and development are often picked up in the rhetoric of educational change, although the connections between them usually remain implicit and unexplored. The present collection, however, goes some way to spelling out these links, by suggesting the kind of tasks and activities that are likely to generate the appropriate knowledge, attitudes and skills for the development of thoughtful practice.

So the improvement of home/school relations is portrayed here as a major task, for which responsibility should be actively sought and widely shared. Within such a view, there are important roles right across the education service for the Government and the DES, for local education authorities (LEAs) and their services; there are clear, joint responsibilities for those institutions and agencies that are concerned with teacher training and professional development, in both the initial and post-experience phases; there is a crucial role for individual schools and teachers, on whom much depends for the development of positive attitudes and for the success of new ideas and practices.

Finally, it goes without saying that although the developments that are envisaged might be professionally led, there can be no real change without the genuine involvement of parents and families themselves, for the improvement of home/school relations calls, by definition, for the education service to become more responsive to the needs, wishes and experience of parents and children and for the development of an honest partnership that recognizes important differences as well as shared concerns. This applies equally to the pattern of relations between individual parents and their children's schools and to the range of groups and organizations that represent parental interests in different ways.

Home and school relations: some special features

The previous section highlights some of the parallels that exist between the development of home/school policy and practice, and the general, collective experience of trying to bring about educational reform and change. This applies both to the nature of the experience itself and to ways of handling it. So much of the language and thinking has a familiar ring to it – strategic issues, planning and resource problems, attitudinal obstacles or those that relate to the need for effective implementation and continuing support.

It would, however, be extremely shortsighted if the price that was paid for these links, was an inability to recognize that as a field of study and practice, home/school relations also has its own distinctive features and salient concerns. Whilst these are explored more extensively in the first volume, 'Perspectives on Home–School Relations', both in the Introduction and in individual contributions, perhaps a single example can serve here to illustrate the general point.

Relationships between families and schools, between parents and teachers are, by definition, not contained within professional perspectives and values. Parents are one of a number of 'external audiences', with their own characteristic perspectives and experience. Secondly, and perhaps paradoxically, parents as a constituency are not, in any useful sense, an undifferentiated group with standardized views of the world and shared expectations of it. The truth, which can be empirically supported, is that parents constitute a diverse range of people who have widely differing views, personalities and experience. Any contemporary account of home/school relations needs to pay due regard to this, and the other special features that give it its own characteristic flavour.

This collection of material also acknowledges the important influences upon home/school relations of working in different settings. For example, it is necessary to recognize that the changing nature of children's experience as they grow up has implications for schools and families alike. In a similar way, a dynamic, developmental view of pupils' careers needs to take account of the ideological and institutional differences (many of which have unavoidable consequences) between the different phases and sectors of the education system, from pre-school through to school-leaving, or to the ways in which special needs are currently defined and met.

It is also necessary (particularly in England and Wales where there is *still* a strong degree of decentralization) to acknowledge the importance of social and professional contexts in the working out of home/school relations. For there are inescapable implications to be drawn from the differences between rural, suburban and inner-city schools, between mono and multi-cultural settings and for working in different regions, which need to be taken into consideration in adapting policies and practices to local needs and circumstances.

Different 'versions' of home/school relations

In the field of home/school relations, as elsewhere, there are widely differing, competing traditions of study and practice. These different 'versions' of the field represent the ideas and activities of different ideologies and interest groups, different professional groupings and institutions, different agendas and ways of working. For teachers, like parents, are a very amorphous and mixed bunch!

Whilst there has not been any deliberate attempt to identify or illustrate these in any comprehensive or systematic way, several of the examples that do emerge, can stand as representative of the wider picture. Needless to say, they are examples that are drawn from the present collection.

The selection of accounts for this collection, for instance, embodies a tension between academic and practical perspectives. Such a tension can be detected in particular accounts and in the selection as a whole; it is often creative, attempting to bring the two to bear on each other in a productive way, but occasionally negative and limiting. It can appear in both the content of particular accounts, and as a feature of its form. A characteristic example of this problem might be the tension between presenting an orderly account which is intellectually satisfying and contributes to the growth of understanding and the knowledge and skills needed to identify and implement a programme of effective home/school action.

A similar path could be explored by tracing through the contrasting perspectives of policymakers and practitioners. This can take many forms such as the lack of mutual understanding between 'the office' and the school or, say, between heads and class teachers. The tension here is between different concerns, perceptions and priorities – with the problems of regulations, strategies and resources, on the one hand, and with finding practical ways in which something can be done, on the other. It can also be characterized by a social and professional distance between 'managerial' and 'good practice' approaches, with their different implications for inter-professional relations.

Finally, the different versions of thinking and practice in the field can be illustrated by juxtaposing two contrasting development strategies. In the first, 'better' home/school relations essentially involve parents and teachers (and sometimes pupils). They focus upon the processes of schooling and the role of parents is seen in relation to this. This more limited and sharply focused version is essentially concerned with the inter-relationships between family and school, particularly as they concern the outcomes of the latter.

Such a tradition can usefully be contrasted with a wider, looser view of home/school relations, which sees parents as inextricably linked to their wider community. It focuses upon the productive links between schools, families and neighbourhoods and concerns itself with the widest possible range of learners and educational needs. As such, the development of more effective home/school links takes place as a key strategy in a broader policy for the development of community education.

'From Policy to Practice': form, content and organization

'Perspectives on Home-School Relations' consists of a series of extended, self-contained accounts, illustrating a number of key issues and perspectives. It is essentially concerned with the study of home/school matters, with different ways of conceptualizing its central problems and with the interpretation of evidence. Although it is sympathetic to the development of more effective practice, this is not its overriding concern.

'From Policy to Practice' shifts the focus to the formulation of policy and its implementation and to the development and evalua- tion of practice. This is reflected in the nature and range of material from which the collection is drawn, which itself illustrates the processes of development. In doing this it draws, in more or less equal proportions, from previously published material, from different kinds of reports that have either had limited circulation or which deserve a wider audience and from specially written material based on current developments.

In this way, the material illustrates:

- the implications of research findings;
- the recommendations of working parties and study groups;

- conference papers and reports;
- documents which outline proposals for discussion and decision-making;
- the critical evaluation of existing experience.

Such accounts also embody a range of styles and forms from the numbered paragraphs of committee-speak, through the flair of educational journalism to the concreteness of first-hand experience and autobiographical recollection.

The material has been organized around key themes and processes (as illustrated earlier in the Introduction) which form the basis of its structure and organization. In order to maximize the benefit from this arrangement each section is introduced by a short preview which raises a number of general editorial issues, as well as illustrating the range and flavour of its contents.

Finally, there are profound changes taking place in the educational system, which focus upon the very heart of its institutions and processes! These involve the nature of curriculum experience, the organization and management of schools, the nature of teachers' contracts and the relationships between providers and consumers. Whilst it is not clear yet what the consequences will be, it is certainly the case that any collection of material which aims to capture the flavour of contemporary events and developments must be both tentative and provisional. This is particularly true of home/school relations which currently occupies a pivotal position in the minds of politicians, professionals and parents, albeit in very different ways.

Part One

The Formulation of Policy: A Wider View

Editorial Preview

The opening section in this collection brings together several accounts that, in different ways, take a very broad view of family/school relationships. Each provides a 'macro' view of its issues, seeing them against a general background of social processes and institutions, against the shaping influences of educational policies or in relation to the processes of socialization in a post-industrial world.

The first contribution is taken from an important accountability study, which examines the workings of the education service provided by LEAs. Through a focus upon 'policy-relatedness' (illustrated in the Introduction), it examines a range of issues and concerns, at both LEA and school levels, such as:

- the nature of professional authority and responsibility;
- relationships at local authority level, between different parts of the education service;
- relationships between 'providers' and 'consumers';
- the needs of 'external audiences' in general and parents in particular.

The Sussex study provides a useful launch for the collection, both for its contribution to the exploration of key concepts and for providing a framework for looking at the field as a whole. It then uses this framework to carry out an applied analysis of current attitudes and practices, before making suggestions for improvement and reform. The study takes as its point of reference, not so much legal requirements and obligations, nor 'custom and practice', but the more constructive purpose of contributing to the continuing development of a more responsive and effective education service.

Andy Stillman's contribution draws upon the interplay between parents, politics and the education service, from his involvement with a national project set up to explore the implementation of the 1980 Education Act. He writes against a political and administrative background, describing different attempts to regulate and manage 'parental choice' within an increasingly dominant market ideology. The account uncovers a wide range of responses from LEAs that shape and influence the nature and extent of choice and the possibility of successful appeals being made by parents.

The account explores some of the tensions between the rhetoric of politicians, the expedience of LEAs and the needs and wishes of parents. Above all, it shows the need (increasingly under threat from government intervention) to balance the needs of the nation as a whole, in providing education for all as a public service, with the wishes of parents in respect of the individual child.

The extract from Sheila Wolfendale's book illustrates two general themes which recur throughout the present collection. Firstly, it illustrates the role of policy in the development of more effective educational and welfare systems. In particular, it outlines an approach in which the formulation of policy is responsive to identified needs. This, in turn, enables the 'caring professions' to provide the more sharply focused delivery of appropriate services.

Secondly, and in sharp contrast to the perspectives of educational politics, the formulation of policy is built around the primacy of the child and focuses upon his or her changing needs, in a range of settings. Her broad, integrated view is a salutary reminder that compulsory schooling is only one, in some ways rather limited, form of educational and developmental experience.

Aspects of Accountability

Sussex University/East Sussex LEA

In the original project report, we were concerned with reviewing the armoury of techniques and procedures which schools and LEAs respectively can deploy in the context of accountability. We now turn, in the concluding stages of our analysis, to a consideration of the different purposes which these techniques and procedures may be called upon to serve.

Three points deserve to be borne in mind by the reader in working through the arguments we shall now rehearse. The first is that accountability can have a positive as well as a negative aspect. It need not be seen simply as a burdensome necessity in meeting external obligations. If properly designed and implemented, an accountability policy can also provide a defence against outside attempts to limit autonomy and the enjoyment of legitimate rights and powers. Such attempts might take the form of political encroachments on freedom, or the unjustified erosion of financial entitlements, as well as campaigns to undermine reputation through the media or to destroy it through libellous gossip.

Second, accountability – as we have come clearly to recognize in the course of our study – is a two-way process. Any LEA, in satisfying its external obligations to maintain proper educational standards, must also see itself as answerable to its teachers and its schools, and must strive actively to sustain its supportive relationships with them.

The third point leads on from these. It is possible to approach accountability as a process of mutual negotiation, in which something is conceded – say, some professional prerogative which contemporary values call into question – and something gained – perhaps a firm declaration of public trust, a renewed guarantee of essential autonomies, or an insurance against future encroachment. Such an approach must call for a gradualist and long-term strategy, based on careful consultation between the Authority and its schools.

It could be expensive in time and effort, and could risk exasperating public patience. But the alternative, of imposing an apparently cheap, quick and easy solution, against the wishes of the schools, might in the end prove a hollow victory. It would at best achieve conformity without conviction; at worst it could lead to the general debilitation which now characterizes many school systems in North America.

Six modes of accountability

In the attempt we now make to knit together the diverse strands of our analysis and to give them a coherent shape, we have inevitably had to oversimplify or sharpen a number of familiar distinctions as well as to introduce some new ones of our own. We wish to acknowledge the crudity and occasional artificiality of the barriers which we have found it necessary to erect in marking out the terrain for further exploration. We recognize and welcome the fact that they will be transcended by the subtleties of future political debate.

It is possible to distinguish three facts within the broad meaning of the term accountability: (1) *answerability* to one's clients ('moral accountability'); (2) *responsibility* to oneself and one's colleagues ('professional accountability'); (3) and *accountability* in the strict sense to one's employers or political masters ('contractual accountability').

These distinctions are exemplified in different ways by schools on the one hand and Education Committees on the other. Schools are primarily answerable to parents, but legally accountable to the LEA (in some circumstances directly, in others via their managers). Education Committees are answerable to their schools, but constitutionally accountable to the electorate (either directly, or via their governing Council). Both have also to acknowledge certain responsibilities to their own professional consciences and to their peers.

We have earlier remarked that accountability must meet two basic, interconnected demands: (1) the preservation and, where possible, enhancement of overall levels of performance through *maintenance* procedures; (2) the detection and amelioration of individual points of weakness through appropriate *problem-solving* mechanisms.

Taking these two sets of considerations together, we can distinguish six different modes of accounting, as follows:

1. Answerability for maintenance
2. Answerability for problem-solving
3. Responsibility for maintenance
4. Responsibility for problem-solving
5. Strict accountability for maintenance
6. Strict accountability for problem-solving

Between them, these six modes serve to draw attention to the demands which might – in principle if not always in practice – be made on schools and LEAs. We shall accordingly use them as the basis for our subsequent discussion. First, we shall look at the pattern of possible expectation as it relates to schools, taking this to be a matter of legitimate interest also to the Education Committee and its officers. After that, we shall sketch out the set of requirements for accountability which might be levied on the Authority itself.

The elements of school-based accounting

There is a variety of possible ways in which the schools might elect to meet their answerability to parents for the maintenance of standards – the first mode in our list. The parents' awareness of what their children's schools are doing may be promoted through regular communication on individual pupils' progress, or by allowing ready parental access to classrooms and teachers, or by encouraging a general atmosphere of open inquiry. Other forms of provision would include explanations of curricular aims and teaching methods, accounts of overall policy, and reports on general standards of performance.

The second mode concerns the school's potential problem-solving strategies, and especially its means of responding to matters of parental concern. These may include early disclosure of problems – whether affecting individual children or relating to wider issues – where this seems appropriate in averting later crisis; and the prompt acknowledgement and investigation of – and subsequent response to – expressions of parental grievance. All parents have a right to know what the appropriate procedures are within the school if they wish to raise a complaint.

The professional responsibilities which might be exercised by schools in the course of their own internal maintenance – the third mode in our list – could be expected to include the development of good relationships with parents on the one hand and the Authority on the other, alongside various forms of domestic monitoring of standards and the regular review of staffing, curricula and teaching arrangements. Schools may also – in so far as their reputations are interdependent – be called upon to exercise professional responsibility towards one another. Junior and Middle schools must, moreover, share responsibility with the Infant and Secondary schools to which they are linked, for the long-term interests of their pupils.

The fourth mode, relating to internal problem-solving, would include – on the institutional front – being aware of and taking steps to rectify incipient points of weakness, and the vigilant anticipation of potential crisis; and – in relation to individual children – the sensible use of screening procedures (such as pupil records and diagnostic tests) to identify and give remedial help to those at risk.

The fifth mode – strict accountability for maintenance – is concerned with the accountability of each school to its LEA for overall quality of provision. Here, one might note its explicit obligation to observe mandatory and constitutional accounting procedures and to meet centrally-agreed specifications. Implicit expectations would include the school's openness to informal visitation by authorized representatives of the Authority, its readiness to justify (if reasonably called upon to do so) its curricular goals and methods and its overall policies, and its similar readiness to account for below-average levels of pupil performance.

The sixth and last mode focuses on the ways in which the schools do or should account to the LEA with respect to problem-solving. In this context, they have a clear duty to report on all such grievances or complaints deriving from external sources, and all such internal difficulties, as they are not themselves able to resolve satisfactorily within a reasonable period of time. They would also properly be expected to develop, on their own initiative, appropriate means of anticipating and dealing with such problems as may in fact arise.

These various elements of school-based accounting are summarized in Table 1. We have not attempted to mark out the distinctions between those items which are universally applicable, those which are common practice, and those at present observed by few schools or none. We have not made any of the subsidiary differentiations between informal and formal, mandatory and constitutional procedures. Nor have we attempted to single out those particular policy options which remain presently available to schools. All such categories are dependent on context: the demarcation lines between them will vary from one time and one place to another. Any reader who wishes to define them for his own purposes will, we hope, have no difficulty in doing so.

The elements of authority-based accounting

It is possible to categorize the different components – both actual and potential – of an Authority's programme of accountability in much the same way as we have just done in relation to a school's. The same list of six modes will serve for this, and we shall examine them in the same order as before.

The first mode, in this setting, concerns an Authority's answerability to its schools for the quality of its maintenance activities. Among the possible items under this head, we may note the obligation of an Authority to provide each school with the resources appropriate to carry out its essential tasks and to meet the reasonable expectations made of it. The LEA will also have a general responsibility for the quality, morale and well-being of its professional teaching staff (one particular expression of this, noted earlier, might be the institution of systematic forms of personnel development). Authorities may also be expected to support their schools as institutions, both by accrediting (and, where appropriate, publicizing) good practice, and by coming actively to their defence – in general or in particular – when their overall standards are subjected to demonstrably unjust or unreasonable criticism. Schools, it may be argued, have a natural right to seek an explanation of their Authority's policies on accountability.

LEAs are, as our second mode suggests, also answerable to schools in regard to problem-solving. That is to say, they have a

Table 1: Elements of school's accountability

	Answerability *(to parents)*	Responsibility *(to self and peers)*	Strict Accountability *(to LEA direct or via managers)*
Maintenance	**1** – Regular communication on individual children's progress (via written reports etc.) – Accounts of overall policy (via prospectus etc.) – Explanation of curricular aims and methods – Reports on general standards of performance, academic and other (via open days, speech days etc.) – Encouragement of better parental awareness of school's activities and endeavours (via ready access to classrooms and staff, atmosphere of open enquiries and discussion)	**3** – Domestic monitoring of standards – Regular review of staffing, curricula and teaching arrangements – Promotion of good relationships with parents (via school social occasions etc.) – Promotion of good relationships with feeder and receiving (secondary) schools – Promotion of good relationships with managers, Advisers, and LEA as a whole	**5** – Observation of mandatory and constitutional procedures – Meeting of centrally agreed specifications – Openness to authorized visitation – Readiness to justify curricular goals and methods and overall policies – Readiness to account for pupil performance standards
Problem-solving	**2** – Notification to all parents of complaints procedures – Prompt acknowledgement and investigation of parental complaints, confirmation of action taken – Early disclosure to parents, where appropriate, of problems (i) relating to individual children (ii) involving wider issues	**4** – Screening of individual children at risk (via internal reporting, pupil records, tests, etc.) – Provision of remedial help to children in need – Awareness of incipient points of weakness – Anticipation of potential crises	**6** – Reporting of unresolved external complaints and grievances – Reporting of unresolved internal difficulties – Development of effective means to deal with problems arising

NB The entries above are not intended to be comprehensive. They are meant only to indicate possible expectations or demands in each category. They should *not* be taken as indicating policies which are necessarily feasible, desirable or deserving of priority at the school level.

moral duty to help schools both to identify potential difficulties and to tackle practical issues for which external support is likely to be necessary or desirable. The former obligation is commonly met through testing programmes designed to pick out areas of weakness – or through the types of diagnostic visitation procedure discussed. Issues serious enough to call for outside help may involve individual children, particular teachers, or the institution as a whole. The forms of response will vary accordingly: they may include intervention by the Area Office, the temporary presence in the school of Advisers, the decision to make extra resources available, or – in the last resort – the transfer or dismissal of staff or even the closure of the school. Furthermore, when a particular complaint registered by a parent or other outside agent (including the press) can be shown to be without basis, the school or teacher concerned may have a right to expect the Authority's full backing in contesting it.

An Authority's professional responsibility to keep its affairs in good order constitutes the third mode in our list. It is discharged in part by fostering good relationships with its schools and teachers (not to mention its own Advisory and administrative staff), and in part by cultivating and enhancing its relationships with the public. Good housekeeping will imply an effective set of procedures for evaluating and reviewing current policy: it can also crucially depend on the ability of officers and members to work together, and the forcefulness of the arguments they are able to muster in their annual bids to Council for resources. The demands of mutual responsibility between different Authorities, and between local and national administration, could also be included in this general category.

Turning next to internal problem-solving by the LEA – the fourth mode – we reiterate a point made by one of the officers we interviewed during the course of our study. Committee members and their staff, besides responding to problems which have already arisen, or acting on issues which they can identify as likely to arise, are called upon to accommodate rapidly to unforeseen political pressures from outside the educational arena and to devise swift and effective ways of meeting them.

Our fifth mode concerns the accountability of elected members to their constituents for the maintenance of overall standards within the education service. This is familiar territory, invoking many of the considerations already explored. Particular forms of certification include Authority-wide testing designed for general monitoring purposes, routine visitation programmes with the same ends in view and the specification of general aims and curricular policies. An important, but generally neglected aspect of this form of accountability is the public disclosure of the nature and extent of the maintenance procedures adopted by the Authority in respect of its schools.

The final mode – the sixth in our list – draws attention to the Authority's obligations to account to the public for the effectiveness of its problem-solving. In this context, its general abilities to predict, handle and rectify problems come under critical scrutiny. Such problems (whether relating to children, teachers or schools) fall into two groups: those which arise externally, in relation to a particular grievance, or to some unforeseeable quirk of circumstance; and those which are generated internally, as a result of malfunctioning or maladministration within the system. If either type of issue is inadequately handled, the LEA must ultimately take the blame. Hence the potential importance of making widely known what measures are in fact available to deal with both eventualities. A closely related obligation is to notify the public of the most appropriate forms in which to register possible complaints. Over and above this, the Authority will be expected to ensure that any actual complaints are properly acknowledged; that they are carefully investigated, and (where necessary) dealt with; and that the fact that this has been done is duly notified to the original complainant.

In concluding this summary review of the elements of Authority-based accountability, we must rehearse the caveats expressed on accountability at the level of the individual school. The considerations set out in Table 1 take no account of time and place, the state of existing practice, or the key policy areas awaiting further consideration. Our concern has been with identifying possible forms of demand for accountability – which we take to be a proper function of policy analysis – rather than with evaluating the significance of those demands in practice – which constitutes a first stage in the formulation of policy proposals as such.

Accountability in the wider policy context

We shall conclude our Report with a brief consideration of the place of accountability in the overall scheme of things – in the whole policy

	Answerability (to schools)	Responsibility (to self and peers)	Strict Accountability (to electorate, direct or via Council)
Maintenance	1 – Provision of adequate resources to enable schools to meet LEA's expectations – Promotion of quality and morale of teaching staff (e.g. via personnel development schemes) – Support of schools (in general or particular) by (i) accreditation and dissemination of good practice; (ii) defence against unfounded general criticisms by members of public or press – Justification of Authority's own policies on accountability	3 – Development of effective member/officer teamwork – Preparation of convincing proposals for resources – Systematic evaluation and review of current policies – Promotion of good relationships with schools – Promotion of good relationships with public (via encouragement of better general awareness of schools' activities and endeavours)	5 – Certification of overall standards (via monitoring tests and visitations) – Specifications of agreed general goals and specific curricular policies (via manifestos, guidelines etc.) – Disclosure of nature and extent of LEAs maintenance procedures
Problem-solving	2 – Assistance in identifying potential difficulties (via screening tests, diagnostic visits etc.) – Assistance, when appropriate, in tackling problems relating to (i) individual children; (ii) particular teachers; (iii) school as a whole – Defence against unfounded specific complaints by parents, public or press	4 – Continuing improvement of strategies for identifying and responding to problems – Awareness of incipient points of weakness in system – Enhancement of abilities to accommodate and respond to unforeseen political pressures	6 – Effective handling of externally-generated problems (serious/unresolved complaints, unforeseeable crises) – Effective handling and rectification of problems generated within system – Disclosure of LEAs available measures for problem-solving – Wide notification of grievance procedures – Prompt acknowledgement and investigation of public complaints; confirmation of action taken

NB The entries above are not intended to be comprehensive. They are meant only to indicate possible expectations or demands in each category. They should *not* be taken as indicating policies which are necessarily feasible, desirable or deserving of priority at the LEA level.

framework of a school and an Authority. One way to approach the question is to reflect on what we, as members of the research team, have learned in the course of our two years' work on the Project.

Although we tried not to let our preconceptions influence the course of our inquiries, we certainly had some sketchy notions at the outset of where the investigation might lead us. One of these was that the schools probably held the key to some of the more crucial policy choices, and that school-based accountability procedures were likely to be the focal point of our attention. Another was that accountability would transpire to be closely concerned with the development of good public relations, and that we might need to give particular attention to this aspect. A third was that accountability might begin to emerge as a new heading in the LEAs budget, and that any policy proposals would have to justify their costs alongside competing claims on resources. As our work developed, we found ourselves forced to recognize that we had got each picture out of focus. It was not that we were plainly mistaken in our vision, but rather that we had caught a blurred and slightly distorted image of what was there to be seen. In each case, the reasons – when we hit on them – were instructive.

Schools are undeniably important components in educational accountability, but our hope of building up a policy framework on the Every School for Itself principle was foredoomed. What we at first failed to realize was that, in terms of accountability, the ruling principle must be that No School is an Island. Public reputation presupposes interdependence, not independence – the one school with a bad name contaminates the ninety-nine with a good. So while each must do the best it can in its own cause, the collective interest must in the end be protected by the Authority (which is there to guard it) rather than by the schools (who are there to serve it). That is why our Report has turned out to be as much about the Authority's options as it is about the schools – though we did not start out with that expectation.

As our many interviews and discussions over the past two years have shown, it is also clearly the case that the successful discharge of accountability must involve the education service in more open dialogue, more vigorous publicity, a more conscious promotion of public relations, than has been its practice in the past. But to equate accountability with communication skills – as we were at first inclined to do – would be to overlook a host of other activities which we now recognize as relevant to our theme. They are those which concern the internal well-being of the system: the identification and amelioration of problems, the proper exercise of professional responsibilities, the efforts at self-appraisal, the enhancement of existing skills, and many others we have touched on in the course of our Report. In the long term, these may turn out to be more important than mere improvements in the techniques of presentation, persuasion and pacification, for they can have a catalytic effect in the regeneration of morale and self-respect, and hence in winning the respect of others. The best way of all of earning public confidence is the most direct: namely to be clearly seen as doing a good job. Again, therefore, while we have no wish to repudiate our initial concern with improved communications with parents and others, our explorations have taken us a long way beyond that point.

At one stage in our thinking, we toyed with the idea of presenting some kind of cost-benefit exercise which could match accountability against other areas of policy. We felt that our analysis would be incomplete if we were not able to present some rationale, however sketchy, to enable the Authority to decide whether it wished to commit new resources in this area, and if so what scale of commitment it might sensibly make. We soon came to realize that the task was self-defeating. The elements of accountability are so diverse, multifarious and pervasive that there is simply no way of separating them out and displaying them as a separate entry in an inventory of tasks or commitments, whether at the level of the Authority or at that of the school. Accountability, far from being – as our initial preconception had it – an element among others in the system, is an important aspect of the way the system itself works.

Very few of the activities with which this Report has been concerned – take school prospectuses, pupil records, County-wide testing schemes, or formal inspection – were the product of William Tyndale or Mr Callaghan's Ruskin speech. They were there – albeit undisclosed, unnoticed and unnamed – long before accountability became the political fashion; and they will doubtless long survive it. What that fashion has done is to call for a more explicit framework of expectations – summarized in Tables 1 and 2 – a framework which may clarify priorities and show the interconnections between activities hitherto separately conceived.

The time may come when accountability becomes a major influence on policy decisions. If so, it may perhaps serve not only to encourage the critical review of existing policies but also to identify the new initiatives which may be needed in response to changes in external circumstance. Such speculation, however, lies at the margins of our present understanding. All we can now say with confidence is that our initial presupposition was mistaken. Accountability – to revive a once much-quoted catchphrase – is not so much a programme, more a way of life.

Parents and Politics: Choice and Education

Andy Stillman

Introduction

The term 'parental choice' means different things to different people. For some it represents the improvement of educational standards through the operation of 'market forces' in a school economy, that is, where children represent 'currency', and 'wealth' is determined by the numbers of pupils on roll. In this context the terms 'good school' and 'popular school' tend to be synonymous. For others, however, parental choice conjures up images of schools seeking popularity rather than educational ideals, the return to selection and, through an unequal access to mobility, a form of middle-class elitism which inevitably develops hand in hand with a growing deprivation in the schools the mobile parents leave behind.

Of course, at the individual family level, increases in parental choice might represent the only way of getting your child into the school you really want, but for every child that secures a place in an overcrowded school, one or more others are denied access if extra resources are not then made available. Parental choice legislation is basically concerned with opening up the discussion about who gets access to which places: it is not directly concerned with increasing the number or quality of the school places. Perhaps not surprisingly there seems little evidence that either the main parent organizations or the major lobbying groups are particularly keen to argue its case.

In 1983 the National Foundation for Educational Research (NFER) sponsored a two-year research project to investigate what was then the most current piece of legislation bearing on parental choice, the 1980 Education Act. The research was designed to look at what LEAs and schools did and why they did it, as well as discovering the parents' responses and reactions to the legislation as they saw it. As such, the researchers explored the issues with education officers, headteachers and parents, as well as delving into the parliamentary history of parental choice and talking with some of the politicians and administrators concerned with the legislation. The 'Information for Parental Choice' project carried out its research from 1983 to 1985 and produced two main reports, *Choosing Schools: Parents, LEAs and the 1980 Education Act* (Stillman and Maychell, 1986) and *The Balancing Act of 1980: Parents Politics and Education* (Stillman, 1986).

This chapter commences with a brief look at the historical and political background as we found it and then ties it in with some of the underlying philosophical considerations. This paves the way for a summary of the rest of the research evidence to be presented in context. In progressing through the chapter, and in considering the implications of parental choice, there are three clear questions which seem relevant throughout and which should help towards reaching an understanding of the processes at play.

(1)   How effective is the 'parental choice' legislation in bringing about the educational improvements that its proponents claim for it?

(2)   Have the politicians and media decided whether the term 'parental choice' refers to the global sum of parental choice, that is, the sum of all the parents' choices, or is it considered to be the amount of 'choice' individuals are entitled to if they are prepared to use it?

(3)   What is the relationship between parental choice and what parents actually want?

Historical and political perspectives 1944–87

The early beginnings

As we conducted the research, many education officers and headteachers told us that the origins of parental choice lay firmly within the 1944 Education Act. A good number added that in many respects the rights of parental choice already existed prior to the implementation of the 1980 Act (GB. DES, 1980), and for some, the implementation had actually reduced the amount of choice available to parents.

Section 76 of the 1944 Act (GB. Ministry of Education, 1944) required the Minister of Education and LEAs to have regard to the general principle that so far as was compatible with the provision of efficient instruction and training, and the avoidance of unreasonable public expenditure, pupils were to be educated in accordance with the wishes of their parents. Over the years and in one way or another this section has been used by many parents seeking to get their children into their preferred school. However, although in legislative terms it had been taken on its face value, there was never any intention for it to offer choice between *like* schools, i.e. between two or more schools which, in major respects, might be similar. According to Lord Butler, who effectively steered the original Act through Parliament: 'The objective of that settlement and of section 76 was to give Roman Catholic and Anglican parents a choice of school' (House of Lords Debate, Volume 353: Column 590, 10th July, 1974). That is, as the 1944 Education Act brought Anglican and Catholic Schools into the state system, this was the section that attempted to guarantee Anglican and Catholic parents the right to send their children to the appropriate religious school if they wished. In the context of its parliamentary debate there was no need for the religious element of Section 76 to be other than implicit when it referred to the choice between schools: away from that context it has been given a far broader interpretation.

Within only two years of the Act being passed the Ministry of Education under a Labour Government became sufficiently concerned about the nature of parents' appeals to the Minister under sections 37 and 68 of the 1944 Act that it published Circular 83, 'Choice of Schools' (Ministry of Education, 1946). This was done to offer clarification to the LEAs about how the Minister would consider the arguments in such appeals – the intention being that LEAs might like to adopt these guidelines themselves. In 1950 the Ministry slightly amended the grounds and republished them in its 'Manual of Guidance: Schools No.1' (Ministry of Education, 1950) again entitled 'Choice of School', which was not finally withdrawn until 1980. This manual would seem to be the first time that a government had opened up the range of what may be chosen, and whilst it commenced with the qualification: 'At the onset it should be noted that section 76 does not confer on the parent complete freedom of choice', on the very next page it offered: 'Section 76 is not limited to choices made on denominational grounds. Nor does it apply merely to the initial choice of school.' The leaflet went on to list what it described as three 'strong' reasons for accepting parents' wishes when choosing a school (denominational, the provision of specific types of work and the linguistic medium used, i.e. Welsh or English) as well as a further five which LEAs might properly take into account.

Whilst increasing the number of acceptable reasons for choosing a school, or at least, whilst publishing the reasons the Minister would be likely to accede to in the case of an appeal (and thus very much offering suggestions to LEAs as to what they too might like to take into account), the Minister also saw fit to strengthen the LEAs' administrative arguments against accepting choice. Here in effect we encounter the first references to the idea of parental choice and the LEA's management of education needing to be treated like a balance with the arguments for each side being 'weighed' against each other. But the idea of there being a 'balance' between the needs of the LEA in providing education for all and the wishes of the parent in respect of the individual child needs exploring. Obviously there is the clear idea that one can evaluate or weigh up the relative strengths of the two sides' arguments in order to decide who should 'win'. But patently this cannot be easy, and when we consider the 'approved' arguments we can see many difficulties; for example, one reason for rejecting a parent's choice is 'the avoidance of unreasonable public expenditure'. But just what is 'unreasonable'? How is an LEA to know what the Minister might regard as 'unreasonable', and how does the Minister assess feelings in different parts of the country? The factors which the ministerial guidelines and the later 1980 Act suggest should be considered when reaching a balance between the parents and the LEA lend themselves to variable interpretations and outcomes. What is more, the strengths of the two sides' arguments are also dependent upon the political and social climates of the time. In considering the goals of the legislation it would seem that central government is trying to legislate in conditions where the arguments' relative strengths will vary not only from time to time, but also from one local authority to the next, from one division to the next within an LEA and even, according to our research evidence, from one appeal committee sitting to the next!

For all the difficulties of assessing the overall balance it would seem that it now favours parents probably more than it did in the 1950s, although this is not necessarily universal across all LEAs.

Perhaps surprisingly, however, over the years there have been few changes in the 'approved' arguments which LEAs and parents use, with most for both sides being traceable back to the 1944 Act and the 1950 Guidelines. Thus, if the amount of choice has really changed, this cannot readily be attributed to changes in the legislation so much as to changes in attitude which have influenced the weightings locally afforded to the various arguments in the balancing process. Of course, one can relate changes in attitude and social climate to political and legislative initiatives, but which is a result of the other? Has the change in attitude come about as a result of the legislation or has the legislation followed it? Furthermore, if the legislation is claimed to result from a change in public attitudes, have the politicians developed the most appropriate legislation and have they been right in their reading of what the public want?

Political solutions in the 1970s

Activity with central appeals remained low until sometime in the early- to mid-1970s when numbers and publicity began to increase. The Department of Education and Science (DES) and LEAs were sufficiently embarrassed with these increasing numbers for them to feel that some form of action was necessary: a mechanism was needed for central appeals to be either stopped at source, or at least diverted back to the authorities from whence they came. One result of the increase in appeals and the sensitivity to them is that it can be argued that had the 1944 Act not allowed parents this right of appeal to the Minister, then it is conceivable that the 1980 Act would never have come about, since the evidence suggests that much of the concept of there being a demand for parental choice only came into existence as a result of these central appeals (Fowler, 1986). We should note, however, that for all political significance ascribed to these central appeals, from the parents' point of view they were rarely effective and the number of successful appeals was consistently very low. In 1977, for instance, only two of 1,124 Section 68 complaints and 24 of 40 Section 37 complaints were upheld!

Other changes were also taking place and by 1976–7 there were three recognizable pressures bearing upon the Labour Government: (1) there was the *perceived* growing demand for parental choice, which stemmed from, (2) the embarrassing problem of the large number of central appeals; and, (3) there were imminent falling rolls. It should also be recalled that these three pressures all arose at a time of serious and increasing economic problems.

The Secretary of State for Education and Science, who, at that time was Shirley Williams, offered potential solutions to all these points in the 1977 Consultation Paper, 'Admission of Children to Schools of Their Parents' Choice' (DES, 1977). Amongst other things the Paper suggested that parental preference should be regarded as having a degree of intrinsic validity which should be given a channel of expression to allow it consideration in the alloca- tion procedure, that LEAs should be able to plan the operating capacity of their schools and be able to refuse a child a place at a particular school if the school was 'full', and finally that each authority's arrangements should also include a procedure for local appeals and that in future, questions of admissions to schools would be specifically excluded from ministerial consideration under Section 68. Overall, although it has been suggested that these proposals would have strengthened the parents' case (Williams, 1985), in reality they appear much more likely to have offered a method to legitimately emphasize and strengthen the LEAs management role.

For the most part, the 1977 recommendations appeared in similar form a year later as the 1978 Education Bill, but, with the election in 1979 and the Tories being returned to power, this Bill never reached the statute books. Not surprisingly, the incoming Conser- vative Secretary of State for Education was still faced with the same three problems, but within the Conservative party there were other pressures for parental choice and these, combined with the fact that the Conservatives had been in opposition when the 1978 Bill had been going through the committee stages, forced the new govern- ment to look for alternative solutions.

In the wake of their electoral defeat in February 1974 the Conser- vatives revised their education policy by toning down their attack on comprehensive reorganization and by introducing the 'Charter of Parents' Rights' which was later put forward as a parliamentary Bill in 1975. The ensuing debates gave an airing to a number of Conservative arguments in this area beyond that of believing that choice was a good thing in its own right. For instance, from the right of the party came arguments suggesting that through the process of parents being allowed to make choices, popular schools would grow and prosper while unpopular schools would either have to recognize what was good and mend their ways or eventually close due to lack of custom.

The issue of diversity of provision was also raised since there are many who would argue that choice between good and bad is no choice at all and that if 'real' choice is to exist then it must be between different styles and characteristics. In line with this came discussion on the provision of the information parents would need to make these choices. How, after all, could parents make informed choices if they knew little of the schools concerned? Less attention seems to have been given to the issues of transport, the minimum number of schools required to constitute a choice, the reduction in choice if some parents wanted schools that were forced to close because of the action of others, the processes by which schools were supposed to learn of the parents' wishes, and the issues of how parents might influence a school once their child was in attendance, although in some ways this was later rectified by parallel moves to increase parent representation on governing bodies.

The 1980 Education Act

In putting forward the 1979 Bill, which later became the 1980 Education Act, we can see that the Secretary of State was responding to the same three pressures that faced his predecessors as well as adding elements of Conservative ideology. For all this, when the Act came into force it would seem that, initially at least, there was little practical increase in choice and possibly even some decrease since LEAs were still able to argue at (the local) appeal that an extra admission would break their planned admission limit for that school. There were, however, some clear changes from Labour's 1978 Bill. The two most important were: the new and compromise solution to the central appeals problem (which was to set up 'independent' committees which would hear and settle parental appeals at LEA level); and the rejection of the idea of allowing the LEA to determine a fixed and binding operating size for schools.

The Act also differed from the 1978 Bill in that it contained no reference to overriding the parents' wishes if there was any conflict with comprehensive principles, although unlike Labour's proposals, the Act did set out to protect the principles of grammar and voluntary aided schools. The Act also made no reference or distinction between the efficient provision of education *in the area* and that *in the school* although this is a distinction many LEAs have subsequently made to protect individual schools within clusters. Under the 1980 Act LEAs were allowed to reduce the 1979 size of schools by up to 20 per cent without permission from the Secretary of State, that is, they were able to announce reduced intended intake figures and to argue at appeal that to allow one school in a group to take in more children would produce deleterious results either financially or educationally in one or more neighbouring schools. As soon as the intended intake figures were given less importance in appeals (see below) the LEAs' arguments were forced to rely upon the efficient and effective provision arrangement.

Since the 1980 Act came into force we can plot four significant developments. The first of these was a judicial review of a statutory appeal in May 1984 (Regina v South Glamorgan Appeals Committee). This review suggested the need for major changes in the way educational appeal committees interpreted cases and in the way evidence was presented. Although the effects of this judgement took a while to be incorporated into practice across the country, as evidenced by the many Ombudsman reports which have mentioned this since that date, it was an event which, perhaps even more than the introduction of the 1980 Act on its own, moved the balance towards the parents.

The second occurred in the 1986 Education Act (GB. DES, 1986) which for the first time requires LEA admissions procedures to come on to the school governors' agenda (Sections 33(2) of the 1986 Act). However, having done this, it is difficult to see what is meant to happen as a result since no action appears to be required as a result of the consultation.

The third development occurred under Section 6 of the 1986 legislation, the 'Repeals and Revocations' section, where a reduction in the amount of choice open to London parents has been brought in. Section 31 (7) of the London Government Act of 1963 can be interpreted as having required London Borough LEAs to treat children in neighbouring boroughs in the same way as their own in respect of admissions to school. This section has now been repealed and as such parents' access to out-borough schools has been reduced.

The final development relates to a speech by the Secretary of State for Education and Science (May 1st, 1987 in Nelson, Lancashire

– referred to in Meikle, 1987) in which he proposed to bring in new legislation to stop LEAs refusing admission before a school reaches its full 1979 roll – a figure that harks back to the days of very full schools. Initially this sounds like a positive move in favour of choice, but perhaps one should ask just who gets more choice and what are the costs involved in those already in the school and to those attending declining schools. This reverting to the 1979 figure for the maximum number on roll basically raises the issues surrounding the second of our initial three questions, i.e. have we increased the global amount of choice for all or is this just an increase for the few?

This last issue also provides perhaps one of the best examples we have of legislation for parental choice being instigated for a number of possible reasons of which the direct improvement of schools and education might only be one aspect. (In this instance there is a strong case for seeing the proposed legislation as being concerned with the political removal of power from the LEAs.) The reality is that education exists in a wider context in life and we should not thus be too surprised when legislation is brought in from this wider perspective, but this is not to say, of course, that the broader perspective in itself improves the educational effectiveness of the legislation.

A framework for research into the 1980 Act's implementation

In order to structure the research, the question arose about what was meant by 'choice' and what were the prerequisites for it to be available. Basically, for educational choice to operate it can be argued that there need to be two or more schools within reach, a diversity of provision, and no restrictions on parents' rights of access, e.g. transport costs, enforced catchment areas or difficult administrative hurdles. But if choice is to mean more than just who goes where, that is, if choice is to have the potential to bring about any educational benefits, then there are several further features which must also be taken into account.

First, if the process of choice is to be able to increase the parents' involvement in their children's schooling, then the choice procedures themselves will need to either initiate and/or further encourage this involvement. In some way or another they will need to encourage parents to respond actively to the issues of what they want for their child and which school he or she should attend – passive acceptance of a predetermined LEA decision is hardly likely to draw parents into the issues.

Secondly, if choice is to have the potential to improve the match between the needs and characteristics of the child and what is offered by the school, then the procedures will require accurate and relevant information about both the child and the school to be available to parents so that they can make appropriate and informed choices. The same levels of information about the school will be needed if greater accountability is to occur and if the stimulation and improvement of schools are to be encouraged through the operation of market-forces effects. If schools for their part are to be able to respond to parents' wishes in more subtle ways than just counting heads, then there must be channels of communication which allow them to become aware of the parents' views and to react to them if they wish.

In outlining these arguments for what the processes of choice might achieve it is accepted that they are all contentious issues and that the effects of choice are open to debate. However, from the research point of view the way each part of the process might be implemented presents a useful framework for mounting the inquiries.

The methods used in the research allowed the project team to identify and describe the different procedures employed by LEAs around the country. One of the main findings was that the large differences between the choice procedures offered by schools around the country was rarely determined by the schools themselves. School choice procedures were basically similar within an area, but there were considerable differences between areas, and as such it appeared that the differences lay with the LEA. It would seem that as regards choice, LEAs differed considerably one from another both in their stated educational policies and in their administration of school allocation, and that even within an LEA, the match between the stated policy and its implementation was not always particularly coherent.

Part of the variation between LEAs seemed to lie with social and geographic factors such as size, whether they were urban or rural and whether they used divisions or were centrally administered from a single education office. But the research also detected the strong influence of the LEAs' individual pre-1980 practices and how enthusiastically and coherently the subsequent 1980 procedures had then been superimposed on to what they were doing.

In looking at the differences between LEAs, various features of practice were identified as being particularly instrumental in determining the type and amount of choice available. The most influential of these features included the provision of transport, the difference between a school's actual physical capacity to seat and teach children and the LEA's intended intake figure for that school, the LEA's policy for reducing surplus places, the specific published admissions criteria and how readily they seemed 'user friendly', the LEA's outward attitude towards parents' wishes, and finally, its encouragement of uniformity or diversity between its schools. Overall it seemed as if the amount of choice on offer by different LEAs could be viewed as a continuum with unhindered free choice at the one end and minimum choice brought about by tightly controlled catchment-area policies at the other.

But within those authorities operating catchment-area policies there was still a fair variation in the amount of choice on offer. Factors such as the requirement for a reply from all parents, as opposed to just from those who wished to state a preference for an alternative school; the sending of a proforma for stating preference rather than the requirement of a formal letter of application to be written by the parents, and the assurance to parents of a reserved place at the catchment-area school whatever other school they might apply for, instead of the practice of some LEAs of 'threatening' the withdrawal of the right of access to the local school if the parent should request another – all have the potential effectively to increase the viability of choice within a catchment-area LEA.

By the same token, in those authorities that operate without catchment areas, choice can still be limited, even to the extent of there being potentially less than might be available in an average catchment-area system. One of the major factors here is the actual number of schools a parent can choose from, and in parallel to this, the issue of whether transport is paid, or even available, to all, some or just the one 'local' school. Similarly, having perhaps set up an open choice system, the actual criteria used for assessing children's rights of access to popular schools can effectively reduce the amount of choice to that of a rigid catchment-area approach. If the main selecting criterion is distance from home to school, then choice as regards popular schools can be seen to be catchment-area based.

If the admissions and information procedures for all LEAs are compared by LEA, then it seems as if the authorities appear well spread out along the continuum of choice described earlier. However, along this continuum a certain amount of clustering was visible and three distinct, though not necessarily discrete, groups seem recognizable. The first group appears to offer parents a genuine choice between all the schools in the division or area and this group we termed the 'optimal-choice' group. At the opposite extreme another group of LEAs seemed to hold the ideal of community schools and community education as being more important than parental choice, and indeed, an ideal whose interests should override those of parental choice if necessary. This might be termed the 'minimal-choice' group. The last cluster of LEAs combined elements of choice and community education and is perhaps best identified as the 'hybrid' group. It is notable that although geographic features influenced these divisions, they were by no means overriding, and the project encountered minimal-choice LEAs in totally urban settings as well as optimal-choice LEAs in green countryside. In some instances, and somewhere off the minimum end of the choice scale, there were, of course, one or two geographic regions where the distances between schools were sufficiently large to deny the possibility of any choice ever being offered.

Differences in how LEAs approach choice can also be seen in the quantity and quality of the information they and their schools publish for parents. The legally required provision of printed information falls into two categories: that provided by the LEA, usually in the form of a booklet which, among other things, describes the admission procedures across the division or LEA and gives lists of schools and the addresses of neighbouring LEA offices; and that put out by the LEA or the school in the form of a brochure which serves to describe the school and provide certain mandatory information – exam results, uniform costs, curriculum details and so forth.

The distribution of the LEA booklets was fairly uniform across the country and most parents would have received their copy. This is not to say, however, that either the content or quality was as uniform, and overall, these booklets were seen to range from being friendly and informative to being terse, legalistic and minimalistic. Some of them almost seemed designed to put parents off the idea of choosing any school other than that which the authority had already recommended and in many cases there would have been parents with difficulties in understanding what was written.

Smith in 1982 had shown that most LEAs should produce translations for those parents whose first language was not English, but in collecting the LEA booklets for our research we had found very few translations available, and Beck, in his 1984 study of the choice procedures operating in London Boroughs (Beck, 1986), could only find three London boroughs which were involved in this work. Putting foreign languages to one side, he went on to comment on the actual readability of the English language used, and, with all the necessary caveats about the difficulty of interpreting the results of readability tests, showed the London Boroughs' booklets to require reading ages which varied from 12 to somewhere in excess of 22 years!

The provision and distribution of the school information and brochures again differed between LEAs and in practice was found to relate closely to the amount of choice on offer. In areas of minimal choice, school brochures were usually available only upon request and open evenings or talks were rarely held prior to the date for expressing preference. Even when these occasions were held, the invitations were often only passed on to catchment-area parents – but then many schools took the view that they should not actively try to attract (poach) other schools' pupils! This attitude clearly supported a view that schools have certain territorial rights over their 'local' parents.

In contrast, in optimal-choice LEAs pre-choice open evenings were more common, though by no means universal, and different schools' information was much more readily available. Unfortunately, whatever the degree of provision, the quality and usefulness of the information in the school brochures was frequently marred not only by poor presentation with difficult language, but also by a fairly common LEA requirement for all its schools' brochures to be presented with uniform formats which concentrated solely upon the common elements. Whilst one can understand an LEAs desire that its schools should not be chosen or rejected solely on the differences in their brochures, where the common format was linked to maximum economy, the brochures did become unnecessarily unattractive and difficult to use.

Four years later there is now an interesting footnote to add to this analysis. Having commented in its report about the difficulties inherent in using school examination results to choose schools, the

NFER project then observed that the legally required publication of school examination results was often sporadic – there appeared to be a reluctance amongst heads and education officers to publish this information. The new 1986 Act seems to have taken up this latter point and these same sets of exam results now have also to be annually published to *all* parents with children in the school by the school's governors in their annual report.

The parents' responses

The observations so far have related to the policies and administrative procedures employed by schools and LEAs. However, the research also sought the complementary information from parents using both interview and questionnaire techniques in the four case-study areas where we knew what the schools and LEAs offered. One of the most striking features we found was the degree to which the parents endorsed the idea of there being varying amounts of choice in different LEAs. In the case-study area which offered the least choice according to the criteria already described, the parents were in no doubt: when asked if they felt they had been offered a choice of school, 66 per cent (543) said no with only 27 per cent saying yes. At the opposite extreme, in the case-study area which best fitted the 'optimal choice' characteristics, 84 per cent (538) of the parents said yes to this question with only 12 per cent saying no.

In the research we asked parents what things they considered important when choosing a school. Across the 2,740 responding parents there was a tendency to attach most importance to educational standards and academic record, but the respective popularity of these reasons varied considerably from school to school. Closer inspection of the relative positions of these reasons showed that whilst they were influenced by the individual school this was not always directly in line with its relative academic standing. When we couple this result with what parents said in interviews, there seems to be a possibility that parents were not actually choosing schools because of their 'high standards', but rather that they would not allow themselves to choose a school which did not have sufficient standards. In other words, they had to be assured that the school had good enough standards before they could choose it on other grounds. The other reasons parents gave were very varied, again fairly localized and often reflected a specific image or aspect promoted by the individual school.

Another feature which emerged was the apparent link between the amount of perceived choice and the level of the parents' activity in the choice procedures, i.e. in their attendance at open meetings, the number of brochures they read and the number of people with whom they had discussions about the secondary schools. It seems that the more choice parents perceived they had, the more they engaged in this type of pre-choice activity.

In investigating the various social factors that might influence the parents' activity in the choice procedures or even the choices they finally made, it would seem that both the child's sex and its position in the family exerted a small influence on these matters, with the parents of girls and first children reporting using marginally more information than the parents of other children. Parents of first children also appeared slightly more likely to send their child to a school which was not the nearest, an aspect which suggested that they were being more selective. Parents of first children also felt there to be marginally less choice available than did other parents.

Although these particular influences were fairly small, the majority of children still appeared to exert a considerable impact upon the choice of school. Sixty-five per cent of the responding parents reported that their child felt strongly about their prospective secondary school. Of these 1,792 responding parents, 78 per cent felt their child's opinion was 'very important' when choosing the school, and a further 20 per cent felt it to be 'fairly important'. Given the size of these figures and the enormous influence and importance of the child's feelings in this matter, one cannot help but wonder whether the information for parents might also be properly addressed to children – an aspect that does not yet appear in the legislation. (See National Consumer Council, 1986.) The child's sex and position in the family had little impact on how important the parents felt the child's feelings to be.

The parents' own education and employment were also found to be influential. The longer their full-time education and the higher their job classification, the more information they used and the more likely they were to choose a more distant school. However, although the data showed considerable variation in participation from one end of the social scale to the other, members of all classes participated if there was any point and if they were given the opportunity.

The outcome of the choice procedures was also of interest. From our questionnaire to LEAs it would seem that in both 1983 and 1984 some 91–2 per cent of all parents gained access to an acceptable school at the initial allocation. On the other hand, for about seven to eight per cent of parents the initial income of their interaction with the LEA was one of conflict – the parents wanted a place in a school the LEA was unwilling to concede. Once this state had been reached there normally followed a period of discussion, review and/ or quasi-appeal. Whilst the first two of these might be endorsed as being sensible ways of seeking solutions and understanding each other's positions, the third is slightly more difficult to accept since if an internal appeal sets out to do anything more than review whether the LEA has operated its criteria properly then there is the risk that it will change its admission criteria for specific parents and therefore operate double standards. If, however, it sets out to do no more than review its procedures, then the idea of it being an appeal hearing is perhaps misguiding to parents. One way or another, the outcome of these procedures was that about a further six per cent of parents were offered acceptable places.

Under the 1980 Act if a parent is unhappy about the place offered by the LEA then he or she can take up their right of a statutory education appeal. For each of 1983 and 1984 we estimated there to be approximately 10,000 statutory appeals, though for a variety of reasons these numbers are very difficult to determine accurately. One way of considering the number of appeals is to view it as involving just about 1½ per cent of transferring pupils. (It has been estimated that the 10,000 appeals have an annual cost of about two million pounds.)

Although space forbids a more detailed examination of these new statutory local appeals, there are three points which are worth mentioning here. Firstly, in looking at how appeal committees operate, there appears to be some confusion as to whether or not they are an actual part of the LEAs normal allocation procedures, then from time to time we see appeal committee chairmen asking the officer in charge of admissions for a wide range of cases to be put forward so that some will be 'successful' and some will 'fail'. The committee wishes to be seen as both human and fair and thus it wishes to be able to 'give in' to some cases. Furthermore, they will ask for a number of school places to be left vacant, again so that they can be seen to be fair and to 'give' places to a number of parents. In other words there seems to be a tendency for the appeal committee to become the last stage in the LEAs process and to decide who gets what in the difficult cases.

However, if the committee were to operate independently and outside the system, then the LEA would initially have to fill all its places according to its published criteria and the appeal committee would exist solely to place those parents whose cases were sufficiently extreme to fall outside the normal LEA procedures. Although it is easy to understand why appeal committees might find it easier to operate as part of the LEAs system, this fits very uncomfortably with both their 'independent' role and with the LEAs statutory duty to accede to any parental request while they still have vacancies – i.e. while any places remain vacant it must be wrong to hold back requests for the appeal committee to decide since the LEA has no right to hold them back.

The second issue concerns the idea that the number of appeals is directly related to the demand for choice. In reporting Kenneth Baker's speech on 1st May, Meikle (1987) described him as wanting more places to be freed for choice with one of the grounds for this being the large number of appeals. Contrary to this, however, it would seem that the number of appeals will increase where parents are more involved in the choice procedures. Almost inevitably we can see that the more choice that is offered, the more parents will be involved and in absolute terms, the more school place choices that will have to be refused. Far from reducing the number of appeals, if Mr Baker's action is to increase choice, it is also likely to increase the number of appeals.

The third issue takes us back to the beginning of this chapter where it was argued that one reason for the legislation being brought in was that politicians were very sensitive to parents' central appeals and that the demands of just a few people were influencing the procedures for the rest. In many ways the statutory local education appeal can now be seen to be as influential, for although it only applies to a small number of parents, probably just about 1½ per cent overall, LEAs are very sensitive to their appeal committees' thinking and we were aware of officers trying to avoid having decisions made against them for the same reason two years running.

A tentative conclusion

In reviewing the changes the Act has brought about we see that for all the appeals might influence the LEAs, they would still appear to bring about few extra places in the initial allocation. Their main influence is on the LEAs procedures for deciding who has access to which schools, and in essence, where schools are full, this is what the whole Act is about. If there are 120 places in the first year of a secondary school, the procedures simply determine which parents have priority in getting their children in. If one system is changed for another, a different set of parents gains the priority. With this in mind one can understand why the majority of LEAs have 'distance from home to school' as the major deciding criterion since not only is it easy to measure and therefore a relatively easy way to rank the requests, but it also encourages local involvement in the school and reduces transport bills. Of course, where there are spare places or where there are several schools with different characteristics or where distances are not too large, then the Act does appear to have given parents a number of extra rights. Where these conditions persist we can see that the global amount of choice in an LEA or division may well have increased if the LEA was not already offering choice before the Act came in, but then, many LEAs were doing so.

Where there is more choice, we might look for evidence of improved or improving schools, but it may be that we are asking too much of the procedures. For instance, one might look for parents to be expressing their educational requirements when they state their preferred school, but for very practical reasons LEAs have chosen to emphasise non-educational grounds as the criteria for admission to school – criteria such as health, siblings, distance and so forth – and the use of these criteria is likely to receive greater emphasis in future years following recent requirements in DES Circular 8.86 (*op. cit.*). Unfortunately it is difficult to see how a school might be sensitive to the parents' educational wishes with these criteria. Furthermore, most of the admissions procedures are dealt with at divisional or county office level and most schools never see the application forms, just lists of new pupils. It would seem that the 1980 Act procedures are unlikely to aid educational improvement other than in a rather gross head-counting way, and even that can be influenced by so many other factors as to only make it a reliable indicator in extreme conditions.

Where there are few spare places and the popular schools are as full as they ever were, then it is difficult to see how the Act gives more choice either in global or individual terms unless the LEA changes from a catchment area system to one of open or free choice, but this was not what we saw. In fact, a number of LEAs argued that with the introduction of the 1980 Act they had had to revert from a relaxed approach to choice, to an enforced catchment-area system in order to cope with the planning of the published intake limits.

It seems appropriate to end this discussion by looking at the last of the three questions raised in the introduction, that of the relationship between parental choice legislation and what parents actually want. In terms of 'choice' itself, one way of looking at this is to ask whether the 1980 Act and the subsequent 1986 additions have allowed more parents to get the schools they wanted, or alternatively, are there now fewer 'unhappy' parents? Given that we found about 60 per cent of the annual 10,000 appeals were given in the LEAs' favour, we may deduce that some 6,000 or more parents per annum are unsatisfied with the school to which their child gets sent. This is over three times the number of central appeals we saw in the mid- to late-1970s, but of course this sort of statistic tells us little since the context has changed, there are fewer pupils and places now available and we may well expect the legislation and media attention to have raised parents' expectations of their entitlement. Unfortunately, these expectations have become increasingly difficult for authorities to meet without spending extra money on maintaining empty places in schools, and this goes directly against the government's other wishes.

As for parental choice actually improving education, what one might regard as the other part of the relationship between the legislation and what parents want, from our analysis of the processes employed so far it is very difficult to see how this might have happened. This is not to say that parental choice cannot bring about improvement so much as that as yet there are few methods and processes being consistently used which could allow any improvement to happen.

'Choice' and 'Preference'

It is acknowledged that the 1980 Act only entitles parents to the expression of preference, and not choice *per se*, but since parents can choose the school to be listed in the preference, it seems more useful to consider the legislation in terms of choice whilst recognizing the real limitations.

Acknowledgements

The author acknowledges with gratitude the funding and support provided for this project by the National Foundation for Educational Research. The author would also like to express his gratitude to all those teachers, heads, education officers and parents who so willingly helped the project, to the Steering Committee and Margaret I. Reid who guided the research so carefully and to the author's colleague and co-researcher, Karen Maychell.

Parental Partnership in Education – A Case for Policy

Sheila Wolfendale

A case for policy

What would a policy for parental partnership in children's development and education amount to, in general terms?

The following assertions are intended to apply as general principles to the settings were the focus of the report – namely schools, pre-school, multidisciplinary team work, the area of special educational needs, community *milieux*, and the home.

Such a policy, it is suggested, is neither the preserve nor the prerogative of particular local authority or community institutions or groupings: the philosophical elements in which the principles are embedded are applicable within and across settings. It would be up to participants in any sphere to combine or emphasize any or all of these principles into a format for practice.

A policy for collaborative parental partnership

This could be based on and incorporate the following principles:

(a) Abandoning the client concept to evolve towards parents as partners in sharing exercises;
(b) Consulting of parents in the same way as professional views and specialist opinion are sought, and for parents to have a voice, a forum, or a means of expression – as professionals do.
(c) Mutual setting of objectives, for example, in curriculum process, learning programmes, special education provision, parent education programmes, aided self-groups.

(d)   Central involvement of parents in the process (provision or 'treatment').

(e)   Parents and professionals to take joint responsibility for outcomes, to be mutually accountable, as well as accountable to a wider public.

(f)   Mutual and joint involvement in hypothesis-testing exercises and in-built evaluation.

Policy into practice in schools

The grounds for a special focus on schools are perceived to be severalfold as follows:

−children spend so much of their time in school and schools are therefore in a position to be a main influencing medium;

−schools are a major community in the lives of children;

−schools can offer expertise and resources to children, families and communities;

−there is considerable potential for a greater complementarity between school and home, school and agencies, schools and their localities;

−there is a growing groundswell of opinion that with alleged rising levels of social unrest, it is incumbent upon schools to re-align with community institutions in order to effect relevant curriculum and adult preparation programmes for 'disaffected' youth. The disparate worlds for the child of school, home, the world of work have to effect a rapprochement;

−schools have a responsibility to address themselves directly to 'world problematique' issues, to the extent that the definition of 'education' may ultimately have to broaden.

The development and education of children should be the proper concerns of teachers *and* parents and the responsibility of equipping children with cognitive and practical tools for personal competence and survival is a collective one.

Objectives setting for home–school policies

The main practical preoccupations ought to be with what the mutual objectives and purposes are for home–school collaboration, what the desired outcomes are, and by what criteria these can be assessed. The intended benefits to children, to parents and teachers could be used as the basis of negotiable contracts between parents and schools.

The tables below outline objectives and their intended outcomes which could be pre-formulated by schools' staff and parents, via working groups or representative committees (not necessarily or desirably via governing forums, but as offshoots or linked to these).

This hypothetical range of possible objectives and outcomes for children, schools and parents has precedent in actual practice. Many small-scale experiments and projects would be amenable to replication, even generalizability, of some of their features at least. Furthermore, the outcomes could be measured and evaluated in a variety of ways (see later in this extract).

There are so many possible combinations of a comprehensive home–school programme that a companion handbook would be required to do justice to all the practical possibilities. Many of these combinations have remained in the realm of speculation, contained in well-intentioned pamphlets for parents or visionary texts; others are known to have been tried out.

For example, The Advisory Centre for Education (ACE) produces a practical leaflet *How you can help your local school*. An article in Field (1977) proposes that schools should appoint advisers, in contrast with an earlier (1966) suggestion by ACE that local education authorities should appoint advisers with a brief for developing home–school contacts. Johnson (1977) puts forward a set of guidelines or questions for teachers to ask of themselves and each other to help them decide the extent to which they are responsive to parents' needs, and what further potential areas there are for fruitful contact. The Manchester branch of the National Association for Multicultural Education (NAME) includes in its document an *A–Z of good home/school relations*.

In a Scottish report (Macbeth *et al.*, 1980) a list of schemes operating in various countries is provided which illustrates the many ways in which home–school partnership can work in practice in terms

Table 3: Objectives and outcomes for children

To enhance their cognitive development generally and to boost attainment (via parental involvement in curriculum and programme planning; parental participation in teacher-supervised 'home' learning).

To 'catch up' on skill-acquisition in traditional remedial senses (parental involvement as above).

To boost/train areas of developmental delay or handicap (parents involved in conjoint learning programmes as co-trainers; parents involved in 'treatment' process).

To resolve behaviour/emotional difficulties evident at home or in school (parents involved in problem definition and description, 'treatment' plans at school or at home).

To collaborate on career planning (meetings and information-seeking).

To feel a sense of well-being and ease that school and home share to the fullest possible extent, common concerns and aspirations for their welfare (home visiting by teachers, parents into school, forms of written communication).

Table 4: Objectives and outcomes – for schools and parents

For schools	*For parents*
	← Reciprocity →
To gain knowledge and understanding of children's homes, families, interests and out-of school activities.	To gain knowledge and understanding of function and aims of school, teachers' role and local education authority services.
← Written and verbal exchange →	
Increased accountability (via openness and access) of curriculum and provision.	To gain information regarding progress of children in main-stream and special education provision.
To gain parental interest, support and backing for schools' goals and activities.	To gain opportunities to discuss issues and formulate decisions: to become involved in curriculum process and learning programmes.
← Advocacy in action →	

of home liaison arrangements; traditional and innovatory forms of verbal and written communication; novel ways of ensuring that teachers and parents meet on a regular basis to discuss individual children's progress; the appointment of 'key' parents to act as catalysts and 'middlepersons' to facilitate other parents' responsiveness; collaborative teacher–parent planning and execution of work programmes for which schools' and community resources are used.

One final example of 'good' or novel practice in this area comes from recent reports that the West Midlands local education authority of Walsall is planning to hold special training sessions to enable parents systematically to evaluate schools and to help take decisions about the school curriculum. This is in a locality which has a well-developed policy of community schools.

Towards a taxonomy of home–school partnership: a basis for reciprocity

A system of classification or taxonomy is offered below, which, it is suggested could be used as a starting framework for the generation and evolution of school and parent partnership policies. As with other taxonomies, this is divided into domains, two, in this case. These share a common format, but each has a different emphasis.

Parents into school

This is intended to conceptualize the *areas* for involvement by parents within the school context, with the main *types* of involvement listed against each area and with the particular *focus* of the involvement noted against each *type*. In this domain the perspective and responsibilities of the schools are paramount.

School to home

In this domain the tripartite conceptual framework is identical to *Parents Into Schools* (i.e., with *area, type* and *focus*) but the context and overall perspective is the environment outside the school, i.e.

Table 5: Parents into schools

Area	*Type*	*Focus*
Concrete and practical	basic help with learning fund-raising and support; practical skills; social meetings	classroom and school
Pedagogical and problem-solving	syllabus design and planning, co-tutoring of school and home-based learning (general education, remedial, special education needs) school-based discussion of progress	curriculum
Policy and governing	educational decision-making; parents as governors	school as institution
Communal	groups for parents and children, (workshops, classes, courses, talks, demonstrations)	school and community

Table 6: School to home

Area	*Type*	*Focus*
Information	verbal, written communication – letters, reports, newsletters, booklets, check and recording systems	home and parents
Support	home visiting (inquiry, counselling, relations-fostering) imparting information, discussion of child progress	home and family
Instruction	educational home visitor/teaching brief (handicap, special educational needs disadvantage, preschool)	home, child and parents
Representation	input by schools into rest of community (resource sharing, resource loan, local meeting place, focal place for cooperative learning)	home and community

the home and the wider community. Thus the taxonomic approach here aims to emphasize the extension of schools into this wider world.

From this presentation it can be seen that the initiatives are intended to be two-way, that is, are beyond a Plowden conception that schools are to 'allow' parents into schools. At worst this has meant far more accommodation by parents than schools themselves have been prepared to make.

It is on this basis of two-way initiative (home-community/school) that the principle of reciprocity rests. This has been defined as 'mutual involvement, mutual accountability, mutual gain', and includes these processes:

– the evolution of agreed aims;

– a statement of the means by which the contributions of parents and professionals can be made;

– consensus regarding the criteria for success or failure of the collaboration.

What is being called for in a 'new style' approach to home–school links is a re-examination by teachers of their professional self-concept.

Research and evaluation

General remarks

Any policy or programme adopted for try-out ought to have means of evaluation built in. The taxonomy presented above could be used as a framework, along with the principles outlined earlier which underlie such ventures. True, service-delivery systems need not necessarily be *research* focused if the mandate is a pragmatic one to 'deliver the goods'. However, some of the research pertaining to parental participation needs to be replicated in other settings, especially those investigations which reported really positive outcomes.

A distinction should be made at this point between the *desirability* of research in the form of ideas hypothesis-testing being built into some parent partnership approaches, and the *necessity* for evaluative procedures to be part of any or all such approaches.

At an early stage of a policy, hypothesis testing might be considered to be essential; outcomes from these could determine whether or not certain features then become part of routine service-delivery and incorporated into routine programmes. Even continuing evaluation might cease eventually, once participants felt confident the procedures were worthwhile and working smoothly, although any venture needs some form of intermittent scrutiny.

The essential point to be made here is that advocates of evaluation approaches usually stress how important it is to build in methods to measure the *process* of the project or programme (sometimes referred to as monitoring procedures) as well as their outcomes, or products.

Application of research techniques to parent-participation policies

These various research and evaluation approaches should be relevant to the measurement and assessment of parent-participation policies. Some examples are:

(1) *Exploratory, survey and information-gathering work* could focus around parents' and teachers' attitudes and aspirations, concrete suggestions as to how links should be fostered; practical ways in which participants can get together; what kind of meetings are suitable for what kind of purpose; what forms of accountability should exist; role and contribution of the support services – examples are legion.

(2) *Hypothesis-testing and educational action research* could engage upon the setting up and follow-through of intervention projects, where the focus in school and/or home, both, or other milieux. The potential for 'home' learning where the parent is a co-educator under the supervision of the teacher is one area ripe for research activity.

(3) *Evaluation* of rather more 'routine' apparently humdrum forms of collaboration would be a vital component. Meetings,

working parties, the 'routine' presence of parents in schools, regular duties such as home visiting by teachers could all be subject to evaluation procedures carried out by participants to some extent, and researchers on funded secondment from local institutions of higher education.

Concluding comment

As can be seen from a wide-ranging review of current literature, schools are being called upon from so many quarters to reappraise their role and function in today's world on behalf of tomorrow's adults. Such a review suggests the need to consider changing functions of schools under the following types of heading:

(1) the scientific base for schooling

(2) schools as the community's agents to support the family role

(3) the 'human care' orientation of schools

(4) 'family life' courses

(5) school response to minority family cultures.

In a discussion on education viewed from an evolutionary perspective, Martlew, Smith and Connolly (in Dockrell and Hamilton, 1980) rework the definition of education as they perceive it juxtaposed between its traditional functions demanded by society and the requirements of a technological and fast-changing contemporary society, which call for different skills and competencies. Continued compartmentalism and educational separatism is not likely to guarantee optimization of human potential, nor the ability to flexibly adapt to and cope with change.

Outmoded aspirations for conventional success in formal learning terms will have to give way to the need to develop different kinds of learning and coping skills. Wolfendale gave attention in an earlier publication (1980) to a curriculum which could include the necessary elements; her suggested list is reproduced here:

social competence: self-care, daily problem-solving, skills of inter-relating and empathy, community participation;

knowledge-based: knowledge of the world around us, current affairs at local and national level, basic history, origins of culture, literature;

performance-based: competence in numeracy, literacy, scientific and technological concepts, industrial and commercial procedures;

cognitive competence: problem-solving techniques; thinking and critical skills; anticipatory learning skills; decision-making; taking personal and altruistic responsibility.

No derogation of teachers' roles is envisaged in pleading for radical change; rather the teacher's contribution as organizer, catalyst, facilitator and expert is linchpin. For children's development to blossom, for their education to flourish, society's invitation to parents is for them to be partners in the educational and community enterprise.

From their perspective as lawyers, Coons and Sugarman (1978) argue a powerful and sensitive case for parental control over educational processes, concluding 'to treat education like childrearing generally would be to give the family the basic power to select the child's educational experiences, with the child protected from the harmful exercise of that power through various judicial and administrative mechanisms'. They say that they prefer 'families or familylike units – supported by professionals – as the appropriate locus of the authority over the child's education'.

The last word comes from an extract from the United Nations Declaration of the Rights of the Child:

The best interests of the child shall be the guiding principle of those responsible for his education and guidance; that responsibility lies in the first place with his parents.

Part Two

Policy and Practice in Different Settings

Editorial Preview

The problem of whether and how far the special needs of children and young people should be recognized and met has had a considerable influence upon educational attitudes and provision – and continues to do so. The accounts in this section illustrate, from a wider range of possibilities, the key features of the differing needs of children, the nature of the separate stages of their development and the different phases of the system they pass through as well as the acknowledgement of important differences of social, geographical and cultural background. But the same accounts also uncover a number of issues and problems that are of common concern and for which wider and more integrated policies would be helpful to the education service and more generally.

Teresa Smith's account, which is part of the wider Oxford Pre-School Project, illustrates just this point, drawing from an area which has made an important contribution to the development of home/school policy and practice in recent years. This extract, however, explores some of the interesting and subtle differences between the largely 'professionalized' nursery sector and the parent-led playgroup movement, which lies almost entirely in the voluntary sector.

It compares the different approaches and differing effects of a range of settings, their organization, curriculum and relationships. It does so by focusing on key notions, such as 'partnership' and 'involvement', not as abstractions but as operational realities, with emphasis upon the *experience* of pre-school education (rather than its rhetoric) and the roles of parents and professionals respectively.

The account also serves as a useful illustration of the potential contribution of particular types of research to the development of home/school policy and practice. For the recommendations that are part of this study derive from, and are grounded in, an examination of the real world, viewed as far as is possible through a critical and unprejudiced eye that is, at the same time, sympathetic to the underlying needs and purposes of the pre-school phase.

Daphne Johnson and Joyce Ransom's account is drawn from a broader action-research project which looked at the relationships between families, schools and a range of welfare agencies concerned with the development of children and young people. Whilst it is located firmly in the secondary phase of schooling it is never insular in its approach, examining the interaction between families and secondary schools against a background which considers the earlier experience which families have.

The study also works within a dynamic perspective, which traces a changing pattern of relationships that incorporate the wish of young people (acknowledged by their parents) 'to stand on their own feet' and be increasingly treated as independent young adults. In doing this, it makes a powerful case for the greater recognition of the part that young people themselves play in home/school relations. This contrasts with the rather hollow rhetoric about parent/teacher/child triangles and pinpoints an area where both policy and practice are very under-developed.

Their work also contributes to the development of policy and practice by looking critically at a number of widely-held assumptions and mythologies about home/school relations. Above all, it demonstrates the value of developing an approach which grows out of a clearer picture of what parents actually believe and expect. This sometimes contrasts markedly with the apparent consensus and established wisdom in significant ways.

Although a great deal of lip-service has been paid to the importance of home/school relations in multicultural settings and to the special educational needs of ethnic minorities, very little productive attention has been focused on this area. In an important exception to this, the work of Barbara Tizard and her colleagues at the Thomas Coram Foundation has led to action research which probes the relationship between thinking and practice, between attitudes and behaviour, between purposes and organization.

Their work is hard-hitting and unsentimental in its analysis of the issues and in its suggestions for reform and development, amounting to a practical critique. The implied demands upon schools and teachers, if there is to be improvement, stand in stark contrast to the low expectations that often characterize home/school relations, on the part of schools and families alike.

It would be inconceivable that a section on home/school relations in special settings should overlook the ideas and experience of the 'special needs' sector. For there is a great deal here from which we can all learn. In this area, for example, there seems to be a much more widespread recognition of the essential role of parents and the active support of families in children's education and development; there is also a great deal of practical achievement of general relevance and usefulness, many exciting initiatives and areas of development. Finally, as a cause or a consequence of these developments, there is a greater recognition of the importance of teacher training and professional development, as part of an overall, integrated view of needs and provision.

Parents and Pre-school

Teresa Smith

Definitions of parental involvement

Now that we have considered some of the developments in parental involvement and the research evidence, we can at last commit ourselves to a definition. Explicit definitions are hard to find; the discussion so far should at least have demonstrated the variety of implicit definitions to be found in both practice and theory. We have outlined two approaches to parental involvement as preschool provision has developed over the last 15–20 years: the first educational, and the second participatory. In the first, parents are seen as learners and teachers of their own children; in the second, they are organizers, committee members, policy-makers, as well as consumers.

Gordon (1969) outlines a five-point scale which combines the two approaches:

(1) *Parents as supporters* – service givers – facilitators – clerical, custodial, maintenance, fund-raising, family nights

(2) *Parents as learners* – parent education courses, observation of children with explanation

(3) *Parents as teachers of their own children* – taking home toys and books for use with children

(4) *Parents as teacher aides and volunteers in the classroom* – prepare materials, read stories, work with children

(5) *Parents as policy-makers and partners* – policy-makers, advisory board members.

The Oxfordshire study – types of involvement and group style

Above we quoted Gordon's (1969) five-point scale for parent involvement: parents as supporters, learners, teachers of their own children, teacher aides or volunteers in the classroom, and policy makers. To what extent does this classification reflect actual practice? How does this compare with the evidence from Oxfordshire?

Gordon's first category is our *servicing* category – parents giving help outside the sessions, making and mending equipment, fundraising, looking after the animals. His last is our involvement in *management*. The others are more problematic. His fourth category, teacher aides and volunteers in the classroom, corresponds closest to our category of *involvement with the day-to-day sessions* of the group – but we have made a further distinction here between.working alongside the children in the group and clearing up after them. This is a fundamental distinction if we are concerned with the roles played by parent and professional. Similarly, Gordon's second and third categories of parents as learners and teachers of their own children restrict what we have called the parent's 'educational' role to work with his own child – we are interested in the parent's role in the group as such. So we do not have information in the Oxfordshire study on the parent's role specifically with his *own* child, except incidentally from comments about the carry-over of learning from the group to the home. Instead, we have information about the parent's 'educational' or 'servicing' role in the classroom or playgroups as it compares with the role of the teacher or the playgroup supervisor.

There is a sixth category which Gordon does not include but to which we have given considerable space in this study – parents as sharers or partners in their children's experience. This is not necessarily the same as being a teacher or a learner – both of which require active participation – although they may overlap. This is the category which elsewhere we have considered under the heading of the openness or accessibility of a group – to what extent parents are welcomed into the group and encouraged to see it as a natural extension of the home experience, with shared information between staff and parent and shared experience between parent and child.

Which of these types of involvement ranks highest in frequency in the study of Oxfordshire nursery schools, classes and playgroups?

More than half the parents we interviewed were involved in servicing or support roles – they made cakes for fund-raising events, painted furniture, concreted the playground, collected jumble, mended books. Almost one quarter were involved with the day-to-day sessions – whether working with the children or clearing up after them. Only one parent in nine was involved with management. According to this study, then, servicing activities are the most usual form of involving parents in the work of the group, followed by helping with the day-to-day sessions, with involvement in management a very long way behind. This formulation, however, obscures a further distinction which we found to be important – whether helping with the sessions meant working with the children or clearing up after them. Only one in five parents said they worked with the children. If we take clearing up as another kind of servicing, although in the sessions, then this category becomes even more dominant. Another way of putting this is the fact that in all the groups more parents were involved with servicing than any other form of help.

What can we add to this picture if we look at the information from the point of view of the *groups* rather than the *parents* involved? We can see that more groups involved parents in servicing than any other form of help. (We cannot say anything about the number of groups involving parents in the sessions, as this was our main criterion for selection in the first place; so numbers of parents are a more important guide here.) Three out of the six groups from which we interviewed parents involved them in some form of management or administration of the group. *Type* of group tells us rather more, although we should remind ourselves that the number of groups is too small to give us very reliable information. Of the three types of group, playgroups came out highest on all forms of involvement – servicing (fund-raising rather than maintenance), management, and help with the sessions; playgroups also came out with the most parents involved in working with children during the sessions as distinct from clearing up, and they were least likely to be selective about the activities parents undertook in the sessions.

When we turn to the groups' openness or accessibility to parents, we can see that the nursery schools were more welcoming and open than any other kind of group to parents at the beginnings and ends of sessions; parents came in more with their children and talked more to staff and other parents, stayed more to settle their children, visited more and brought their problems. The only exception to this picture of general welcomingness was the presence of 'non staff' adults in the group – here playgroups came out significantly higher. From the staff interviews, we have seen that the nursery school staff tended to place most emphasis on parents visiting before the child started at the group, and staying to settle him. In the interviews with parents, we asked about four types of contact, all of which could be said to be ways for parents to share in their children's experience – visiting and settling in, access to staff, social events, and parents' committees. Of these, the most important was the process of starting a child in the group and maintaining contact with the staff while he was there; social events were less important, and parents' bodies least important of all. There was not much difference here between different types of group. The one striking exception was a nursery class which consistently had the least contact of any group with parents – whether as sharers in their children's experience, settling them and talking to staff, or as helpers in the group or outside.

More parents, in all kinds of group, had this contact – the process of starting the child in the group and maintaining contact with the staff while he was there – than were involved in either serving, management, or help with the sessions. If we include in the list of parental involvement this basic contact, where the parent shares in the child's experience but is not necessarily an active participant in the group, we can see this will head the list.

If we summarize the information from the Oxfordshire study on the roles played by parents in their children's pre-school groups, we can see that they are, first of all, sharers in their children's experience, with open access to the group, whether playgroups, nursery school or class; second, servicers or supporters – providers of practical help outside the group; third, helpers or 'aides' in the day-to-day sessions of the group; and fourth, 'teachers' in the group working alongside the children in the same way as regular members of staff.

We find that most of the pre-school groups in the study fell into either the 'open/partnership' or the 'open/professional' categories. That is, they were all friendly and welcoming places, with parents visiting and settling in their children, talking to staff about problems and progress, and encouraged to see what their children were doing. Some, however, welcomed parents as partners in the process of educating their child, and encouraged them to work freely in the group with the children. Here the focus was on parent and child together, and there was a feeling of shared territory with staff, parents, and other adults. These were the 'open/partnership' groups. Others thought of the group as primarily for the child's benefit, with parents involved to provide continuity and information about home experience, but not encouraged to participate except to give practical support outside the sessions or to clear up after the children. These groups tended to be staff-controlled and directed, and were not so open to other adults. These were the 'open/professional' groups. We found nursery classes in the first category, nursery schools and playgroups in both.

Fewer groups in our study came into the 'closed/professional' category. None of the nursery schools were of this type. Their professional approach was strongly bound up with a view of parents as sharers in their children's experience and therefore a determination to be as open and accessible as possible to parents. But we find some of the nursery classes; and also some of the playgroups, and other forms of private groups – particularly those with regular helpers rather than parents on rota, and without a parents' committee.

But two of the groups in the study did fall into the 'closed/partnership' category. This is perhaps surprising – that a group where parents were seen as partners or where the focus was on parent and child together rather than the child on his own should discourage parents from settling in the child, say, or from free access to the staff. Both these groups restricted parents' access, although they intended to operate as partnerships rather than focus on the child alone, and one had parents helping in the group with clearing up after the children. One of these groups was a crèche set up for working mothers, the other a playgroup. But we do not have sufficient information from the study to see whether these groups were atypical in other ways or to explain why they fell into this category.

Parents who were not involved

This study has little to say about working mothers or ethnic minority groups – two groups picked out in the literature on pre-school policy as in need of special attention (CPRS, 1978; CRC, 1975). Yet this in itself is important. Half the mothers we interviewed were working, most part-time – yet there were no apparent attempts on the part of staff to think through the question of how to involve working parents. We heard a number of comments about mothers working with young children, or going back to work 'too soon', or groups not being in business to cater for mothers to 'dump' their children. Working parents often regretted the difficulty of being involved, or felt guilty about not putting in their fair share of effort. Several spoke of the negative attitudes of staff – one had felt harassed to pick up her child on time. With groups dependent on parent help to keep open, like playgroups, some parents felt increasingly guilty about 'not pulling their weight', and staff acknowledged the increasing difficulty of maintaining a parent rota.

Immigrants or overseas visitors formed a small proportion of our sample of parents. Nevertheless, it is important to note that they consistently came out lower on any dimension of involvement. At times it was clear that parents did not understand what staff required or expected, far less the educational objects of the group. One Pakistani father explained that his wife had attended an open day but had understood nothing. Staff felt that immigrant families were less willing to be involved; on the other hand, there were clear indications that the parents were willing but did not understand that they had ever been asked.

What of the parents who were not involved and wished to be? In the groups that did not involve parents except for servicing, two in three parents would have liked to be involved in some way or other, and half of these had not been approached. In the groups that did involve parents with the sessions, 12 out of 30 would have liked to be more involved than they were; some were obviously withdrawing for the moment because they were pregnant or had young children to cope with, but others had developed new ideas through being involved. That is, more than half the parents in this study would have liked to play a larger part in their child's group and share his experience more closely. This is the strongest possible indication of the waste of interest on the part of parents – interest in their children's experience and development that could have been built on for both parent and child.

Shared experience or an educational role?

Recent research on pre-school programmes suggests that involvement of parents with their children as active teachers and learners may be one of the key ingredients of success in affecting children's achievement and intelligence over the long term (Fantini and Cárdenas, 1980) or changing parents' attitudes about education and their own role with their children in the short term (Armstrong and Brown, 1979). Critics of the 'parent education' approach argue that the flavour is far too didactic – learning, whether for children or adults, should be gently assimilated through active experience, rather than *taught*. However, our evidence suggests that it may not happen like this – at any rate, not all the time or not for the parents we interviewed. We found remarkably few examples of parents being aware of pre-school as a specifically educational experience for themselves – a place where they could learn about child development, how children learnt – or of a specifically educational role for themselves with their children. We did find examples of parents gaining ideas for activities to carry out with the child at home, watching children with fascination, extending their understanding of children's needs and capacities. But we should have expected far more examples of this kind, if indeed parents were learning through simple exposure. It is also true that we have no evidence about parents' actual practice with their children, as distinct from what they said about it; and we do not know whether parents would talk about an educational role which they then failed to put into practice, or change their approach to the child and be unable to express this in words.

The emphasis on involving parents, as we have seen from both the parents' and the staff's interviews, was overwhelmingly on sharing the child's experience as a natural extension and continuity of the home experience and as a vital support for the child. Learning for parents was part of shared experience with the child, rather than a separate activity.

The notions of 'parents as learners' or as 'teachers of their own children', in Gordon's phraseology, look somewhat uneasy in the British context. None of the groups we studied contained a home-teaching component, as do many American programmes; nor did they explicitly instruct parents to work with their children – far from it, indeed, as many staff expected parents to work with other children rather than their own if they stayed to help in the group. Yet there were staff who spoke of parents learning in the group about child development, and parents who talked of learning how to carry on the work of the group with their child at home. The emphasis, though, was informal rather than formal, and not always couched in educational terms. Asked about their role in the group, parents tended to talk about 'general support', 'taking an interest', or 'shared experience' with their child. When they did talk about 'learning' or 'teaching', it was to give specific examples of something that had struck them – the fascination of watching children working with lego or finding new words, of learning to stand back and observe their own child, or of 'getting ideas for what to do at home'. Only occasionally were there comments of a more general kind – 'learning about children's reactions or behaviour', or 'explaining' the importance of different kinds of play to parents.

So it was unusual to find parents acknowledging an explicit learning or teaching slant to their role, and even more unusual to find this put in educational language. But if we turn to what staff had to say about the parents' role, we find a more explicit statement of educational aims. When asked about the value to parents of involvement, staff were more likely to say that it gave them a better understanding of or a different perspective on their child. Perhaps staff and parents have similar things in mind, although the language they used was different.

Did the explicitness of parents' educational understanding vary with the type of group? Were parents more likely to think of their role in educational terms in groups where they were involved more closely with the work of the group, where they helped in sessions alongside the children rather than in servicing or chores, where staff were more explicit in their attempt to involve parents in educational partnership? Certainly there seems to be a link. Parents were more likely to give examples of situations that had struck them in those groups which put most effort into involving parents with the day-to-day sessions, and particularly where parents worked alongside the children. In the case of the playgroup with a strong democratic orientation, it is strikingly those parents who were 'in on the network', rather than those for some reason outside it, who spoke of their role and involvement in this way.

Two points stand out here. The first is that parents – and staff – were most likely to see the role of the parents in educational terms in groups where parents were most closely and actively involved and where there was least barrier between staff and parent. This cuts across all types of group. The second point is that this understanding of the role of parents was not at all formally expressed. Nowhere did we find a formal 'programme' for parents. They were not instructed in child development, or in activities to use at home. The nearest approach to anything formal was a meeting, sometimes held at the beginning of term, when the organization of the group was explained to parents and they were encouraged to become involved. But this was the exception rather than the rule. Not that an informal approach by staff was any more usual. Although staff might hold the view that involvement was a means of learning for parents, there was very little discussion between staff and parents about the group's activities or objectives. We noted in the observations that discussion was comparatively infrequent, and what little there was of it tended to happen more in nursery classes than either nursery schools or playgroups.

So we might say that in the Oxfordshire groups we studied, parents operated as teachers or learners more by accident – a happy, spontaneous flash of insight, as it sometimes appeared from parents' accounts in the interviews – than by deliberate, carefully planned design.

We have here two different views of learning and how to foster it. One is the view associated with traditional English nursery education, with its emphasis on free play, enriched environment, and learning through exploration. On this view, parents will learn simply through exposure – through sharing their children's experience in the group. The other is a structured programmed teaching approach, where teachers teach and parents or children learn. On this view, parents need a structured 'parent programme'. But there is a third way, which combines both structure and learning at the learner's own pace, when opportunities for learning are created or picked up and then developed. On this view, staff should take the parents' experience in the group and make the learning explicit.

We do not know which of these views of parents learning is the most effective. It may be that exposure and shared experience is simply too low-key, and not sufficiently explicit, for parents to learn as much as they could about how to foster their child's development. Our evidence certainly suggests that opportunities were missed to build on parents' excitement or flashes of understanding and insight, or their desire for more information. We should note Barbara Tizard's comment (Tizard, 1978) that parents' greater knowledge of what went on in the group did not necessarily bring with it any greater understanding of these activities. But is this so because parents fail to understand, or because staff do not build on the opportunity to help parents learn?

Yet we know that the parent's role in his child's development, and his encouragement of the child's learning, is crucial from the point of view of the child's long-term life chances. Most groups in our study in Oxfordshire were concerned to welcome parents as sharers in their children's experience in the sense of observing what they did rather than participating more actively. If parental involvement is to mean more than communication or sharing information on the Plowden model, then we must work hard for a more participative approach. We must recognize the boundaries and barriers that exist between the roles of parents and professionals in many groups, whether subtly or openly, and experiment far more boldy with different ways of putting the partnership between parent, child, and professional into practice.

Family and School –
the Relationship Re-assessed

Daphne Johnson and Joyce Ransom

This account has given voice to the views and feelings of some parents about their children's secondary school years. The typicality of their views, and the factual accuracy of the family and school experiences on which their feelings are grounded should not be taken for granted. Some of the reservations which must be borne in mind about interview material and its interpretation by researchers are discussed elsewhere, but the insights which these research data give into what the idea of a home/school relationship may look like from outside the school cannot be ignored. In this chapter we shall reiterate what we believe to be the 'messages' of our research with parents – messages which were briefly heralded earlier. And we shall consider what may be the potential of a relationship between home and secondary school as new cohorts of children live out their school days in the 1980s.

The principal insights arising from the research have, we believe, been: that parents and teachers have different views on the benefits of a home/school relationship; that teachers' expectations derive from primary school models of parent/teacher contact involving the dependency of the child, and that teachers evaluate parental support for the secondary school by the extent to which they visit the school.

To take first the question of how the success of home/school cooperation is assessed by teachers, it was evident from the literature reviewed, and also from the research discussions with teachers, that the most accessible criterion is the readiness of parents to come to the school. Yet parents' accounts of the backing they gave to their children's secondary education included many home-based forms of support and interest which were unseen by teachers. And the reasons which prevented many parents from visiting the school were not solely those of apathy or conflicting priorities. Many parents positively took the view that it was better not to intervene in the developing relationship between the pupil and his secondary school. The child was learning to stand on his own two feet, and the teacher was bringing his professional skills to bear on the child's development. Unless something was going seriously wrong, the appearance of parents on the school scene might disrupt rather than help.

The teacher's definition of the cooperative parents as the visible accessible parent is linked with the assumption that cooperation between secondary school teacher and parent is potentially similar to cooperation between primary school teacher and parent. Essentially, the basis for cooperation is the perceived dependency of the child, and the need for adults around the child to work together for his benefit. Yet we have seen that, from the parents' point of view, many of the benefits which may be gained from personal acquaintance and contact with the child's primary school teacher cease to operate when the secondary school years are reached. Teaching has moved beyond the basic skills of reading, writing and counting, progress in which the lay adult can readily appraise, and feel able to assist. Secondary school subjects are perceived as specialized and constantly updated by new knowledge and teaching methods. If the child can cope with them, well and good. If not, no amount of contact between teacher and parent is likely to help.

Nor is the child's health any longer a non-controversial subject of contact between parent and secondary school teacher, as it may well have been during the primary school years. With the onset of puberty the adolescent's demands for physical privacy make him main custodian of his own health. If parents or teacher see cause for concern, they may try to persuade their son and daughter to accept advice or treatment, but to go over the adolescent's head and debate his physical problems and practices with another non-medical adult is rarely seen as appropriate. For the parent, the relevant professional is now the doctor rather than the teacher.

Sometimes, the contact between home and primary school has been particularly close. Parents have found a part to play in the day to day life of the school, or have gained personal enjoyment from the witnessing of children's display activities. Or, because of their child's initial reluctance to go to school, parents may have come alongside him at every opportunity, to give a sense of security and encouragement and share with his teacher in the allaying of his fears.

With the move to secondary school, parents often review their own behaviour and attitudes. This is the time to make a break, or to step up the phased withdrawal which has been taking place over the early school years. The perspective now is forward to employment and independence rather than backward to pre-school years and dependency. From now on, the role of the parent in relation to the schoolchild becomes a more self-effacing one, so far as the provision of security is concerned, but also perhaps a more coercive one in terms of making progress towards economic independence. Neither development is obviously served by being hand-in-glove with the teacher (although a new role may be perceived for the teacher to which we shall presently turn).

These themes about the parent's perspective on the school, together with the folk-dance of relationships within the family, which bring parents and child now closer together, now further apart, have seemed to us to underlie much of what parents had to say about the secondary school years.

What are the present forms of home/school contact actually achieving?

Analytic and descriptive literature about the partnership between family and school, written from the point of view of the educationalist, has in the past pursued three main themes: the question of welfare, the question of values, the question of accountability (Johnson, 1982). Practising teachers, busy with the year-to-year pursuit of their craft, tend to give emphasis to the definition of home/school relations which prevailed at the time they received their training. In the case of teachers contacted during our research, this was chiefly the theme of values – how familial attitudes might promote or hinder the educational progress of the child. This preoccupation found voice in an expressed desire to learn more about the home, to educate the parents about the benefits of secondary schooling, and to motivate parents to give more support in the schooling of their child. In the schools concerned, the actual opportunities for home/school contact were similarly ossified around the practice of the 1960s, taking the form of parents' evenings, PTA activity chiefly of the fund-raising kind, and publicly accessible functions at the school; and teachers' debates about the objectives of the home/school relationship made little attempt to evaluate what home/school contacts, as currently organized, were actually achieving.

No doubt there are many secondary schools where policy and practice in the development and maintenance of a relationship between home and school is constantly updated and adapted to take account of new ideas and test the benefit of new forms of contact. But we are equally sure that there are many secondary schools like the four we studied during the latter part of the 1970s where, after the upheaval of reorganization on comprehensive lines, the schools were, not unnaturally, concerned to build on routine and regularity, rather than pursue innovation or critically monitor the outcomes of present practice.

We have seen that in the schools studied, the most prominent opportunity for contact between home and school was at the parents' evening. These evenings, it seemed to us, fell far short of meeting the teachers' objective of getting to know the parents and the child's home background, and hence understand the child better. The public and bustling nature of the evenings was hardly conducive to the development of an acquaintanceship between teacher and parent, let alone to the developing appreciation by the teacher of the pattern and preoccupations of family life in the pupil's home, and how these impinged on his schooling.

We have already discussed at some length the many reasons why parents did not make frequent contact with their child's secondary school. But when they did make contact, what were they hoping for?

Broadly, it can be said that, compared with teachers, parents were expecting more from home/school contacts, but accepting less. They seemed to look to the parent/teacher relationship (a more personalized concept than that of a 'home/school' relationship) to enable mutual help in the handling of their particular child. It is in this sense that they expected more than the teachers did. They acknowledged that both parties had work to do for the child, for which they were variously equipped; and they anticipated that the teacher's professional knowledge of children could be applied to their own child in such a way as to offer expert enlightenment about his individual capacity and potential. As the child moved up the school, the question of what he would do after leaving school became increasingly central for parents. But all the way through parents were aware that their child was developing and changing, and they seemed to look to the teacher to give them clues about what they could anticipate from the child in the years ahead.

A pattern of home/school relations chiefly structured around parents' evening at the school did not match with parents' expectations any more than with teachers' objectives for the encounter. Nevertheless, the parents' evening seemed to some extent appropriate for what parents had in mind, and this may be why most parents essayed the encounter at least once. Ritually the occasion met the desire of parents to see the teacher face to face, to talk about their particular child. But aside from the fact that the meeting took place while other parents were nearby, with both teacher and parent under pressure to be brief out of consideration for the needs of others, the actual focus of discussion might not be what parents had in mind. Their orientation was towards the child's future, while the teacher proposed to review the successes and failures of the child's immediate past. This was what the teacher knew about and had prepared himself to discuss, in a marathon of retrospection about each of his pupils in a particular class over the past year. Small wonder that his comments of guidance for the child's future were usually confined to advice about remedying past error. 'He'll need to pull his socks up, and apply himself more, if he's going to get anywhere.' If there had been no noticeable past error, the teacher might have little to offer, from his exercise in retrospection. Hence the comment, 'Nothing wrong there' to the parents of an unobtrusive child, or the would-be complimentary but irritating comment, 'You're not the ones we want to see' to the parents of a successful child.

In such encounters, the parents' hopeful expectation of psychologically based and expert assessment of the implications and possibilities of their child's skills and behaviour dies the death, perhaps never to be resurrected. Some parents accept the teacher's definition of the purpose of the occasion, and conclude that if there is 'nothing wrong', there is no need to go to the parents' evening; others conclude that if there is something wrong they are not going to get any help during such a brief and crowded encounter. Not a few parents continue to make a ritual appearance every year, but recognize that it is for the most part a ritual event, at which they and the teachers can find little to say to one another, but can 'talk about the weather'.

The parents' objective of picking the teachers' brains about their particular child can however more readily be achieved if the parents make an approach to the school as individuals. Many schools, including those studied, make every attempt to respond to parents' requests for ad hoc interviews. But the very fact that such encounters are by definition not institutionalized and 'laid on' means that parental initiative is needed to bring them about.

Some parents can only bring themselves to approach the school when they have built up a head of steam about some grievance, and are determined to 'have things out'. Unaccustomed to taking the initiative in social or business encounters, a number of parents gave us vivid accounts of how they had surprised themselves by tackling a teacher in a blustering and aggressive fashion quite unlike their usual demeanour. Such an approach must have been counter-productive to the parents' real aim of sorting things out, and if a high-handed approach triggered an equally high-handed response, it is not surprising that in at least one case teacher and parent came to blows. In their calmer moments, however, diffident parents were well aware of the teachers' wide ranging tasks and responsibilities, and expressed themselves as reluctant to 'trouble' the school about matters which people with a more activist outlook on life would have taken up without delay.

What pattern of contacts would best meet the varying objectives of teachers and parents for a home/school relationship?

One answer might be a home-based rather than a school-based encounter, in fact a visit by the teacher to the pupil's home. If teachers really want to get to know the parents and appreciate the child's home circumstances what better way to do so than by visiting the home? And if parents want the teacher to give thoughtful consideration to their child's future, would not the teacher's attention be more appropriately focused in the child's home rather than in the school?

The objections to home visiting are manifold and well-rehearsed by teachers. To the outsider, some seem less well-founded than others. Given the stated aspirations of the schools we studied to foster home/school relations, it was perhaps surprising that home visiting by teachers was frowned on as a matter of policy. It was suggested that by calling on parents at home teachers would be exceeding their responsibilities, invading parents privacy, and probably laying themselves open to circumstances with which they were not equipped to cope. A senior teacher with wide experience of families with problems commented specifically that the young middle class female teacher would be clay in the hands of the manipulative parent, alert to gleaning personal advantage.

Whether teachers would in fact be exceeding their responsibilities in visiting the home seems open to debate. If parents and teachers are to some extent partners in child rearing, during the school-age years, with alternating responsibility for the child at different times of day, there seems no obvious reason why it is more appropriate for teacher and parent to consult together at the school rather than in the home.

At the school however the parent sees the teacher in his place of employment (although, for the most part, outside his 'working hours'). But the home is a private domain, and access to it must always be individually negotiated. The contention that home visits would constitute an invasion of privacy is therefore, perhaps, tenable in principle. But principles are not necessarily confirmed by practice. Parents we interviewed had, in a few cases, been called on by teachers, and without exception these occasions were mentioned appreciatively. Whether the teacher had called to bring homework for a sick child, to escort a child home from an outing, or (despite school policy) to discuss a problem of the child's attendance, behaviour or achievement, parents, in spontaneously mentioning these events, expressed their pleasure that the teacher had 'taken the trouble' to come round.

Another slender indication from our data of likely parental approval for home visits came from those parents who had recently immigrated to this country. Asian and West Indian parents alike had experience from their own childhood of teachers visiting the home, sometimes to lay down the law in no uncertain terms about how the child should mend his ways at school. They were surprised that teachers in Britain did not make similar approaches, and seemed to take for granted a closely shared evaluation by teacher and parent of the child's best interests.

Although only a few parents had actually been visited by teachers, some few more had been contacted at home by some other emissary from the school, from an education welfare officer offering to arrange a meeting between the parent and the concerned senior teacher, to a representative from the parent/teachers association rounding up support for functions at the school. Diffident, retiring mothers (who in our experience greatly outnumber the scheming, manipulative mothers referred to by the senior teacher) were particularly grateful for the encouragement and moral support which such approaches offered. One mother had never been contacted in this way, but wished that she had. If someone were to get in touch with her about events at the school and offer to meet her on the corner so she did not have to walk into the meeting on her own, it would make all the difference, she felt.

The welcome given to researchers calling to conduct home interviews is also relevant here. Although it was stressed that researchers were not *from* the school, but calling with the school's agreement and approval, parents frequently imputed a liaison role to the researcher, looking to us to explain the school to them and them to the school.

There is, we suggest, no doubt that considerable scope exists for strengthening home/school understanding by making some arrangement for parents to be individually contacted, from time to time, in their homes. But does all this imply that teachers should make regular home visits?

In fact the most practical and fundamental objection to such a proposal has not yet been raised, and was not put forward by teachers collaborating in the research. No teacher roundly stated that to undertake home visits as a matter of regular practice would be far too much work for teachers to undertake. The school policy of discouraging home visits perhaps freed teachers from the necessity of articulating this objection, but it is an entirely valid one. The thousand or so pupils in a comprehensive school come up from perhaps 800 homes. The 80 teachers who make up the staff of such a school might, without too much difficulty, visit ten homes each in the course of a year. But not all the 80 members of staff would be appropriate callers, if the purpose was to discuss with parents their particular child. Some specialist teachers know only a restricted group of children who take their subject. Other teachers have wide-ranging administrative responsibilities, but little classroom contact with pupils, while yet others have overall pastoral and disciplinary responsibilities for a sizeable section of the pupil population, but close acquaintance with only a few children, exceptional in some way or another.

Moreover, even if teachers did each undertake to visit a number of pupils' homes, this could not render parents' evenings superfluous, since on the latter occasions parents can speak, however briefly and superficially, to a number of teachers each of whom has some intermittent contact with their child. So the teachers, in undertaking home visits, would be taking on an additional task rather than replacing the evenings spent talking to parents at the school with time spent in pupils' homes.

This brief exercise in head counting does however indicate that if schools were to have a policy of arranging for some teachers to make occasional home visits, perhaps twice in the pupil's school life, this might not be quite so impossible to carry out in practice as would at first sight appear. Some schools do have such a policy, and however rare the visits they do obviate the continuing anonymity of parents. In the schools we studied there were parents who, although they had four or five children attending the school over a period of ten or twelve years, were as unknown to the teachers as the parents of any first born to attend the school.

This book is not an account of research on the scientific model, where a high degree of objectivity and detachment is incumbent on the researcher. Within the constraints of time and our own capacity for understanding, our aim was to enter as fully as possible into the eye-view of those researched. In an earlier work (Johnson *et al.*, 1980) we have described and reflected on the teacher's eye view of the comprehensive school and its external relations with other groups and institutions involved with the secondary school child. In this book we have adopted the perspective of the parent, and discussed the schools and their children's secondary school years from the parents' point of view. In conclusion, we sum up by giving our own views on the potential for an appropriate relationship between home and secondary school, in the light of our research as a whole.

It seems to us that both teachers and parents are to some degree mesmerized by the conventional wisdom and rhetoric of the campaign for closer relations between home and school which has been uncritically espoused for the past 20 years.

Even so, parents are perhaps more realistic than teachers in what they look for from the relationship between home and school.

Parents recognize that such a relationship may have to meet different needs at different times during their relationship with the school, because the child is the only reason for home and school to be involved together. As the child changes so the needs which a home/school relationship might meet will change. Teachers, on the other hand, can theorize about and make administrative arrangements for home/school contacts without having particular children in mind. Understandably, they sometimes see 'parents' as a *body* of people, a client group, rather than the mothers and fathers of Tom, Dick and Harriet.

But although we consider parents' ideas about the home/school relationship to be more flexible and down to earth than those of teachers, we concede that many parents are unrealistic in what they expect to get from talking with teachers about their child. Whatever the circumstances of the parent/teacher encounter, whether at crowded parents' evening or during a visit to the home, the teacher cannot offer a psychological assessment of each child's emotional, intellectual and vocational capacity. What the teachers can fruitfully tell the parents, however, is 'this is how your child gets on in the institutional context of the school'. This is valuable information for parents to have, as a supplement to their own longer term knowledge of the child in the context of the family. Nevertheless, there may come a stage at which parents decide to do without that information, in recognition of the young person's growing autonomy and independence. When the school-leaver goes to work, he will have to learn to get on in the new environment without benefit of consultations between parents and employer as to his progress. For some young people the final years at secondary school provide a sheltered workshop for trying out the role of independent adult.

This developmental aspect of the secondary school years seems to be overlooked in the home/school literature, and indeed in the administrative arrangements made for parents to visit the school. Whatever arrangements are made for parent/teacher contacts at particular schools tend to be consistent throughout the secondary school years. These arrangements do not take account of the growing maturation of young people during their time at school.

The wisest parents, we contend, are those who are most sensitive to the phases the child is going through, in handling their own relationship with the school. The child is in any case an unheralded third party to the parent/teacher encounter in that, with very few exceptions, parents subsequently tell the child what has been said. Increasingly, as the child gets older, the relationship is appropriately a three-way one in which the child must figure. Eventually the pupil himself becomes unequivocally the teacher's client. The parent, still the legal guardian, must still be called upon for specific authorization and confirmation of plans agreed between teacher and pupil. But parents are no longer part and parcel of the school's dealings with the child, as they were in earlier years.

Adolescents are frequently ambivalent in their attitude to parental support, and the young person's progress towards autonomy is rarely smooth and continuous. But parents, rather than teachers, can best appraise what their child's needs are for parental participation in his school affairs. Teachers who comment 'I never see the parents' seem to be awarding a black mark to the family as a whole. Yet the parents may be making a sensitive assessment of what is an appropriate amount of contact for them to have with the school at a particular stage in their child's school life. Our advocacy here is for the child, and his right to influence and modify the amount of contact between home and secondary school. But even the most dedicated of parents and teachers cannot always be child-centered in their activities. They may want to get something out of parent/teacher encounters for themselves. What is the viability for a relationship of general acquaintance and/or friendship between parent and teacher? Many PTA activities are predicated on the assumption that parents and teachers can do and enjoy each others company. Is this assumption borne out in practice?

A study such as our own, which focuses on the role of the adult (whether parent or teacher) in relation to the child, necessarily underplays the propensities and the self-interest of the adult as an individual. Yet parents, and teachers too, are people, with their own sensitivities. Role-playing cannot fill the bill for an encounter between parents and teacher on an ostensibly social occasion such as a cheese and wine evening. In the absence of their child, it is unnatural for adults to take the role of 'parents' in conversation with other adults, the teachers. Yet it may not be easy for either parents or teachers to muster the social skills necessary for more general conversation with comparative strangers. It is easier for both parents and teachers to get along together as equals when there is a task to be shared, such as running a stall, or building a swimming pool.

Whether or not particular parents and teachers actually get on together socially is more or less fortuitous. Some of the parents interviewed were unequivocal in their comment that social events involving teachers had no attraction for them. But in recognizing the right of parents to say that teachers are not the type of people they feel at home with, one must also recognize the teachers' right to admit the same about the parents of their pupils. More than any others, arrangements for this social aspect of parent/teacher contact must leave room for individuality of need and approach, so that possibilities for parent/teacher camaraderie are neither ruled out nor rigidly institutionalized.

One further aspect of the scope available to parents in their relations with the secondary school remains to be discussed. This is the question of whether parents, as parents, can play a useful part in the government of schools.* At the time of writing this is a matter of live debate, and considerable further research is needed to establish both the parameters and the potential of the parent/governor role.

We have already indicated that our research did not encourage us to see a viable role for parents as representatives of other parents. Two of the parents interviewed already were members of the governing board of the schools their children attended. They found the work rewarding in its opportunities for the expression of their personal and politically affiliated opinions, but the extent to which they could confidently represent the views of other parents seemed in doubt. And those parents who had no experience of participatory democracy, but discussed the role of parent/governor in the abstract, seemed dubious that parents as a body had sufficient in common to authorize specific parents to speak on their behalf.

The 1980 Education Act has however now provided for each school, whether primary or secondary, to have its own governing body, which is to include two parents of pupils at the school. In addition, the act envisages a greater degree of choice by families in which schools their children attend, and the publication of information which will enable that choice to be made from a position of some knowledge about the school's record in recent years.

* This topic, and a wider set of issues related to the government of education are the subject of research by Johnson and other members of the Educational Studies Unit, Dept. of Government, Brunel University. (*School Governing Bodies* Project, 1980–3.)

As we write, the date at which the sections of the act providing for the election of parent (and teacher) governors will be brought into effect for all schools has not yet been announced. The first pupils to be subject to the new admissions procedures will be the cohort of 1982.

Onlookers to social life sometimes claim to perceive a 'new generation' of young people, who, for better or worse, differ in their characteristics, beliefs and behaviour from those who have gone before. It may be that a new generation of parents will be identifiable, who assume and exercise the more active and critical role in relation to their children's schools which the 1980 act envisages for them. Taking a longer view, however, the dictum that 'the more things change, the more they are the same' seems a convincing one. Opportunities for school government and critical consumerism during the secondary school years will, we predict, be grasped by some parents but will elude the detached majority, whose ideas about relating to the school take little account of educationalists' interpretations and reinterpretations of what the partnership between school and home might be. Yet these parents, like many of those we interviewed, will have aspirations for their children's secondary schooling, and hopes about their children's personal development and achievements. They will try to impart these aspirations and hopes to the child himself, and leave it to him, as part of his growing up, to do what he can to come to acceptable and effective terms with his school.

Cannot the secondary schools drop their preoccupation with 'the home', cease to lament the parents they do not see and concentrate on working effectively with the young people they do see? Such a relationship would leave the family where they want to be, in the background, and establish a more realistic partnership between secondary school pupil and school.

Involving Parents from Minority Groups

Barbara Tizard, Jo Mortimore and Bebb Burchell

Many teachers find it very difficult to involve parents from minority groups in their children's school education and in the general life of the school. Yet such involvement is essential if schools are to educate all children for a multi-cultural society, profit from the diversity of cultures among the children and parents, and provide equal oportunity for all children.

It will be apparent that much of what we say in this applies to all parents, and all schools. However, there are specific factors which tend to prevent teachers and parents from minority groups developing closer relationships. And in many schools, where the 'minority group' in fact constitutes the majority, the need for parent involvement is particularly pressing.

Some teachers, seeing the poor response of minority group parents to overtures from the school, conclude that the parents are not interested in their children's education. Others argue sympathetically that the parents are so burdened by social problems, poverty, poor housing, long hours of work, and so forth, that it is unreasonable to expect them to become involved.

There is, however, much evidence which suggests that the opposite is the case. For many parents the wish to obtain a good education for their children was a major factor in their decision to emigrate. In general, truancy rates are lower, and the proportion of children staying on at school after 16 higher, among minority group children, and their parents tend to have high aspirations for them. The establishment of supplementary or 'Saturday' schools within minority communities, which provide not only mother tongue teaching, religious knowledge, cultural and traditional activities, but also in many cases supplementary teaching in literacy and numeracy, suggests dissatisfaction with state schooling, and real concern for and interest in their children's education.

Problems of teachers and parents in multi-cultural schools

If the interest is there, why is it difficult for teachers to involve and work with minority group parents? There is no simple answer to this question, not least because of the diversity among minority groups. With some parents, for instance the Spanish and Italian, the main difficulty may be the lack of a shared language; with others, for instance Pakistanis and Chinese, there may be not only language obstacles, but others arising from communicating with people whose cultures are very different and distinct. Communication with West Indian parents is not usually hindered by language differences, nor by the existence of an obviously distinct culture. Instead a major barrier, present also with Asian groups, may be fear and suspicion, bred by racist experiences in our society. With all these groups there are also likely to be cultural differences in the widest sense – in child rearing practices, and in attitudes to education and schools – which contribute to the difficulty of understanding and communicating.

The most easily identified of these obstacles, which we will return to later, is the 'language barrier' – it is hard for teacher and parent to communicate without a common language. But more subtle difficulties arise from cultural differences which affect parent-school relationships. Minority group parents' expectations of the school are frequently at variance with school practice. Parents tend to expect a formal relationship between teacher and child, when the teacher offers an informal one. They expect that their children will be made to sit still, and address the staff politely, and that serious punishment will follow lapses in discipline. They are also accustomed to regard schooling as a matter to be left to the teacher, and puzzled by requests to work in the school. On the other hand, in their country of origin the teacher was likely to be no stranger to them, but someone who lived within their community and with whom they were in daily contact outside the school. The British situation, in which parents are expected to visit and even spend time in the school, but the teacher tends to hurry away from the neighbourhood as soon as school finishes, is unfamiliar to many minority groups.

Despite their inclination to leave schooling to teachers, minority parents are usually puzzled and often antagonized by the 'learning through play' methods of British nursery and infant classes. For example, when we asked the parents in our project if they knew why certain play materials were provided in nursery schools, we found that the majority of Asian and West Indian parents had either no idea, or had developed their own explanations much at variance with the teachers – for example: 'Water is provided so that children will lose their fear of water,' 'Sand is provided to remind the children about the seaside, which English people are so fond of.' In some minority groups a high value is placed on children looking clean and tidy, and parents' hearts do not warm at the sight of their children wet from water play or covered with paint. West Indian parents often particularly object to the provision of sand, because of the difficulty of brushing it out of tightly curled or plaited hair.

Asian parents are often disappointed and bemused by the apparent absence of systematic English language teaching in most nursery schools. In our project, many Asian parents said that they had sent their children to school to learn English. Not unreasonably they did not all accept the teachers' argument that their children would learn English in the course of normal nursery activities, particularly when the majority of children in the class were non-English speaking.

Not only the teaching methods, but the teaching aims are incomprehensible to many parents. They expect their children to progress as rapidly as possible with reading and writing, at a time when the teachers are intent on developing creativity, imagination, and the provision of varied perceptual language and motor experiences. Attempts by teachers to explain their aims and methods tend to leave these parents unconvinced. Everything in their own experience and culture leads them to believe that their child's future success depends on his acquiring habits of hard work, and on diligent attention to formal skills.

Other difficulties may be caused by schools having inadequate, incomplete or incorrect basic information about children, their families and their lives. Names are sometimes misspelt or changed, teachers may not know, or may be misinformed about what language the parents speak, what language is spoken at home to the child, where the parents come from, or what religious beliefs they hold. Additional information about the cultural backgrounds of the children may not be collected or assembled in a very useful way by the school – for instance books about minority cultures are often not available for teachers in the staffroom, and the dates, names, and meanings of religious festivals are not always known. While complaining that minority group parents do not come to the school, very few teachers visit them at home, spend time in the neighbourhood, for instance in the local shops and cafes, or visit the temples, churches, or social centres which play an important part in the lives of the families.

If to this is added the mono-cultural, ethnocentric character of most British schools, the disregard for and tendency to devalue other cultures (in respect of choice of books, pictures, stories, songs, toys, interior decoration, food, clothing and festivities), it is hardly surprising that many minority group parents will feel excluded, unacceptable, puzzled and even hostile towards their children's schools.

Staff-parent relationships and sensitivity to racial issues

At this point it is necessary to raise the question of whether one component of minority group parents' reluctance to take part in the life of the school is a suspicion that teachers are racially prejudiced. Very few teachers would admit to such prejudice, and indeed most would regard racist sentiments as morally wrong. But, despite this, teachers like the rest of society may display an insensitivity to the point of view of minority groups which can cause deep resentment. One example of this is the common use of the term 'coloured', with the implication that people of the most varied language, culture, and indeed, colour, can be grouped together by virtue of the fact that their skins are not 'white'.

Teachers may also be insensitive to the way in which minority groups are depicted in the school's story and textbooks. Because most of us have grown up with books and comics in which the 'white man' is portrayed as civilized and noble, the 'black man' as savage, primitive or comical, we tend not to think about the effects of these portrayals on black children's sense of identity. But West Indian and African parents do not view Little Black Sambo with affection. They are quick to notice if black people are depicted in the schools' books and pictorial material as semi-clothed savages living in huts, if people in Third World countries are generally depicted as in need of charity – the 'Oxfam image' – or if their children are taught that America and Africa were 'discovered' by Europeans.

Infants, and even nursery children, are frequently called 'wog' or 'paki' by white children, especially in the playground. Teachers often believe that this name-calling should not be taken too seriously, since it seems to them no more or less insulting than such taunts as 'four-eyes' or 'midget'. There is, however, good research evidence that by or even before the age of five both black and white children are well aware of the derogatory attitudes to minority groups held by much of society. To be called a 'wog' is not therefore simply perceived by the child and his parents as personally offensive, but reinforces their awareness of the hostility of the wider society towards their own group. For this reason staff need to have a clear policy, known to children and parents, for dealing with racist insults.

Some teachers who would not countenance racist insults claim that they are 'colour-blind', and treat all children in the same way. This policy, albeit carried out with a real concern to be fair, may in fact be damaging to black children, and appear to parents to be racist. This is because, while stating that 'all children are the same', the school in fact operates as though all children were white. The children, and their parents, see no recognition of themselves in the life of the school. To a large extent of course, this is even more true of society at large – black children in this country have to grow up in the knowledge that the cult-figures of childhood, whether spacemen, TV stars, or fairy-tale characters, are almost invariably white. Schools, however, have the opportunity to point out to both white and black children the contributions that have been made by many different cultures: they are in a position to develop a positive policy aimed to help all children towards an appreciation of, and respect for, ethnic, cultural and linguistic diversity.

A somewhat different problem is the tendency of some teachers to allow attitudes to individual children and their parents to be influenced by stereotypes about the characteristics of minority groups. Thus any negative features of the child may be 'explained' in terms of his own or his parents' group membership – for example, some teachers almost expect children of West Indian origin to be aggressive and to be low achievers. In consequence, factors in the school situation which might have a bearing on the child's poor behaviour or low achievements are overlooked. Or little effort may be made to discuss educational issues with Asian parents because they are believed to be illiterate, and uneducated, when a closer knowledge of the family might reveal their intense concern with their children's education. Any multi-cultural school which sets out to discuss these issues with its parents is likely to find the parents very aware of racial stereotypes, and anxious lest these stereotypes should prejudice the treatment of their children.

Ways of working with minority group parents

Aims

- To facilitate the contribution of minority group parents to the life of the school by adopting a multi-cultural approach

- To enable minority group parents to contribute their knowledge of their children and their culture to the teachers

- To enable teachers to consult minority group parents about their children's education, and discuss educational issues with them

- To help teachers to explain their aims and methods to minority group parents

In the course of our project we made some steps towards involving minority group parents in the life of the school. In one school, where two thirds of the parents were from minority groups, 80 per cent attended film shows about their children's activities at school. This attendance rate was achieved by repeating the films at hours to suit shift and night workers, giving parents information in their own language, and inviting them to bring other relatives. In the same class, mothers from a number of different cultures made illustrated books for the class, in their own languages, relating tales from their own childhood. An essential prerequisite for this contribution was probably the fact that the research officer concerned visited each family at home, explained how they could contribute and why it would be of value to the child and the school, brought the necessary materials, and discussed in detail with the family how to make the books and what might go in them. International social evenings also took place in this school.

In another project school, serving a largely Sikh population, individual appointments were made for mothers to visit the school and watch the class in action; mothers were invited to the school to make Asian sweets with the children; parents helped the school to celebrate Guru Nanak's birthday, and evening meetings at which the head explained the schools' aims and methods were attended by about 50 per cent of the families.

These steps were useful beginnings, but they often failed to achieve the aims for which they were set up. An occasional international social evening does not necessarily increase goodwill – it may instead confirm existing attitudes that the English are stand-offish, the West Indians noisy, that Asians eat 'peculiar' food, and so on. Nor is it enough to increase the numbers of parents going to school meetings, unless at such meetings parents freely put forward their own points of view. It cannot be assumed that because parents have spent time in the classroom they have understood or sympathized with what the teacher was trying to achieve. When we asked Asian mothers whether seeing what went on in school had helped them to understand the school better, 60 per cent of them said no. This was not because of the mothers' inability to understand, but because their attitudes to children, play, schools and education were very different from those of the staff. Unless teachers make determined efforts to understand these attitudes, consult the parents, and listen to their points of view, a parent involvement programme can leave teachers feeling very frustrated. It may seem to them that they have made considerable efforts, and that these have not been adequately appreciated by the parents.

This situation, like all those we have outlined above, is not peculiar to schools in multi-racial areas. It is also the case that many white indigenous working class parents are puzzled by 'learning through play' methods, find the concept of parent involvement unfamiliar, would like their children to make an early start with the 'three Rs', and find the culture of the school alien. (Compare the books, pictures, decoration and furnishings of a modern primary school with those chosen by working class parents in the locality for their own homes.) Moreover, just as teachers may have false and devaluing stereotypes about ethnic minority cultures, they may also believe that white working class parents have little to offer to the school.

Our interviews suggested, however, that these problems existed in a much more acute form in multi-cultural schools and that it was correspondingly more difficult to achieve any real teacher-parent partnership in these schools. For minority group parents to have the

opportunity for full involvement – that is, to contribute their knowledge of their children and their cultures – and to be consulted about
the way they are educated, radical changes would be necessary. The
school would have to make exceptional efforts to respect, and to be
seen to respect and understand, the cultures of the families it
served. In effect, what would be required would be a bi-cultural or
multi-cultural school.

The contribution of parents in multi-cultural schools

There is an obvious and readily accessible source of help for schools
who want to respond to the needs and reflect the culture of minority
groups. In-service courses, special advisors and advanced diplomas
for teachers are important but the children's parents and the local
community leaders can also advise the staff about educational aims,
religion, customs, festivals, stories, music, food, games and decorative
materials. The undoubted fact that at present minority group
parents tend to stay away from schools reflects, in our opinion, the
parents' belief that they cannot contribute to their children's education, and also that they are often unsympathetic to the school's
approach. But how many heads and class teachers have asked these
parents for help in contributing to the curriculum and in making the
school truly multi-cultural, or have consulted with them about
whether the school is meeting the needs of their children?

Our experience in one multi-cultural nursery class was that, when
personal relationships had been established with the parents by
visiting them in their homes and seeking their views on education,
they enjoyed contributing their own experience to the classroom by
writing or telling stories about their childhood, and the teacher was
delighted with the result. But in order to forge real links with the
community, it seems likely that teachers must make the first move,
by going out of their school – visiting the children at home, using the
local shops and cafés. They could ask for invitations to visit the
families' churches, temples, and social centres, and discuss the
possibility of holding school meetings and exhibitions in them.
Teachers are often understandably nervous about establishing links
with what seems to them a very alien culture, and sometimes find
the initial steps easier with the support of one or two colleagues. (A
similar nervousness is often felt by parents when visiting schools.)

It is, perhaps, important to point out that home visiting, like any work with parents, does not necessarily result in improved parent-teacher relationships – its effectiveness depends on how and why it's done. There is a danger that home visiting by teachers can become a form of social work from which the teacher returns mainly impressed by the absence of toys and books in the home, or the evident difficulties in the lives of the parents. Such visits would not lead to an increased contribution by minority groups to the school, or to an increased respect by the teachers for the families, and could even be counter-productive. For this reason home visiting, in our opinion, should be arranged with specific educational aims – to discuss a child's progress at school, and to seek information and help from the parents. It should also be seen as one among many ways in which teachers move out towards the community.

As well as trying to get to know individual families, there is much to be said for an additional way of establishing links with parents, in which the parent body is approached as a group. This is certainly feasible in a school with a substantial number of children from one minority group. Representatives of minority group parents, staff and other members of the community can form a group to look at all aspects of school life, to help promote a multi-cultural approach, and to help the school explain its aims to the minority groups and respond to their needs. If the group concerned is non-English speaking, it can undertake other functions – for instance arrange for interpreters and translators, and classes for parents to learn English and for teachers to learn the minority languages.

Areas of conflict between staff and parents

Open discussion between staff and parents is likely to reveal the kind of disagreements on aims and methods which have already been outlined. Two other areas of potential disagreement between teachers and minority group parents are the role of punishment in the school, and the amount of emphasis that should be given to formal teaching.

We do not underestimate the difficulty of explaining modern teaching aims and methods to parents from a very different culture. Nor do we suggest that teachers should – or indeed would – accede to parental wishes which were totally at variance with their own approach. But unless schools are prepared to discuss such issues with parents, explain their approach, listen to the parents' points of view, and go some way towards meeting them, they cannot hope to enlist parental support for their work. Teachers might think it worth considering whether, because of their intimate knowledge of a child and his environment, his parents' opinions about his educational needs should be taken seriously. For instance, if parents are worried because 'modern maths' seems to have superceded mental arithmetic, a teacher might consider supplementing her mathematics curriculum with mental arithmetic, or showing parents how they can help their child to learn it at home.

The objections of parents to sand and water play may disappear if they receive an adequate explanation of why the teacher considers the materials important, especially if the children are provided with suitable protective clothing – like hats for sand play, and waterproof overalls for water play. Alternatively, the teacher may decide in the face of entrenched parental objections that sand and water play are not educational essentials. If parents are concerned that their children are not being taught English systematically at school, the staff may have a fresh look at what is known about second language teaching for young children, and the comparative effectiveness of different methods.

It is not, of course, likely that one meeting or discussion with parents will be very effective in improving mutual understanding. This is only likely to develop over a period of time, in which teachers have shown in a variety of ways that they respect the parents' culture, want to listen to their opinions, and are willing to take their points of view seriously.

Mother tongue teaching

A difficult and controversial question is that of whether the school should undertake mother tongue teaching, both oral and written, for children from other cultures. Many minority group communities organize 'supplementary' schools for this purpose, and they may well prefer to undertake the teaching of their own language and culture themselves. But it could be argued that a multi-cultural school, particularly in an area with a high concentration of families from one culture, should be bilingual, or at least advance all the children's education in both cultures. Such a policy would, of course, require the employment of a substantial proportion of minority group staff. It would certainly seem appropriate to raise these issues with parent groups, since they are ones of deep concern to many minority group parents.

It would also seem important to discuss with parents whose native language is not English the question of the best language to use with their children at home. We have found that some parents, anxious to help their children's education, speak to them only in English, even when their own command of the language is poor. Teachers need to be aware of this practice, and its possible disadvantages for the children, and discuss the question with parents.

The language barrier

For many teachers in multi-cultural areas the most easily identified problem in working with parents is 'the language barrier'. This problem could be considerably eased by a local authority's determination to employ members of the minority groups on the staff, or to employ interpreters for schools, or to assist any English staff who wanted to learn the minority languages. In a school where the children spoke many languages, their situation would be eased if there were at least one teacher who had some knowledge of each minority language. At a much less ambitious level, we have found that parents are very appreciative if a teacher makes the effort to learn to greet them in their own language.

Where funds are not available for interpreters, and minority group members are not on the staff, we have a number of suggestions to offer which involve making the best use of the resources that are at present available.

Interpreters and translators

Whether a school has only one parent with whom communication in English presents problems, or whether it has 90 per cent, an interpreter should be available to both parents and staff. Often some member of the family, even an older child, can play this role;

it is not a good idea to rely on other parents to interpret (though it may occasionally be necessary) because of considerations of confidentiality. Local minority groups may be able to supply interpreters, if the school has made efforts to be involved in these groups. Resentment can easily be built up when schools appear to be restricting their contact with minority group agencies and organizations to the occasions when they require a service from them. On the other hand, in an atmosphere of mutual respect and goodwill, much help may be forthcoming.

For translations of prospectuses, newsletters and notices similar sources of help, including parents, can be used. Parents will be especially helpful in examining materials for appropriate content relevant to their cultures, checking that dates do not clash with a religious celebration, and that the information given covers points which parents are likely to be concerned about.

Holding meetings for parents who do not speak English presents schools with a rather greater problem than finding interpreters for day-to-day individual conversation. The obvious approach is to have translators available at meetings to translate sequentially what is said. But this is inevitably obtrusive, difficult, and time consuming, and prevents the natural flow of discussion. In schools where at least two languages are spoken by large numbers of parents one solution is to provide the same meeting separately for the different language groups. This is at first sight a divisive practice, but if the main priority is for communication to take place between staff and parents then it may be acceptable as the only solution. Opportunities for all parents in the school to get together may be more appropriately provided by less verbal occasions – such as socials, outings, picnics or concerts.

Another approach is to suggest that parents organize for themselves bilingual representatives who can mediate between staff and their language group. Parents can then approach the school through the bilingual committee, suggesting topics for meetings and arranging interpreters. The committees can meet as a group to discuss and report to all other parents about meetings held, discussions, decisions and so forth.

Commentaries for films can obviously be made in the required languages and shown at different times to parents speaking different languages. Reports can be kept of discussions, and a meeting held for all parents when questions and answers could be given, using interpreters.

Partnership between Home and School

Peter and Helle Mittler

It is now widely accepted that the education of handicapped children must be seen in a broader context than that of the school alone. Since the influence of the home is clearly fundamental, partnership with parents should be considered a central component of special education.

The range of relationships between parents and teachers is very wide. It can extend, at one extreme, from merely formal communication about dates of terms to open access to all reports and records on their child, to participation of parents in classroom teaching, discussions of school policy and curriculum and selection of teachers as members of school governing boards.

Many schools are now re-examining their practice, just as many parents are pressing for a greater degree of participation in the development of plans and programmes for their own child. In particular, parents who have had positive and successful experiences of collaboration with professionals before their child went to school represents a new generation of articulate, well-informed and highly skilled parents. Once their child moves into full-time special education, they tend to ask questions about the school's policy for partnership with parents. 'How are we going to work together in assessing my child's strengths, weaknesses and needs? When do we discuss selection of priorities for teaching and what kind of communication link are we going to set up to keep each other informed?'

Our Manchester survey explores home-school links at three stages – when the child first enters the school, while he is at school and at the time of preparation for leaving. It also invites suggestions from headteachers on ways in which parents can and do contribute to the life of the school and asks for examples of successful and less successful attempts to involve parents. As a result of this exercise, some headteachers approached parents about their own experience of collaboration with schools and invited suggestions from them on how home-school links could be improved. One new headteacher designed her own 36 item questionnaire and personally visited all the families of children in her school and is modifying school practice in the light of parents' responses (Boucher, 1981).

Among the questions that might be considered by each school, the following may be useful starting points.

A. Entry into school

Home Visits:

Does a member of the school staff visit the family at home before the child starts school?
Such visits enable the head or class teacher to get to know the whole family not just the mother, and to see the child in his own home setting. They can help teachers to learn something of the child's behaviour at home, and to begin to build up a picture of his strengths and needs, as well as the priorities of the family. An initial visit can also help to identify the best ways for the child to start school – e.g. by periods of part-time attendance, the extent to which a parent could stay with the child, any special difficulties about eating, toileting, medical problems and transport.

One of the aims of a home visit is to begin to discuss with the family ways in which home and school can establish a working relationship. This will obviously take time to negotiate and will depend on the resources and priorities of the family, but visits to the home can begin to lay the foundations for a realistic discussion of what will and will not be possible. This is also a good moment to make it clear that parents are welcome in school.

Assessment

The 1981 Education Act formalizes the rights of parents to be involved in decisions concerning their child's special educational needs. These rights are summarized in DES Circular 8/81, but further regulations and guidance are promised. Amongst the changes in the new Act are the following:

(i)   LEAs must notify parents of their intention to make an assessment and provide information about assessment and procedures. They must also notify parents of the results of the assessment. Parents must be given the name of an officer from whom they can obtain further information and be informed about their rights of appeal to the Secretary of State.

(ii)   Parents must receive a draft of the LEAs statement of special educational needs and have a right to an interview with an officer of the LEA and with anyone who gave advice to the LEA about their child's statement of needs. The LEA must consider any representations made by parents.

(iii)   Parents have the right of appeal to a local appeal committee against special educational provision specified in a statement. Although the appeal committee can refer an appeal for the reconsideration of the LEA, they do not have the power to overrule the LEA. In this case, or if the appeal committee agree with LEAs judgement, the parents can appeal to the Secretary of State if they are not satisfied with the LEAs decision. He has the power to confirm or amend the statement or to direct the LEA to cease to maintain the statement.

(iv)   LEAs have a duty to comply with requests for assessments made by parents, 'unless it is in their opinion unreasonable'. Parents may appeal to the Secretary of State if they feel aggrieved by the LEAs decision not to make an assessment.

(v)   Parents are required to present the child for any examination felt necessary to enable the Secretary of State to determine issues arising from the provisions of the Act.

Once the child is in school, collaboration between parents and teachers is a matter of good practice rather than legislation. The question can therefore be put as follows:

How are parents involved in the assessment of their child's skills, abilities and needs?
The answer to this question will depend on the kind of assessment procedures used in the school. Some schools use published

developmental checklists, others have developed their own checklists. In either case, it is worth considering ways in which parents can provide information based on their own expert knowledge of the child's behaviour. Some schools go through a checklist with the parents item by item, others leave a copy of the list with the parents and ask them to fill it in (perhaps each parent doing so independently); others leave the parents to study the questionnaire and then go over it with them either at home or at school.

Discrepancies between the assessment of parents and teachers can form a productive starting point for discussion, since it is not uncommon for certain behaviours to be more in evidence in one setting than another; for example, a child may put on his own shoes at home and not at school, or vice versa. Several studies have shown that parents' and teachers' assessments correspond fairly closely when they use the same instruments. A number of checklists were originally developed for the use of parents but are now in fairly general use by professionals as well, e.g. the PIP Development Charts (Jeffree and McConkey, 1976) and Pathways to Independence checklist (Jeffree and Cheseldine, 1982). In addition to developmental checklists, teachers have developed a range of observation methods and records.

Do parents see records or have an opportunity to comment on the observations of teachers towards the end of the initial period of assessment and before their implications for further teaching are considered by the school?
Once the school has completed its initial assessment, perhaps sometime during the first term, parents should be given an opportunity to discuss the interim findings, to contribute their own observations and to comment on anything which they feel might give a misleading impression of their child's behaviour. Where there is genuine disagreement about some aspect of a child's behaviour, the parents' observations should be recorded and noted, with their knowledge.

Full involvement of parents in the initial process of observation and assessment and in the resulting formulation of the child's programme is of the first importance. Parents should have the opportunity to identify and discuss their priorities for the child and to share with school staff the methods that they have found helpful and unhelpful in their own experience of the child at home. This is also a good time to discuss ways in which teachers and parents are going to continue to communicate and to keep each other informed about the child's progress and further needs. It is this initial period that lays down the foundations for later collaboration and trust. It is only if parents know and understand what their child is learning and doing at school that they can support and work productively with teachers.

B.   During school years

Collaboration between parents and teachers can take a very wide variety of forms during the child's years in school. The nature and quality of collaboration will vary with the changing needs of the child, the parents and the teachers. Relationship between home and school must therefore be flexible and must be able to respond to changing circumstances and the different responses of different families. There is clearly no set formula for partnership.

The questions and suggestions that follow merely represent some examples of current practice. We are not suggesting that all of them should apply in every school and for all children. But we do suggest that each school should consciously think out its policies and practices in relation to the development of partnership with parents.

Access to school staff

Many headteachers say that 'parents are welcome in my school at any time'. What does this mean in practice?

Can they go straight to the child's teacher or are they expected to talk to the headteacher first?

What about access to other school staff? Are they clear about procedures for contacting staff? Should they telephone for an appointment at first? What facilities are there for parents while they are waiting to see a member of staff? Many parents find it difficult or even stressful to stand or sit about with nothing to do and this can discourage them from visiting the school.

School meetings

Most schools arrange meetings of parents for a wide variety of purposes. Nearly all parents can visit schools at set times to look at displays of childrens' work and attend Christmas plays but these are really open days rather than meetings called for specific purposes – e.g. to discuss children's work and progress, sometimes following the preparation of the school report.

Meetings are held to provide opportunities for parents to meet visiting specialists such as physiotherapists, speech therapists, psychologists or doctors, not only to talk about their child but also to learn more about the work of these specialists and how they relate to teachers. Some schools also hold meetings to discuss important educational issues, such as possible changes in the policy of the school, aspects of the curriculum, methods of teaching, changes in services or legislation, new developments in services for adolescents or adults.

In addition to meetings for parents as a whole, some schools make it possible for small groups of parents to meet either informally or for a particular purpose. For example, some schools have a special parents' 'den' where they can meet at any time, make hot drinks and simply chat, and where meetings can be held to discuss particular issues. The actual physical arrangements for parents to wait are important if parents are to feel both comfortable and welcome when they visit the school.

Review meetings

Many schools now hold regular meetings to review the progress of each child and some invite parents to attend either the whole or part of such a meeting. Such meetings can be particularly productive where schools have developed a detailed curriculum plan with recording systems which enable both teachers and parents to provide information on the child's progress in reaching specific goals.

Sharing success

Some teachers invite parents into school to see the child at various stages of a programme designed to teach a specific skill. The parent is involved in planning and, if possible, carries on some of the teaching at home. Emphasis on achievements rather than problems can provide a good foundation for partnership between parent, professional and child.

Transport to school

Questions concerned with how the child is to travel to school are clearly relevant to the quality of parent-teacher collaboration. Although the LEA generally provides a school bus or occasionally a taxi service, careful planning is needed to compensate for the greater distance between home and school and the diminished opportunities for direct contact between parents and teachers. The provision of school transport makes it difficult for parents to meet teachers and other parents who are bringing or fetching their children, as is the case in infant and junior schools. Even where a handicapped child is attending a unit in the same school as a non-handicapped brother or sister, they are generally not allowed to travel together on the same transport. Similarly, a parent cannot use school transport to visit the school; in any case he or she would have to make their own way back. Some parents also object to the use of special transport, as it sets the child apart from other children in the family and in the neighbourhood (Rheubottom, 1982).

The flexible use of school transport can help to overcome some of these problems; for example, bus escorts can provide a valuable link between home and school, provided this is consciously fostered by the headteacher rather than being left to chance or goodwill. They can also do valuable work with the children themselves and enliven what can often be a dull and exhausting journey.

Home-school notebooks

Many schools now use some form of notebook or diary which travels regularly between home and school. These may be sent daily, weekly or less regularly. According to Smith (1982) three main purposes can be identified for such notebooks:

(a)   for general information ('we have a student teacher in the class now, her name is X')

(b)   for more specific communications and instructions ('his calipers seem to be rubbing his leg, will you look at them in school today and see what you think')

(c)   for active collaboration on a joint teaching venture (e.g. discussions of specific steps reached on a particular programme, methods of teaching, record of achievement in reaching a particular step, change of plan, reward, etc.).

Some notebooks tend to be largely one-way communications from teacher to parent, others encourage parental comment on the opposite page. These can lead to a follow-up telephone call or visit if necessary.

Reports

The writing of school reports now seems to be much more common than it was some years ago, though no hard data is available on this subject. Reports can vary greatly in frequency, style, organization and information content, from a few brief comments organized along 'subject' lines like a conventional school report in an ordinary school, to highly specific accounts of the child's achievements in attaining goals outlined in an individual programme plan. School reports can be used as an integral part of a continuing dialogue between home and school; where regular home–school notebooks are used, a report can provide an opportunity to step back and review progress and reconsider priorities. Used in this way, a report is not merely a record of achievement but the starting point for a joint approach to the development of a further programme of collaboration.

Asking the parents

There are many ways in which schools can approach individual parents directly.

Most commonly, they may make a special point of discussing a particular problem presented by the child and working out ways in which they can jointly work towards a solution. This can be done by inviting the parents into the school, by a visit to the home or by a combination of the two.

Quite apart from questions concerned with an individual child, teachers may find it helpful to discuss a range of general issues with individual parents. These might concern questions of school policy, organization or curriculum, or a change which is under consideration but which has not yet been decided. Some schools have also taken the initiative in asking parents about their preferences for receiving reports, information from the school, social and informal meetings that would interest them, contacts with school and visiting staff and with other parents. Parents are more likely to feel involved in the work of the school as a whole if staff take them into their confidence about wider questions of policy.

It is also worth asking whether enough opportunities are available for parents to offer any special interests or skills to the school. Some schools wait for the initiative to be taken by the parents, others ask parents directly or make suggestions based on their own knowledge of parents' special interests. The range of possibilities among any group of parents must be very wide – it can include participating in extra-curricular activities, swimming, school visits or a particular skill or interest, such as cooking or carpentry.

Parent workshops

Many parent workshops have taken place in special schools during the last ten years and a number of descriptive reports have been published (e.g. Cunningham and Jeffree, 1971; Bevington, Gardner and Cocks, 1981; Gardner, 1982).

Schools are developing a variety of models and approaches to suit their own characteristics and to fit in with the needs and resources of parents. There is no single 'formula' but the essence of a workshop is that it should include a practical and experiential component in which teachers and parents share their knowledge and skills not only in planning but also in carrying out a programme of teaching with one or more children. In addition, workshops can create opportunities for parents to air a whole range of issues and concerns, to make social contacts and to listen to invited speakers. Even so, the workshop component per se is essentially practical and involves teachers and parents taking part in joint activities designed to help the child to learn new skills or to develop competencies and behaviours.

Cunningham and Jeffree (1975) single out a number of critical issues for discussion:

(i) The needs of parents in attending a workshop are primarily to be able to do something positive to help their child. They look to teachers and other professionals to help them help their child in their ordinary day-to-day interactions with the child. They want to make better use of the time they already spend with their child, rather than spending more time with him, and they are not necessarily receptive to the suggestion that time should be set aside for special one-to-one teaching sessions. But they do welcome suggestions for ways in which they can take advantage of opportunities as they occur casually during the course of their ordinary encounters with the child.

(ii) This implies that parent workshops should aim to help parents to learn principles and techniques which they can use in the future. A workshop may be concerned with the here-and-now of helping a parent to become proficient in teaching a child to use a spoon, put on a sweater or pay the milkman. But these efforts will be largely wasted if the parents are not helped to 'internalise a model' of teaching which they can then try to adapt to a range of other situations both now and in the future. This is one reason why small groups of parents can be such a productive feature of a workshop: parents are not only concerned with learning about approaches to the problems presented by their own child but take part in group discussions to help formulate approaches to the children of other parents in the group. Small group discussions can help parents to derive general principles and experimentally put them into practice in contributing their own suggestions to the problems facing other parents. The tutor or group leader clearly has a critical role in ensuring that the principles are well understood and are being applied relevantly and flexibly, rather than as a standard cook-book prescription . 'If the parents acquire these guiding principles and then set up their own teaching programmes, this not only increases the individuality of the teaching, but provides the parents with a permanent method of treatment in that they are no longer as dependent upon an instructor but might devise their own approaches' (Cunningham and Jeffree, 1975, p. 407).

(iii) The content, structure and organization of parent work-shops vary considerably but a number of features are common to many of the reports. Referring again to Cunningham and Jeffree (1971, 1975), we can note the following components:-

(a) Helping parents to become more skilled and systematic in observing, assessing and recording their child's skills and behaviours. To this end, they may be given a developmental chart and asked to fill it in over a period of a week or so. They may also be shown how to record observations on simple tick-charts. These skills can be demonstrated and then practised in a workshop session by showing a child on video-tape or by a role play session in which a parent pretends to be their own child while the rest of the group record or assess.

(b) Using assessments and observations of the child's behaviour to evolve an appropriate teaching objective which the child ought to be able to acquire over a period of one or two weeks.

This is one of the most difficult changes facing both teachers and parents. It calls for discussion on priorities about which teachers and parents are not necessarily in agreement. It requires careful analysis of the task to be taught so as to ensure that the teaching steps are small enough for the child to be successful and agreement reached on the teaching methods to be used to help the child to learn. Here again, rehearsal and role play can help to make the experience concrete and realistic.

(c) The importance of planning, organization and efficiency in the actual conduct of the workshops cannot be over-emphasized. In particular, course tutors need to meet regularly in order to discuss results and to prepare for the forthcoming workshop. They should also consciously work to fade tutorial support and gradually increase the work done by parents both in discussion and in working out teaching objectives for the children.

Although parent workshops can do much to enhance the confidence of parents in working with their child and can also be very helpful in bringing parents together in joint activities, it is not clear whether they lead to any marked changes in what parents do at home or in the achievements of the children.

This point was emphasized by Gardner (1982) in a recent paper summarizing experience of a range of parent workshops in Walsall. She found that parents were more likely to use the skills taught in the workshop if they were also visited at home between sessions so that they could practice their teaching skills under supervision. She also found that teaching at home lacked direction and consistency until the school had worked out a detailed curriculum for the school as a whole and an individual programme plan for each child. However, we would add that parents can also be involved in discussions about the development of curriculum both for the school as a whole and for their child.

Other types of small parent groups have different advantages. Many schools arrange a regular time for parents to meet over a cup of tea in an informal way. An informal atmosphere can help parents to feel comfortable enough to share both happy and difficult experiences with other parents and with professional staff. This can be mutually supportive and provide useful learning experiences of a less structured kind.

Residential schools

Where a child is attending a residential school, partnership between parents and school staff presents obvious difficulties. Despite the special challenges involved, there is scope for considerable progress.

The number of children and families involved is not inconsiderable. According to the most recent DES statistics relating to the year 1979 (GB. DES, 1981) around one-sixth of all pupils receiving special education in 1979 were in some form of residential school (not counting hospital schools). The majority of pupils in maintained and non-maintained residential schools were classified as ESN(M) (6165), followed by maladjusted (3951), and by either delicate or physically handicapped or both (3708). Comparable figures for independent schools are not available, though it is likely that many of the pupils with special educational needs would be classified as maladjusted.

The number of children in residential schools must be falling rapidly as a consequence of the financial problems facing local authorities. Many LEAs are either closing or reducing the numbers of children in residential schools for which they have a direct responsibility, or are no longer able to pay the fees of children attending schools run by other LEAs or by private or voluntary organizations.

The withdrawal of children from residential schools clearly poses special problems of relationships with parents, particularly where the LEA proposes to return the child to the parental home. If the staff of the residential school and of the placing LEA have worked closely with the parents throughout the child's stay in the school, the foundations for effecting a smooth return to the family home or to a substitute home may well have been laid. Where this has not happened, the upheaval resulting from the closure of a residential school can be deeply harmful both to the child and the family and can adversely affect the development of both.

The 1981 Education Act lays down that in future all non-maintained and independent special schools must publish information on their facilities and curriculum and make that information available both to the LEA and to the parents on request. The Act also stipulates that all schools must have satisfactory arrangements for the involvement of both parents and teachers in the running of the school. The Secretary of State has powers to insist that independent schools meet similar standards to those of maintained and non-maintained schools in respect of premises, qualifications of staff, education and care.

The range of residential schools, the type of children for whom they cater and their patterns of staffing is very wide, as is the nature of the formal and informal relationships between officers of the LEA placing the child and the staff of the school.

The simplest relationship is one in which an LEA itself administers one or more residential schools either in or near its own geographical boundaries, as is not uncommon in the case of some of the larger metropolitan authorities.

In this case, there should be clearly agreed procedures within the LEA and between its officers and the parents about how links between home and school are to be established and maintained. Clearly, the needs of families and children will vary widely, and will also change significantly over time, so that detailed guidelines would not be appropriate. But whether one LEA is involved, whether the placing LEA needs to relate to another LEA in which the residential school is situated, or to the staff of a non-maintained or independent school, the questions that need to be asked are essentially similar.

What then are these questions? We will list merely a few of the more obvious ones here, since most of the issues already discussed in relation to other special schools and classes apply in varying measure to residential schools also.

1. *How far do parents have the information on the range of possible schools at the time when the issue of boarding education is first raised?*

2. *Do all parents have an opportunity to visit possible schools? Who goes with them – a professional person responsible for the placement such as a social worker or educational psychologists or adviser?*

3. *How far are decisions on the choice of school in the hands of administrative staff?*
    In that case, what opportunities are there for parents to discuss choice of schools with them?

4. *When parents visit the school to discuss possible placement, do they meet the whole range of staff or only the headteacher?*

5. *If the child's admission to school is likely, does a member of the school staff visit the family at home? If so, do they also liaise with staff of the child's previous school and the agencies responsible for the placement – e.g. school psychological or child guidance service?*

6. *Once the child is in school, what kind of communication links are envisaged between home and school?*

7. *Is there a step-by-step plan either to return the child to his family or to make alternative arrangements (e.g. fostering, hostel)? In the latter case, how are the parents informed of a decision to seek alternative forms of care?*

8. *While the child is in residential school, who works with the family – is it local staff (e.g. school psychological, child guidance, social services) or staff of the residential school or both?*

9. *How do those responsible for the placement decision monitor the child's progress and the appropriateness of their recommendations and choice of school?*

10. *How does the placing and paying LEA satisfy itself that the school is meeting the needs of the children they have placed there? Do they regularly visit the school or do they ask an officer of the LEA in which the school is situated to do so? Who visits – psychologists, teacher, social worker, administrator?*

11.   *Within any one residential school, what arrangements have been made to develop effective communication concerning the needs of the child and how these will be met jointly between teaching and residential care staff? Are all school staff responsible to the headteacher or are residential care responsible to someone else, either inside or outside the school? To what extent do residential care staff help to share in decision making and planning – e.g. through case conferences and review meetings?*

Part Three

The Development of Practice

i) At the LEA Level

Editorial Preview

Much of the home/school literature and reported experience in this area appears to operate on the assumption that the onus for the improvement of family/school relations lies more or less exclusively with schools and teachers. The present collection, by contrast, has given considerable emphasis to the view that real progress with regard to such a large and complex task needs the support and the experience of the education service as a whole. Here, there are important roles for national government and the DES, for LEAs and their agencies, for training institutions and last, but by no means least, for schools and teachers.

In this section, I have deliberately brought together in adjoining chapters a range of examples to illustrate the distinct, though overlapping contributions of LEAs and schools respectively. In doing so, it is implied that each has an important, complementary contribution to make. LEAs, for instance, are best placed to assess local needs, to provide guidelines and support and to undertake particular types of initiative and projects.

By contrast, schools are capable of enjoying special relationships with the neighbourhoods they serve, and operate through the interaction between individual families and the school system. Above all, it is at the school level that the opportunities and problems of improving home/school relations are experienced most vividly and sharply.

(i) The development of practice at the LEA level

Inheriting the legacy of Eric Midwinter's work in Liverpool, Coventry has probably got the longest established and, in some ways, the most developed experience of any local authority committed to the improvement of home/school relations. It has done so by establishing an authority-wide development project, selectively funded and located and intelligently adapted to local needs and circumstances.

It operates through a strategy which attempts to combine general direction through an agreed policy providing guidelines and identifying areas for development, with considerable scope for variation and freedom in each of its neighbourhoods. It does not have a narrow or limiting view of home/school relations, seeing them rather as an important element in a policy for community education and development, alongside pre-school provision, parent and adult education, the need to develop relevant curriculum and the movement towards community schools – a truly broad front.

The present extract provides background to a study of the effects of parental involvement in and support for their children's reading, which gives the extract a sharper edge. It also shows how a number of project schools have gone a long way down the road and face, not so much the problems of developing the basics, but the very different, second order problems of institutions that have already opened-up considerably.

Alwyn Morgan's account, based on his work with the Clwyd pilot project, is also linked to a broader community education strategy. But there the similarities end! For Clwyd provides very little in the way of formal, declared policies, reports or other official statements – just a co-ordinator with a roving commission and a high degree of commitment.

This LEA strategy is based upon a small-scale, low-budget attempt to develop good ideas and positive experience in three sharply contrasting communities and to support their wider diffusion across the authority as a whole. It very much depends upon the identification and dissemination of 'good practice', and upon mechanisms and networks to make this experience available to others. In this respect, it provides some striking examples of the value of working with other institutions and with the support services and of the value of interprofessional links in the development of new attitudes and new ways of working.

Finally, this account (like the others in this section) shows how far home/school relations has moved its central concerns from the margins of educational life closer to the heart of the key processes of teaching and learning. Here, parental influence on the curriculum is seen not in a negative way but as a potent resource and an influence towards relevance and positive curriculum development.

In recent years the Inner London Education Authority (ILEA) has published a number of reports concerned with home/school relations in its schools and is currently involved in interesting initiatives in this area. But none have made such an impact as the Thomas and Hargreaves Reports, on the state of London's primary and secondary schools respectively.

Not surprisingly, the home/school focus is diminished somewhat by the broader focus of the reports as a whole. But it has generated enough impetus in this area, for a later group of inspectors and seconded teachers to pick up and be thinking through a number of the questions that are raised here and to relate these to the further development of policy and practice.

From the established base of a survey carried out in a cross-section of its schools, the ILEA reports have set out to:

- encourage participation in the process of institutional and professional development, via a critical review of existing attitudes and practices.

- to identify guidelines – general principles and values – which individual schools can interpret for themselves.

- to consolidate a number of trends and general achievements; to establish areas of growth and development.

- to identify and endorse their support for a number of interesting initiatives.

The Hargreaves Report, in particular, from which this extract is taken, offers a potent reminder of some of the pressing needs and intractable problems that are the daily concerns of many of those living in our larger cities. It is also concerned with getting the basic foundations of London's education service right, not in any narrow, pejorative sense, but in terms of fundamental values and the practical arrangements that these require. In the home/school field this focuses increased attention upon the need for positive attitudes, improving communication and the development of effective linking mechanisms.

Reflecting, perhaps, its role as Britain's largest education authority, is the implicit model of an administrative and policy-making centre, presiding over a diverse collection of individual schools. In spite of this, however, the underlying change strategy appears to be 'normative' rather than coercive or centralist, attempting to persuade teachers that what is presented is normal and unexceptionable, to be taken as a baseline for future development.

Supporting Work with Parents

Paul Widlake and Flora Macleod

The Community Education Project since 1975

Coventry, unlike some of the other local education authorities which took part in the community development projects*, has sustained innovation and given it a permanent place within its Education Service (despite changes in political control with the City's Council). The nature of its origins, its endurance over more than a decade, the consistency of its stated objectives and the steady support it has enjoyed from the Education Committee: all these factors make the CEP a very unusual institution in English education.

The establishment of the CEP was in line with the CDP objective 'to increase the capacity of relevant services (in this case, Education) to respond by providing help which is more acceptable, intelligible and lasting in its effects' (Firth, 1977). Naturally, over the next eight years, individual teacher-advisers and the Project Leaders have extended and deepened their interpretation of this objective by encouraging:

– greater interaction between schools and their communities

– deeper understanding within schools of the social and cultural environment in which they work

– development of new patterns of teacher organization and communication in order to create an educational environment which will enable the development of skills of community participation.

---

* Coventry was one of 12 LEAs which took part in the national (Home Office) Community Development Project (CDP), established in 1976 to revive communities in disadvantaged areas.

In its infancy the CEP consisted of a small team placed in an infant school in the heart of the City's multi-ethnic and disadvantaged area. Its work ranged over twelve primary schools and a nursery centre and involved the Sidney Stringer community school. The team provided additional support and innovative services to teachers, pupils and parents in the area by:

- developing a programme in schools designed to encourage home/school and community/school links

- developing in-service training and support programmes for teachers in
  - the use of the latest teaching techniques;
  - development of communication skills;
  - understanding of the culture of people in the inner-city area;

- supporting teachers in their first year from college

- developing an adult programme seeking to respond to community needs rather than present the community with additional education possibilities offered from an institution

- establishing a home tutoring scheme for immigrant mothers

- assisting with the extension of pre-school provision.

In 1975 the idea of a 'decentralized' team working with a group of schools and encouraging them to cooperate across an area was replicated in four other areas of the city. These areas were selected on the basis of degree of disadvantage suffered by the pupils in the schools, thus retaining the original 'positive discrimination' policy in the new areas.

Community education strategies have developed in each area, and differ in detail, but all regard home/school relationships as a priority.

HOME/SCHOOL – strategies and supporting materials have been developed which have widened, deepened and informalized parental involvement in many of the schools concerned. Parents are being accepted as genuine partners in the educational process. The following list gives some idea of the kind of activities which are occurring right across the city:

Parents' rooms	Do-it-yourself evenings
Family Clubs	Film nights
Dressmaking	Discos
English lessons	Social evenings
School Youth Clubs	Lunchtime concerts
Subject evenings	Craft Club evenings
(e.g. modern maths)	Keep-fit classes
Tea afternoons	

PRE-SCHOOL – development of mother and toddler groups in many schools, ready-for-school groups, and a wide range of home visiting strategies. The training element in these strategies has laid the foundation for adult education work.

In March 1973, the Bernard Van Leer Foundation in Holland provided a grant for an experimental scheme using local mothers, trained and supervised by qualified teachers, to run annexes to the Hillfields Nursery Centre. Three years later the Foundation offered to provide sufficient additional funds to enable the scheme to be extended to a second area for a three year period.

Pre-school work has been stimulated by CEP in a variety of ways: for example, by a booklet 'From Home to School' used in all five areas which enabled the education visitors to reinforce the ideas contained within it; mothers and toddlers clubs in schools, toy libraries, module displays of toys and materials and the active encouragement of play groups run by local mothers.

ADULT EDUCATION – From informal beginnings, dealing with a content mainly concerned with the development and education of young children, a more formal provision has developed. Courses on local history, simple graphics, Indian dancing, and GCE 'O' Level English are examples of provision made at several primary schools. Many adults attended regular classes in day schools to study for 'O' and 'A' Level examinations.

Leadership courses are also being run to train some parents to take over the leadership of a wide variety of groups in schools. This generation of self-help skills is further exemplified by the training of a multi-racial group of parents who carry out home visiting duties in their school catchment area. These visitors work under the direction of the school Headteacher and in close liaison with Health Visitors and Social Workers.

Some schools are now beginning to evolve a parents' syllabus from their home/school programmes. Each school's syllabus is structured to ensure that during their time with the school, parents will be given a share in most aspects of the curriculum side by side with their child's progress through the school.

Regular radio broadcasts by CEP staff on educational matters are backed up with specially prepared materials across the city.

The Gulbenkian Foundation also provided funds for two short term appointments: i.e. the appointment of a 'young person development officer' to work with all the children resident in a particular section of the Sidney Stringer catchment area, and an 'artist-in-residence' who was attached to the Sidney Stringer School and Community College but who worked closely with the teacher-advisers in the video field.

CURRICULUM – materials have been devised to encourage situations in which parents, children and teachers work together on the development of observation, analysis, diagnosis and social action skills in terms of the local environment.

Four of the five areas have seen the influence of the community on the curriculum as a priority which is exhibited in several patterns – using the local community as a resource for learning, taking the local community as a starting point for wider urban studies, or taking a particular aspect of the community as the basis for developing a specific curriculum strategy. The publication of various teaching kits have evolved out of these initiatives. Particular interest has been centred on the teaching of reading skills and has resulted in the production of a highly structured and monitored scheme to measure and describe the effects of parental involvement in a school-directed reading programme, pre-school reading material, a booklet specifically designed to stimulate parental involvement in a school reading programme, and reading books containing children's imaginative stories.

Home-tutoring services for Asian adults have been operating throughout the period under review, 1971–77, and families in many parts of the city are in receipt of regular help. In addition there are a variety of afternoon and evening classes, which are regularly attended by 120 women but with many more attending occasionally as and when other commitments permit.

Other activities of the Community Education Project include the provision of in-service training for teachers, the publication of regular communication links with schools – bulletins, news-sheets, staffroom folders etc. and holiday play-time schemes engaging the practical support of students attending Lanchester Polytechnic and Warwick University.

CEP: school and community: aims and objectives (1984)

It will be of interest to record the most recent statement of aims and objectives (1984) and to note their consistency with the original, CDP-inspired, statements.

(i)   Objectives at school level
    (a)   Commitment to a developing home/school programme
    (b)   Acceptance of a pre-school role in the area
    (c)   Acceptance of an adult education role
    (d)   Concern for the children outside normal school hours
    (e)   Having the school reflected in the community
    (f)   Having the community reflected in the school
    (g)   Commitment to improvement and development of all aspects

(ii) Objectives at in-service level
    (a)   To develop teachers' confidence with adults
    (b)   To develop a positive attitude towards parents on the part of teachers
    (c)   To develop teachers' empathy with people in the area
    (d)   To develop parental confidence in dealings with teachers
    (e)   To promote a welcoming climate in the school
    (f)   To encourage provision for adults in the school

(iii) Aims at area level
    (a)   To promote equality of opportunity

(b)   To adjust educational provision to the needs of the people of the area

(c)   To promote education as a lifelong process

(d)   To promote constructive discontent concerning the school and the community

(e)   To maximize information between the education system and the community

(f)   To develop the school as a resource in its area

Practical implications of these aims and objectives for each school

(i)   Home/school

(a)   Developing family curriculum. Home involvement and classroom involvement on offer in each main teaching group. Most aspects of the curriculum being dealt with during the seven year primary span.

(b)   Social events both regularly and one-off

(ii)   Pre-school

(a)   Home visiting of next year's pupils

(b)   Ready for school group

(c)   Mother and toddler groups

(d)   Links with local playgroups, etc.

(iii)   Adult education

(a)   At least one class on offer e.g. 'O' Level, keep fit, OU, etc.

(b)   Links with local community college for taster session and other recruitment exercises

(c)   Self help group meetings in a room provided

(iv)   Children out of school

(a)   Out of school activities e.g. chess club, country dancing, etc.

(b)   Junior youth club perhaps in conjunction with local community college

(c)   Links with local youth clubs for advertisement and recruitment

(d)   Holiday playscheme on site or links with local playschemes

(e)   Latch-key programme

(v)   School reflected in the community
    (a)   Work displayed at various local sites
    (b)   Community service activities carried out by children
    (c)   Newsletter
    (d)   Occasional 'happenings' in catchment area
    (e)   Education comes to town cooperation

(vi) Community reflected in the schools
    (a)   Curriculum includes study of local community
    (b)   Local people offer skills and memories in classroom activities
    (c)   Books on the locality in the library
    (d)   Books written by residents. These are then included in school libraries and resource areas.

Conclusions

As a consequence of deliberate policy-making over a period of 12 years, community schools have grown up in many parts of the city and a tradition of parental involvement has been established in Coventry such that most primary schools take the presence of parents for granted, and they are included in many activities. In some parts of the City, two generations of parents have now worked in partnership with teachers. Through support from schools, parents have been encouraged to take direct action in relation to their own lives as well as making a positive contribution toward the psychological and educational development of their children. In short, children have been socialized into a school system where there are few barriers between the home and the school.

Observations of a representative sample of Coventry primary schools leave an impression of highly effective organization, using varied and flexible methods within an overall commitment to community education, in contrast to Raven (1980) who found that specific attempts to alter parents' behaviour were in danger of being crude, insensitive and more likely to increase their sense of helplessness than diminish it.

Coventry has allocated extra resources to schools designated by normally accepted criteria as disadvantaged, and has supported these schools, predominantly through its Community Education Project. It can be stated from the results we obtained that this form of provision is associated with good results in reading, writing and oral language skills, with lively and adventurous curricula and with an unusual degree of parental participation.

This is certainly very encouraging for those who have pioneered and implemented this policy, and maintained it under political control by different parties. Of course, such a survey cannot establish the causes of good results, but there is a great willingness on the part of politicians to draw negative conclusions about the efficiency of policies if the results are bad, as happened to the Headstart programme in the USA when early evaluations did not support the programmes.

The implementation of a policy of positive discrimination in Coventry appears to have avoided the most obvious pitfalls and to have met some of the requirements suggested by Lodge and Blackstone (1983), particularly in regard to central direction:

> Clearly rectifying educational disadvantage will take a long time and will require sustained action by powerful administrative agencies. But the very apparatus of the educational priority programme suggests a lack of commitment. Far from being located at the heart of the policy-making system, where policy concerning educational disadvantage must be placed if it is to be taken seriously, it has been relegated to peripheral outposts. (p. 128)

In Coventry this policy *has* been located at the heart of the policy-making system, and the study of its operation in primary schools has been a stimulating experience. The educational benefits of involving parents are very obvious, and have been clearly demonstrated. The central message has often been expressed in straightforward terms, especially by community educators in the USA:

> There is a whole book of studies (you know how somebody is always doing a study on something or other) that makes very interesting reading. Fifty-five pages of short versions of studies that say when parents take *any* interest in schooling, the kids' ranks go up; even if they only spend ten minutes a day talking about school; even if they only wish the kids a good day and remind them to 'work hard today'.

However, it is time to move forward from broad statements of this kind, a strong lead having been given by community schools in Coventry where a clear linear relationship was found between the amount of parental support for their children's reading and the reading scores obtained, confirming the observations of the Haringey study conducted by Tizard and his associates (1981b). There can be no doubt about the effects of involving parents in their children's reading, but the significant differences between the schools which were re-tested also points to the school's crucial role in this process. Further studies are desirable to explicate these school/parent variables.

Clwyd Community Education Pilot Project: Some Lessons Learned

Alwyn Morgan

Clwyd has a proud history of community schools which dates back to pre-local government reorganization days (1974). The present Authority comprises the former counties of Denbighshire and Flintshire, which covered a geographical area in North East Wales stretching from the Dee Estuary and Cheshire border in the east to the Conway Valley and the coastal resort of Colwyn Bay in the west. The enlightened pioneers of the community schools within these two authorities were the respective Directors of Education, who have received virtually no national recognition for their work in this field.

In Denbighshire, under the Directorship of T. Glyn Davies (1958–70) the Education Committee worked with village hall committees to establish four purpose-built rural community primary schools, opened between 1966 and 1971. However, it was in his previous post as Director of Education for Montgomeryshire (1943–58) now Powys (Mid-Wales) that he conceived the idea of the rural community primary school – three such schools were opened, the earliest in 1950 (Morgan, 1983). In Flintshire, by contrast, the Director, John Howard Davies (1970–74) sought financial support from the County and former local councils to provide seven high schools and three primary schools with impressive community facilities.

Following the amalgamation of the former counties, the policy of providing schools with community facilities was continued by the new Authority of Clwyd under the leadership of John Howard Davies (1974–85), until increasing financial constraint eventually brought such a policy almost to a total halt. In the meantime these purpose-built community schools had pursued their goal to enhance the quality of life within their local communities with varying degrees of success. The model of community education generally encouraged at these schools was of a traditional nature, synonymous with practice witnessed in the Cambridgeshire Village Colleges and the early Leicestershire Community Colleges. This work was typified by the formal programme of evening classes, dual use of school facilities by local clubs and societies, and, in certain instances where it was seen as non-threatening to headteachers, youth service provision.

In 1982, the Clwyd scenario was to change with the intervention of Keith Evans, the present Director of Education, who was then the Deputy. He was concerned that community schools were in a minority and that it was still a matter of earlier geographical accident whether or not the local community had the opportunity to be fully involved with the life and work of the school. As Evans (1985) wrote in *Outlines 2*

> If the Local Education Authority adopts a 'laissez faire' attitude and simply allows a thousand flowers to bloom this very varied picture will continue and the extent to which communities feel that their school belongs to them will simply reflect the varying levels of conviction and motivation of individual heads and governing bodies. It is not surprising that an LEA which wishes to see community education flourish must feel dissatisfied with such a random picture but the key question which presents itself is one of strategy.

After some deliberation on this matter, the LEAs Community Education Working Party decided that a macro approach would be counter productive. It was therefore agreed that the way forward should be to identify three 'families' of schools to pilot a new approach to community education. The three 'families' of schools (i.e. three comprehensive schools and their feeder primary schools) in separate areas of the county, were selected because for a variety of reasons there appeared to be little interaction between the schools and the local community. The schools had not been selected on any pre-determined criterion e.g. level of disadvantage. Quite fortuitously, in retrospect it was noted that the schools in the three Pilot Project areas reflected an overview of Clwyd, with its anglicized urban industrial communities heavily troubled by unemployment, contrasted with the Welsh speaking rural heartland, where the strife of modern day living appears to take a lower profile.

It should be pointed out at this stage that there was little prior consultation with the schools regarding their involvement. A decision was arrived at by the Departmental Working Party and the schools informed at a later date. Moreover, a further factor created a certain degree of initial unease amongst the headteachers concerned. This was related to the fact that this initiative was to be a low-cost project, with only minimal resources available as and when specific developments demanded. No pump-priming resources were to be granted. The only major resource commitment to the Project was a co-ordinator, who, when other LEA duties would permit, would support, guide, advise and encourage the general development of the work. A further inhibiting, or even threatening factor for the headteachers concerned was that for the vast majority, the concept of community education was totally strange.

Having therefore decided upon the Project schools and the minimal level of funding, it was then necessary to draw up, albeit within the very obvious constraints, operational strategies for the participating schools. These suggested areas for development had to be of a nature that would assist the headteachers to improve the service they offered to their pupils, parents and local community. Failure to meet this criterion would make the Pilot Project a nonstarter!

The school curriculum therefore provided an obvious starting point. The one rich resource bank for curriculum development that has yet to be fully appreciated or tapped effectively is the community at large. Over the years there have been many advocates for a community orientated curriculum, one of whom was Eric Midwinter, who stimulated debate as a consequence of his work in Liverpool in the late 1960s. Despite his advocacy for this approach, the community has yet to be widely and readily acknowledged and accepted as an integral part of the school's learning resources. Unfortunately the opportunity to allow pupils to see the relevance of their education within the framework of the community is frequently overlooked. However, it is interesting to note that the GCSE and CPVE examinations are beginning to make small inroads in this direction.

All too frequently pupils have been force-fed on the ancient and distant e.g. the Vikings, Wheatlands of Canada and Sheep Farming in Australia, whilst the potential learning experience within the locality are totally ignored. The Pilot Project consequently encouraged a starting point that was nearer to home and more recent, before opening out to a broader perspective. A practical example of such an approach was a cross-curricula theme entitled 'The Swinging Sixties'. The participating schools (from the Wrexham area) initially looked at the impact of that period of time and the subsequent changes on the local area. A number of people were also brought into the schools to recount their lifestyles, whilst the pupils additionally went out into the community to research information on varying aspects of the Sixties. Having initially stimulated interest amongst the pupils by exploring the local dimension of the project, national and international issues followed.

Other examples of relevant cross-curricula projects that relate directly to the lives of the pupils, include Crime Prevention, Health Education and Consumer Education (a subject that deserves greater prominence in the curriculum since astuteness in such a matter can help to determine future quality of life). Such topics as these also provide the opportunity to explore the local, national and international perspectives. Town, village and country trials have also encouraged interesting opportunities for local cross-curricula thematic initiatives. A further stimulant for curriculum development was the production of a small directory highlighting a wide range of contacts outside the education service that could be called upon, when appropriate, to support the schools' learning programmes and extra-curricula activities. Schools were also encouraged to add to this list with contacts from within their own catchment areas.

The above ideas were put forward in order to commence in a small way, a process of change within the curriculum. The Pilot Project schools were encouraged to make a conscious effort to break down the invisible barriers that often surrounded them and look to the community to revitalize and reinforce the curriculum in a manner that creates enhanced interest, motivation and enjoyment amongst the pupils. Unfortunately this approach is rarely touched upon at either initial or in-service education and is constrained further by the pressures of time, timetabling and examination work.

A second target area for development within the Pilot Project was the working relationship with parents, which has yet to gain its rightful acknowledgement from initial trainers, administrators and teachers. Not only is there a growing wealth of evidence to show that where parents have been actively involved in the educational process, their children have benefited e.g. 'Raising Standards' (Widlake and Macleod, 1984), but also the wider implications of the

1986 Education Act (management, annual report etc.) will put schools and particularly headteachers at their peril if a working relationship is not encouraged. Where parents have been kept at arms length and not given an insight into the present nature of schooling, then future management and Annual Report meetings may not be of a harmonious nature.

Consequently the model of parental involvement developed over the years in Coventry under the guidance of John Rennie and later Terry Bull was examined for possible initiatives in Clwyd. Consideration was therefore given to some of the following

(i)   Improving the quality of home/school communication e.g. handbooks, letters, leaflets, parents evenings, displays of work in the community etc.

(ii)   Providing information about the education system, e.g. parent curriculum workshops, parents in class to observe pupils at work. A successful venture was a joint initiative with BBC Radio Clwyd entitled 'Ask the Teacher'. For twelve months this weekly programme explained to listeners various aspects of education.

(iii)   Parental involvement within the school, e.g. attending and participating in assemblies, general help, skill sharing, running book clubs, assisting on outings etc.

(iv)   Parent rooms to meet educational and social needs of parents. Recreational activities for parents.

(v)   Home visits.

(vi)   Making schools more welcoming to parents.

(vii)   Parental involvement in the curriculum.

It was this latter initiative that presented the most intriguing challenge, because assuming from earlier research that home/school reading schemes can help raise reading standards, then this premise has important implications for parental involvement and support across all areas of the curriculum. If and when such a potentially exciting situation can be attained, parents will be empowered to become a potent force for collaborating with teachers in the education of their children. Up to the present time, the vast majority of parents have been mystified by the nature of the curriculum and modern teaching methods. Contrary to the opinion of many teachers, parents are not apathetic in their attitude towards their children's learning, (most parents want their children to do well at school), they are merely alienated because of all the changes that have taken place since the time they were at school. In the intervening years, teachers have seldom communicated the manner in which schooling has changed effectively or entertainingly. This problem is reinforced by the use of educational jargon and acronyms galore which adds to the general confusion.

The challenge in Clwyd has therefore been to give the parents the means, in a structured manner, to understand and support work in all areas of the curriculum. The break-through for the Pilot Project came almost accidentally with a home/school curriculum devised by an infant school in the Wrexham area. Over a period of 12 months parents were presented with a range of tasks to undertake at home with their children, to highlight all aspects of the curriculum. This approach was also reinforced with informal talks to parents on their children's education. Additionally, the 'Swinging Sixties' cross-curricula project referred to earlier presented primary school parents, irrespective of background and ability, with an opportunity to support their children's learning. Again the format was to set pupils tasks to undertake at home with the active cooperation of parents. This wider approach to parental involvement in the curriculum resulted in pupils often returning to school with twice the amount of work generally expected of them and, additionally, parents visiting school were able to discuss a curriculum initiative with confidence – an infrequent occurrence in the past!

Such was the success of this model of working with parents, that the practice is actively continued. Whereas previously pupils were frequently reprimanded if there was evidence of parental assistance with homework, pupils are now given tasks across all areas of the curriculum to complete with the support of their parents. In this manner, over a period of time parents become acquainted with the curriculum and see for themselves the progress or problems encountered by their children. Parents are therefore given the means to feel part of their children's education and are brought into a more effective dialogue with the school, which can only be of considerable benefit to all concerned. Such a style of working can be adapted with thoughtful planning to most areas of the primary and early secondary curriculum. There is a need to further research this approach in some depth as it could have exciting implications for future home/school relationships.

The third area of development outlined to the Pilot Project schools was that of lifelong education. We now live in a society where education as a 'front-ended' model, i.e. 5–16 years of age, is inadequate preparation for life within a rapidly changing society. Education must therefore be 're-packaged' to be seen and sold as a range of relevant opportunities that are available in a variety of settings in response to a multitude of needs. The past and present middle-class image of education must be discarded in order that *all* people may take advantage of whatever courses may be pertinent to their own needs and interests.

Against this scenario the headteachers were encouraged to make space available for daytime or evening formal and informal learning opportunities that the providing agencies e.g. LEA, OU, PPA, WEA, University Extra Mural Services etc. wished to organize.

Particular use was made of the LEA MSC Adult Education Outreach Workers who are a countrywide team with a brief to establish informal learning groups especially for those who have previously had little contact with the service. Additionally, emphasis was also placed upon learning opportunities for parents. Would the fact that education was seen to be important for the parents have a knock-on effect for the pupils? Furthermore, learning situations were encouraged to cut across traditional age-groupings, with opportunities being presented for pupils and adults/parents to learn together, thus reinforcing the concept of education as a lifelong process. Using strategies such as the above the schools were therefore encouraged to support initiatives commencing with the pre-school field and reinforcing the concept of education as an accessible and continuous service that not only responds to needs but additionally gives people a greater feeling of self-worth.

The fourth and final aspect of the Pilot Project was to reinforce the traditional model of community education referred to at the beginning of this paper. Many schools, whether or not designated as community schools, provide a lively focal point for local groups, clubs and societies. It is also generally accepted that in many areas there is woeful under-use of educational plant. Whilst it is acknowledged that many schools do not provide the ideal premises or conditions for certain community activities, no unreasonable barriers should be placed in the way of a group of individuals wishing to take advantage of school facilities.

The headteachers concerned were therefore urged to make their facilities more accessible for community use, and where possible, encourage the development of new groups. Bearing in mind the impact on schools of falling rolls in recent years, and that many people prefer to go out in the daytime rather than evening (particularly in the winter), emphasis was placed on daytime activities. The majority of the schools had no purpose-built community facilities, but rooms have been adapted or transformed at little cost. Alternatively, the dining hall, a classroom and the hall have been used when not required by the school. As the headteachers were given few resources for the Project, the new clubs that have been established are largely comprised of parents, and this has been a further means to promote more effective home/school dialogue.

A further strategy for this particular aspect of work was to encourage inter-agency collaboration, with links sought with Social Services, Area Health Authority, Library Service, local community workers etc. In such a manner more effective use can be made of school facilities. Additionally, wherever possible some form of interaction would be established between the pupils and the various groups utilizing the facilities.

Having established very broad parameters for the Project it was made known to the participating schools that the direction in which they travelled in order to bring about anticipated change, would be left to themselves, pending available resources, local needs, strengths etc. However, it would be totally unrealistic to expect change simply to materialize without support being forthcoming in many different forms. The following points are therefore an outline of the strategies for development used to support the Community Education Pilot Project.

(i)   Inset

> As stated earlier, community education was totally new to the vast majority of headteachers. There was therefore a very real need to provide the necessary insight into this somewhat bewildering and in certain cases, threatening concept. To this end, following informal meetings for the headteachers, the Project was launched on a formal basis with a large scale one

day conference staged with the support of the Community Education Development Centre. The purpose of this event was to highlight current philosophy and practice and focus on examples of good practice locally and on a nationwide basis. This was followed on a termly basis by seminars or workshops led by well-known protagonists within the field of community education. Unfortunately, for a period of time, industrial action intervened. Less formal school-based in-service was also arranged as requested.

(ii)   Consortium development

Bearing in mind the potential role of headteachers as agents of change, it was decided that the way forward for the Project would be by means of a consortium of headteachers for the three respective Project areas. It was expected that the consortia would be:-

(a)   a forum for the development of community education;
(b)   mutually supportive bodies, where those involved would have the opportunity to establish dialogues for reporting, reviewing, questioning and sharing experiences and practices;
(c)   a vehicle for assisting with the professional development of those involved.

Consortium meetings which have been held on a half-term basis or more frequently, have varied considerably in terms of character from one area to another, particularly in terms of attitude, commitment and level of activity.

(iii)   Project newsletter

A newsletter, which appeared on a termly basis, was used primarily as a record of initiatives, particularly on an inter-area basis, and secondly as a focus on examples of good practice. It also provided encouragement and motivation for those in the field. Other features included news on non-project schools, conference reports, book reviews etc.

(iv)   'Drip-feed' – project literature

To supplement the information gleaned from local, regional and national conferences a wealth of papers and articles on subjects appertaining to community education was distributed to the schools, in the initial stages on a weekly, if not twice-weekly basis. Moreover, copies of the CEDC monthly newspaper 'Network' were provided for the schools, in order that national news, issues and current trends could be brought to their attention.

Consequently, by fully utilizing the school mail service and the current wealth of papers on community education, no school was allowed to forget its involvement with the Project!

(v)   Inter-authority exchanges

This was seen as a further means to support committed head-teachers. A link with Coventry was established and a Clwyd headteacher was given the opportunity to spend a week in the City seeing examples of good practice at first hand. A reciprocal visit was hosted at a later date with the headteacher being given the opportunity to address teachers in different areas of Clwyd on the work within his Authority.

Industrial action constrained the extension of this scheme until recently, when exchange visits have been established with Leicestershire and Nottinghamshire. The intention was to establish numerous exchange arrangements with a number of LEAs and thus develop a resource bank of information within Clwyd relating to actual practice on the national scene.

(vi)   Advisory team links

Pending the initiative, the interest or cooperation of relevant Advisory Officers was sought to support the work of the Project. Close links have always been forthcoming from the Primary Advisers, whilst individual subject advisers have been brought in, as and where necessary. An example of collaboration was seen when a music workshop for all ages was staged over a weekend, in a primary school. This event would not have been possible without the committed involvement of the Music Adviser and his peripatetic teachers. Additionally the PE Adviser attended a demonstration on the potential of indoor bowling mats.

In this manner, not only is a broader base of support being given to the schools from the Advisory Team, but indirectly the Advisers themselves are also being introduced to the concept of community education.

(vii) Clwyd Community Education Association

Within 12 months of launching the Pilot Project a Clwyd branch of the CEA was established, thanks largely to activists not involved in the Project. However, the Pilot Project headteachers were encouraged to attend in order that they could have further opportunity to share ideas and experiences with others involved in community education.

(viii) Liaison with Unions

This has been seen as an important plank for development, as the cooperation of the relevant unions is essential. All too often various misconceptions abound regarding this field of work. Consequently, the local Union representatives have been kept informed of developments in order to maintain channels of dialogue and goodwill between all concerned. It is pleasing to note that the Project's strategies for development outlined above have had some effect as the following list of initiatives shows.

CLWYD LEA
Community Education Pilot Project, Gwersyllt, Holywell and Llangollen Areas

Specific Project Initiatives

1. *Home/school links*

   (i) Curriculum workshops

   (ii) Parent and pupil dance classes

  (iii) Parent/community room in schools

  (iv) Daytime educational classes for parents

   (v) Daytime recreation classes for parents e.g. yoga, keep-fit, badminton, etc.

  (vi) Daytime talks for parents e.g. health visitor, ESW, Children's Librarian, Social Worker etc.

  (vii) Swimming classes for parents

 (viii) Parents attending assembly

  (ix) Parents participating in assemblies

   (x) Home/school reading scheme

  (xi) Home/school brochures

  (xii) Parents football and netball teams

 (xiii) Parental support for school production, e.g. costumes, props, make-up, lighting

 (xiv) Parents concert party

  (xv) Skill sharing by parents in the classroom

 (xvi) Parental support with games, school outings, swimming

(xvii) Parental support for curriculum work, e.g. Domesday Project, Cynhefin Project

(xviii) Parental support for coffee mornings, jumble sales etc.

 (xix) Drama workshops for parents

  (xx) Informal drop-in centre for parents

 (xxi) Video workshop for parents

 (xxii) Evening pop-mobility classes for parents

(xxiii) Home visits prior to admission to Infant School

(xxiv) Home visiting packs

(xxv) 'Moving Up' publication (Infant to Junior)

(xxvi) Daytime visits to new school by pupils, teachers and parents

2. *Lifelong education*

   (i) Parent and Toddler community arts classes

   (ii) Accommodation for Parent and Toddler groups, pre-school playgroups and Mudiad Ysgol Meithrin

   (iii) Daytime adult education classes

   (iv) Adults in daytime 'O' and 'A' classes

   (v) Video workshop for parents

   (vi) Clwyd Dance Project classes

   (vii) Informal learning groups

3. *Curriculum development*

   (i) Home/school curriculum project

   (ii) Swinging Sixties curriculum project

   (iii) Town walkabout workbooks

   (iv) Involvement of adults/groups other than teachers to curriculum options

   (v) Induction courses for community service placements

   (vi) Projects involving the Police, Fire Service, Ambulance Service etc.

   (vii) Visits, e.g. Alyn Fish Farm, Coedpoeth Bakery, Bersham Heritage Centre, Greenfield Valley etc.

   (viii) Use of the elderly as a learning resource

4. *Community development*

   (i) Dual use of school facilities by a wide range of local groups

   (ii) Evening use of the school by the adult education and youth services

(iii) Reprographic service for community groups

(iv) Evening use of school by local IT group

(v) School based senior citizens luncheon and coffee clubs

(vi) After school breakdancing club

(vii) Pupil birthday parties held in school

(viii) Holiday playschemes based in schools

(ix) 'One-off' activities – discos, shows, concerts, fashion shows. It should be noted that some schools within the Authority have even hosted wedding receptions and funeral teas!

(x) Community Concert Party shows

(xi) Indoor bowls clubs.

It is the writer's firm belief that all schools must in time (and sooner rather than later) operate as community schools. The notion that additional facilities are required is totally false; they are merely a bonus. In fact some of the Pilot Project schools are developing into more effective community schools than their counterparts within the Authority that are fortunate enough to possess enhanced facilities, which are used merely for dual-use purposes, with little interaction with the school. Community education is a philosophy and agent of change, which when translated into practice enables schools to become more relevant and humane institutions that want the best for pupils, parents and the community generally. To work towards such a goal requires the philosophy and practice to be reflected *centrally* in the daily routine of everyone employed at the school – it must not be seen as the responsibility of one or two people in peripheral roles.

The manner in which schools are changed into more open establishments is the burning question. In the past it has been seen nationally to come from enlightened headteachers, pressure from parents and the community, or in the case outlined in this paper, authority led. It can be said with certainty that it has not developed in response to any dictum from the Government, in the guise of MSC or the DES. Consequently, we are still in a situation where community schools are in a minority, but interest in working with parents and the wider community is growing rapidly. What lessons can therefore be gleaned from Clwyd's top down model, which is still very much in its infancy?

First, the notion of a Pilot Project to encourage examples of good practice, which can later be replicated in other areas is sound, *providing that it is resourced adequately.* Community education must not be regarded as a cheap option, which will in time affect the credibility of the work. If new practice is to be established and fresh contacts for the schools to be 'networked', then time must be allocated for the work to enable all the ensuing tasks and activities to be undertaken effectively. Unfortunately, to date, community education has relied heavily on goodwill. For the future, the proposed teacher contracts and the 'burn-out' factor often associated with this work will demand that time is provided for the additional tasks of running and managing what will inevitably be a larger operation. No authority should attempt to duck this responsibility.

Other resources that are required include the devolvement of financial responsibility to schools relating to the dual use of facilities, adult education, youth service etc. along with the means to generate an income from these budgets, which can in turn be used to improve the general programme in consultation with a management body. A further small bonus is a room within the school that can be adapted and used as a comfortable and friendly base for a wide range of activities. For such a purpose, advantage should be taken of the falling rolls situation that is affecting many establishments. Schools should also endeavour to signpost the campus effectively both externally and internally so that visitors are able to find their way around the school with confidence.

A means to bring about change and establish a community ethos within schools is by in-service training. Initial training did not prepare teachers to work with parents and the community, and therefore action, in the form of in-service training is essential. This should be of varying duration, take a variety of forms and respond to individual, institutional and authority needs. It is also important that interested parties have the opportunity to attend national conferences and share the valuable experiences of others.

In addition to a range of resources and in-service training, there is a further need for a fairly intense level of community education advisory support if the work is to be taken seriously and the necessary changes encouraged. In Clwyd, the varying levels of advisory commitment to the individual schools has been determined by the responses of headteachers, who, generally speaking, appear to fall into three categories. In the first instance, many headteachers could see the value of the work and responded reasonably confidently and positively. These headteachers in the main required little encouragement, merely a certain degree of guidance and oversight. A second group of headteachers could see the merit of this new, but possibly threatening, approach and consequently required a more demanding level of support, particularly when instigating a new initiative. If this was successful other initiatives would follow. However, if for any reason the activity was judged by the headteacher to have failed, an uphill struggle would be faced to reawaken interest in the Project. Thirdly, there are several headteachers, who for reasons best known to themselves, have not been affected in any shape or form by the Pilot Project. Had a higher level of resourcing been made available in the form of home/school liaison teachers or community tutors, along with area-based advisory teachers to support the schools, such headteachers might be fewer in number.

Finally, where a Project of this nature is authority led, with schools expected to display a community ethos, it is only proper that the officers and administrators from County Hall understand and support the need to work with parents and the community. It is essential that in such a model for change, headteachers who are expected to be the catalysts for action, should clearly see the commitment of those above them.

Improving Home/School Relations in London's Schools

ILEA

The teacher/parent partnership

In this country parents are under no obligation to send their children to school. Under the law, education is compulsory, but schooling is not: the school is one possible choice for parents when they seek to discharge their obligation to educate their children. If parents can demonstrate that they are discharging that obligation by their own provision, they are entitled not to send their children to school. Most parents, of course, opt for the school. Strictly speaking, they have *chosen* the school and in a real sense the school is acting on behalf of the parents with their consent. These facts remind us that schooling and education are not the same thing. Education begins from the moment a child is born and education during early childhood rests largely in the hands of the parents. At the age of five the child is normally sent to school to profit from the formal education provided there, but education continues also to be provided by the home, by friends and relatives, by the community. The school is one part of a much larger educational enterprise, and what happens in school should never be separated too sharply from the education which takes place out of school.

If the school is to realize its aims, it must always connect with home and the community (see p. 132). The effective education of the young is a joint enterprise among several partners and any attempt to improve the education of the young must involve *all* the partners. This is a central theme of our Report. Our brief is to consider the curriculum and organization of the secondary school, but we can do so only by recognizing that what happens in school is a product of a partnership between the school, the home and the community. The school is effective when its work is an expression of a common enterprise.

For very many years we have known, both from well established research findings as well as from common sense, that parental commitment is a cornerstone of the school's success. If parents are interested in their children's schooling, if they are supportive of the school's endeavours, if they act in partnership with teachers, then the children will achieve more in school. When parents adopt this approach, the teachers are delighted, for they see daily the effects of such parental interest. But some parents do not: they are often judged indifferent to the children's progress at school. These parents appear unresponsive to the school's request for help and support: they may not come to parents' evenings, even though it is these parents that the teachers are most anxious to meet. Such parents are more likely to be working class than middle class, though we must not forget that most working class parents are committed to their children's education. There is a range of reasons why some parents do not appear to be supportive. In many cases they are among the poorest sections of our society and are locked in the difficult struggle to survive; they often live in inadequate housing in underprivileged communities; they are badly paid, work unsocial hours, or are unemployed; and, perhaps most significant, they have limited experience of the educational system, their own schooldays were often unhappy, and they may retain a suspicion and fear of teachers.

There is very little the school can do towards removing poverty or improving the adverse social conditions in which many such parents live. Yet if we want children to achieve more, especially working class children, then improved home/school liaison and increased parental involvement must be a top priority. Cooperative home/school relations will enhance everything the school does. No school, however good its pastoral care, can be a substitute for the home. The school must complement and work with the home. In the light of the conditions in many areas of inner London, we are conscious of the great devotion of many teachers to the young people in their charge. Their efforts are, however, limited in potential if they are exerted *in spite* of the home rather than *in association with it*. Most teachers accept that fine principle: the problem is how to achieve it. We open our Report with that exceptionally difficult task because we believe that, whatever the difficulties, it is at the heart of any attempt to reduce underachievement and disaffection; and we do not pretend that there are no natural tensions between home and school. Parents are rightly concerned with the welfare of their own children: teachers are concerned with the welfare of all the children in the school. Parents have their own conception of their children's abilities and qualities: teachers must make their own professional judgements on these matters. Parents have views on what their children should be taught and how it should be taught: teachers too have preferences in matters of curriculum and pedagogy. There is always great scope for difference, misunderstanding and even conflict between parents and teachers. When the school reaches out to parents, it takes risks. But unless the school takes these risks, the proper partnership between home and school can never be established. We begin with some of the basic questions. What are the most effective methods of bringing parents into the school? How welcoming is the school? How does the school communicate with parents? How does the school involve the parents in what the child learns at school?

Bringing parents into school

In most schools most parents attend parents' evenings. In a few schools the number of parents attending, considering the importance teachers attach to these events, is surprisingly low. It is common for teachers to complain that the parents they most urgently need to meet do not turn up. Many teachers feel they have done their best to inform parents about such meetings and their importance, and they become resigned to the continuing absence of some parents. Attendance is difficult for some parents: they may be working in shifts; they may live some distance from the school; it is perhaps a one-parent family with several small children and it can be difficult to find somebody to care for them whilst the parent comes to the school. But some parents who are free to come decline to do so. In some cases the parents may be apprehensive about visiting the school. They feel isolated, insecure and self-conscious in a large room with many parents and teachers. They are oppressed by the queues which form in front of each teacher; they are unsure what to say to the teachers. Most teachers are aware of such feelings in some parents, but they do not always know how to allay their anxieties.

We believe that the apprehension of some parents can be reduced if they are invited to the school for other kinds of occasion when they can feel more relaxed and less 'on trial' with the teachers. Parents who form the habit of going to the school regularly are more likely to attend the parents' evening. Most parents are very proud of their children. The parents of children taking part in plays, in sports teams, in musical festivals or art exhibitions often need relatively little encouragement to come to see and share in their children's achievements. These events are designed primarily for the pupils' benefit, but they often forge an important link with the home. Some schools stage such events regularly, others much more rarely. The greater the variety of such events the school is willing to mount, the more the parents will come to the school. Some schools plan these events very imaginatively, making sure that very many pupils are involved, not just the same talented minority, and ensuring that parents' needs are attended to. They reap the rewards of greater parental commitment.

Parents' evenings and extra-curricular events are usually large occasions. Some parents are more easily involved in the school by occasions which are less formal and more intimate. Two schools we visited have specially invited to the school the parents of pupils receiving learning support from the special needs department. A small social evening to discuss why their children are being withdrawn from some lessons for special help proves attractive and reassuring to many parents, who feel able to discuss the scheme in general, as well as the progress of their own children, in a friendly and unthreatening atmosphere. These are models of good practice which also lay the foundations for better attendance at the full parents' evening.

How welcoming is the school?

To many parents the school is a rather forbidding place. Teachers, who spend so much time in the school, do not always take account of this. There may be no physical barrier between the school and its surrounding community, but there is often a psychological barrier which needs to be broken down. Many schools have several entrances, all of which except one are kept locked because they have suffered from the disruptive attentions of intruders. It is not always clear which is the main entrance. Very few ILEA secondary schools have a 'welcome' sign at the door. Once inside the school, many parents are confused about what precisely they should do next, especially if they have not visited the school recently. Often there are no signs to the general office. These are small matters, but they are important to many, especially working class parents. Most of the Committee were strangers to the 61 schools we visited, but only in some was entry into the school easily negotiated and in most we did not feel welcome until we met somebody. We think it essential that schools take action to make it clear to parents that they are welcome, and that indications of this welcome are made before parents finally meet someone.

One simple method of making the school approachable is to provide a reception desk operated by pupils. In most schools one or two pupils are free at most times of the day, if only because they are excused physical education or games. If a desk is placed near the main entrance, the pupils can welcome any visitors and direct them appropriately. It is also an excellent social education for the pupils on reception duty. In a few schools we visited, one or two pupils were awaiting our arrival and, since we were expected and arrived punctually, we were addressed by name. Our sense of being welcome was immediate and profound.

Nowadays parents often telephone the school, sometimes on quite small matters. It is important that their message is taken seriously and is dealt with. In practice, it is very easy for such messages to be lost in a busy school office, especially at certain times of the day, and when the person who can best deal with the matter is teaching. One ILEA school has organized a system whereby there is always a head of year (or a deputy) on duty to receive telephone calls from parents, or to meet parents who arrive at the school without an appointment. When this teacher is on duty, she or he must be available in their office. There is thus always a teacher with pastoral experience available to talk with a parent, to deal with the problem or to explain why the appropriate person is not available. Parents naturally come to see the school as responsive to them.

In another school, the teachers have an 'open day' each Wednesday morning. Parents are free to go anywhere in the school. Where the presence of parents would be intrusive, a 'No visitors please' sign is displayed. By opening the school in this way once a week, the school exhibits its conviction that it has nothing to hide and that parents are welcome.

How does the school communicate with parents?

Most communications from the school to the home are written. We have been impressed by those schools which have a policy for communicating with the home and thereby co-ordinate the many notices and letters that are sent to parents. It is bewildering to parents if there are too many written communications, or if they receive letters from too many members of staff on different matters.

In recent years there have been a marked improvement in the quality of handbooks or booklets offered by ILEA schools to parents. In the best schools we were impressed by the clarity of these communications, which are free of educational jargon. Some schools sensitively ensure that communications are translated into the mother tongue of the parents: a pupil can usually be found to help with this. Some schools send regular newsletters to the parents. These newsletters permit many of the communications to the home to be co-ordinated easily and effectively, as well as reminding parents of important events in the school's calendar. Parents come to expect the newsletter, which is thus less likely to be 'lost' as is the fate of many communications carried home by pupils. Some schools use 'homework diaries' or 'journals' in which parents can make comments to the teachers. If the form tutor also uses the diary to make a comment from time to time, this can alert the parent to a problem in its very early stages when it is most easily dealt with.

For many parents the most important communication from the school is the child's report. Many schools have greatly improved the form and content of reports in recent years. Yet some schools still issue reports which are too brief, ridden with clichés and confusing. Parents expect more than a very terse comment; they have a right to have grading procedures fully explained; they should be told when there is a problem which requires discussion with the teachers. In many schools the report is closely associated with the parents' evening, for then parents can discuss the report with the teachers when it is fresh in the minds of both. We are in favour of this development. Some schools have now adopted the 'cheque book' style report, whereby each teacher writes the report on a separate page and all the individual reports are stapled into a booklet. This gives each teacher more room for comment, and one major advantage over the single-page report is that, if a teacher makes an error, there is no need for the whole report to be re-written. There should always be room for parents to comment on the report.

How does the school involve the parents in the child's learning?

The content of the curriculum has changed substantially since many parents were themselves at school. It is important that parents know what the children are learning under both the conventional subject labels as well as the newer titles for courses. We were impressed by one school which issues three separate curriculum handbooks, one for first year pupils, one for middle school pupils and one for the sixth form. The handbooks explain the curriculum, and deal with the school's philosophy in relation to equal opportunities, mixed ability teaching, record-keeping and assessment. This is a much more effective form of communication with parents than is possible in a single booklet which aims to cover all the pupils in the school. Such readiness to communicate with parents in relation to their specific needs and interests, depending on the child's position in the school, is admirable.

Again most of the schools we visited now provide excellent booklets for third year pupils explaining the option scheme. This is a transitional stage in secondary education when decisions of great importance are made. The best booklets we have seen explain not only the content of the different options, but also the implications of making certain choices for future opportunities. Thus they prepare parents for the meetings with teachers during this period.

Schools sometimes introduce courses with names which are unfamiliar to parents – *SMILE, SMP, Eclair*. In the best practice the school produces a clear explanatory booklet for both parents and pupils to prevent confusion or worry. It is helpful when booklets are translated, where necessary, into the parents' mother tongue. Parents expect to be informed on curricular matters where they have very strong views or the content is potentially controversial – for example health and sex education, (where their right is, in fact, a legal one) racism and sexism. These are topics which relate to education outside the school as well as within it and parents should be privy to such developments. Parents have a right to be consulted about such curricular matters. A curriculum which is relevant to the lives of young people is likely to contain controversial elements: a curriculum which is entirely uncontroversial will be dull. Schools should not avoid a controversial curriculum, but they should provide parents with real opportunities to discuss it with teachers and to see it in operation if they so choose. Home/school liaison does not mean a passive handing over of children to the teachers; it means a constructive dialogue between home and school.

We think that most schools will not dissent from what we have written on home/school relations. We have been impressed by some of the developments we met in our visits to schools, but there are some ways in which most schools could improve their home/school relations. In our view even the best practice does not go far enough in the light of the importance of parental involvement to any serious attempt to reduce pupil underachievement and disaffection. More substantial changes are needed.

Parents' evenings are seen by parents as one of the most important events in the school calendar, and rightly so. We believe, however, that more needs to be done to augment the contact between teachers and parents. At the point when a pupil transfers from the primary to the secondary school, many schools offer a personal interview to the parents. These meetings are usually valued by parents and teachers. Ideally, such interviews with parents should continue on an annual or bi-annual basis throughout a pupil's career. The problem of time is real for both parents and teachers. Many teachers already give freely of their evenings to marking, to preparing lessons, and to extra-curricular activities, as well as to parents' evenings. As far as parents are concerned, we believe that most parents would make the effort to attend school for a half-hour interview once or twice a year with the tutor and pupil, to discuss progress and identify future educational goals. As far as teachers are concerned, the cost in time for a tutor with 30 pupils would be a maximum of 30 hours per year – about a period a week on average throughout the year. We feel that this is so important a matter that the tutor should be given one such period a week, extra to the normal provision of non-teaching time, to plan a programme of personal parental interviews. Nevertheless, this is asking a good deal of teachers. Yet some schools already do offer such individual interviews to parents. It is a practice we admire and commend to other schools.

Is the traditional parents' evening the only other possibility? We think not. In any event, parents' evenings are not supported by all parents. On these occasions the parents try to see as many individual teachers as they can or as they think necessary. The conversations with teachers are inevitably rather short, and much time can be spent in queueing. There is little opportunity for parents to talk with one another, even though they often have common problems; there is often less opportunity for (say) a form tutor to discuss general issues with a group of parents.

In our view there is a need for a parents' meeting which is smaller, more intimate and less forbidding than the conventional parents' evening covering a whole year group of pupils. The obvious unit for this is the tutor group, especially in schools where the pupils remain in the same group with the same tutor for the five years of compulsory secondary schooling. In the early years, this tutor group is also the (mixed ability) teaching group for several subjects. Parents of the pupils in a tutor group, then, have much in common. We believe schools should establish a *tutor group parents' association*. Twice a year the association would meet with the tutor and the head of year or head of house. These meetings can be very informal. They provide an opportunity to discuss the whole range of common problems: the curriculum, especially subjects or courses with which parents are unfamiliar; teaching methods; standards of achievement; and social relations between the pupils, especially the recurrent problems of bullying, racism and sexism which so evidently require parental involvement if solutions are to be found. Many parents have problems with their children, but often they believe the problems are unique to themselves and they are unsure how to deal with them. The association allows the parents to share these problems and explore, with the teachers, the ways of dealing with them. Parents can offer one another mutual help and support; just as the tutor group affects the friendship patterns of pupils, so the tutor group parents' association will generate friendships among their parents, and this is a sound basis for mutual aid. It might even be possible for such an association to arrange for a crêche during meetings, for it is frequently the problem of caring for young children which prevents many parents from attending. Through the meetings of the association, parents can come to common agreements amongst one another and with the tutor on important school matters. A classic case is homework. If parents can discuss this issue fully, they are more likely to agree with the school's homework policy, and to play the supportive role which is so essential. At the end of the meeting, some parents have the chance of a short, private word with the tutor or head of year, if only to arrange the date for a personal interview. If several tutor group parents' associations meet at the same time, the head of year or head of house can move between meetings as required, thus making a saving on his or her time commitment. Such an arrangement makes it easier to provide a crêche. The cost of all this in time to the tutor is quite small: two evenings a year. But the potential benefits of this investment are, we think, enormous.

The tutor group parents' evening complements the annual parents' evening. We believe it will be attractive to many parents, some of whom currently dislike the much larger and somewhat more formal parents' evening. As such, it can be a stepping stone to greater parental involvement. For instance, the occasions can be used, by teachers or by active parents, to advertise other school-events: personal contact is often much more effective than a written invitation alone. Quite simply, many parents like another parent to go with and the need for company should be acknowledged. In some areas evening transport networks may be poor, or parents nervous of travelling alone after dark. If contact between parents is encouraged and established, there is a greater chance of lifts being offered to those without cars and thus the removal of a deterrent from attendance. The tutor group parents' evening would be, we think, a sound basis for increasing parental involvement. It will be said that the tutor group parents' association will not solve the problem of the parent who declines to come to the ordinary parents' evening. Perhaps so; but if the tutor group parents' association is firmly established at the point of primary-secondary transfer, when parental commitment is particularly strong, we believe that many parents who now become lost to the school as the years pass will be retained for a much longer period. Indeed, it might be advisable to phase in the tutor group parents' associations over a six year period, beginning with the first year.

It is impossible for a committee such as this to take account of all the highly varied needs and conditions of ILEA secondary schools. The people in the best position to generate new ideas for increased parental involvement and better home/school liaison are the teachers and parents in the individual school. Our task is to provide a mechanism by which that can be achieved. We believe there is room for an additional body to act as a 'think tank' for home/school relations, a body which is neither the governors nor the present parent-teacher associations. We propose that governors establish a *home/school council* to undertake this work. It may need to be a new body, or the existing parent-teacher association might be adapted for this purpose. The home/school council has no formal powers: its aim is to advise all the existing bodies, especially the governors, on various aspects of home/school relations. It might wish to refer matters to the governors; and the governors may wish to refer some matters to the council. We believe that the council should consist of:

(i) at least one parent from each year group, these persons being elected from the parents within each year group;

(ii) the head(s) of each year group, with the headteacher and the teacher in charge of pastoral care;

(iii) a representative of the Education Welfare Service; and perhaps

(iv) some governors.

We believe such a body could produce imaginative suggestions for the improvement of the teacher/parent partnership. The machinery we propose looks cumbersome. 'Not another committee', some critics will say! But the need to involve parents more fully is, in our view, absolutely vital to improving the achievement and reducing the disaffection of pupils. It is evident that in each school a senior member of staff needs to be in charge of home/school liaison and the teacher/parent partnership. We consider that the deputy head-teacher or senior teacher with pastoral duties should assume this responsibility, as now obtains in many schools, and be the person to supervise the introduction of the tutor group parents' association and the home/school council.

School governing bodies

The Taylor Report (GB. DES, 1977) recommends that schools' governing bodies should consist of equal numbers of four groups:

representatives of the local authority; school staff; parents; and representatives of the local community. It was clearly intended that parents should have stronger representation among the governors than they have hitherto enjoyed in most schools. We support this principle. If the parents are not adequately represented among the governors, they do not and cannot exercise an appropriate level of participation in the life of the school. If parents and teachers are to act in partnership, parents must be formally involved in the governance of schools.

Some schools do not find it easy to recruit parent-governors. We know schools where parents do not seem to be enthusiastic about attending events which are open to them. Parent associations and parent-teacher associations may involve a relatively small minority of parents. It is also said that parent-governors are not always very representative of the parent body as a whole. An increase in the number of parent-governors might do little to increase parental involvement with the school; it might even exacerbate the problem of the unrepresentativeness of parent-governors.

The force of this argument cannot be denied. Yet the Authority has been a pioneer with respect to the introduction of parent-governors and the effects have been beneficial. This is an appropriate occasion to review the position of parents on governing bodies and build on past achievements. We believe that, as part of a concerted strategy to increase the level of parental involvement in ILEA secondary schools, the number of parent-governors should be increased. In our judgement, parents should constitute one-quarter of the governing body. We recommend that the Authority amend the Instrument of Government for county schools accordingly. In practice this means increasing the size of governing bodies to 23 of whom five (22 per cent) are parents. In our view four of these parent-governors should be elected by and from among the parents of pupils in the school. The remaining parent-governor should be co-opted by the governors to ensure that any minority groups among the parents are represented on the governing body.

Much of this commentary applies to inner London. Some teachers, we believe, misinterpret the parents' trust in the school as a lack of interest in their children's education and such misunderstandings can be removed only by more direct contact between parents and teachers. However, many West Indian (or Afro-Caribbean) parents have difficulty attending events in schools, especially where parents work on shift duties or in the case of a one parent family. We have been told by a group of West Indian parents that many parents feel uncomfortable in the presence of teachers, sometimes finding it difficult to express exactly what they feel. These problems can be severely exacerbated if they detect that the teachers are in any way condescending or patronizing in their approach to them. There is a real danger here that the only time many teachers meet a West Indian parent is when the parents are summoned to the school because a problem has arisen with the pupil, and that is not the best basis on which to found home/school cooperation. We believe that our tutor group parents' associations may be of considerable help here. They provide an opportunity to involve parents in the school from the point of transfer from primary school; they help to cement closer relations between the parents and one member of staff, the tutor; they provide opportunities for parents to exchange ideas, share problems and offer one another mutual support and aid. Most of all, they are occasions when, from the very beginning of secondary education, the tutor can explain in detail the ways in which parents can play an active role in the education of their children. Most West Indian parents have the interest, but they need practical advice on how to express the interest. There has been, in recent years, success in showing parents how they can help their children with reading, but most of this work is confined to the primary school. This approach must, in our view, be extended into the secondary sector. Of course at this level some of the curriculum material will be much less familiar to parents and they may lack the confidence to help their children. This can only be solved if the schools are willing to explain secondary school courses to parents and give explicit guidance, at meetings, and through booklets, on the helpful role that parents can play. We need hardly add that such an approach would be advantageous to many working class parents as well as to ethnic minority parents. The school has to take the initiative here. In the absence of an effective partnership between parents and teachers, the factors of parental frustration and lack of confidence on the one hand, and low teacher expectations on the other, will continue to reinforce one another in a vicious spiral that inevitably reduces the achievement of many working class and ethnic minority children. It is for this reason that we consider home/school relations to be such a prominent area.

Part Three

The Development of Practice

ii) At the School Level

Editorial Preview

In the previous section a brief comparison was introduced between the respective roles of LEAs and schools, as a backcloth to a number of different accounts of LEA strategy. In this section, a fuller comparison becomes possible with the addition of a number of accounts and extracts which illustrate the role of the *school* in the development of home/school thinking and practice.

The role of the LEA has been characterized as concerned with administrative and managerial elements. It is often largely concerned with the formulation of policy, the allocation of human, financial and material resources and their effective organization. The role of the school, by contrast, highlights the range of important variations and differences of philosophy and leadership style or between schools and their neighbourhoods, for example. It revolves around the interaction of individuals, with its focus upon personality and attitude, consensus and conflict, normative pressure and voluntary activity. Above all, it is concerned with the practicalities of policy and with the everyday realities of how to make things work.

The section has been organized around a number of general themes. It opens with contrasting examples of a 'whole school' approach to home/school relations and a mainstream view of development in this area. The focus then switches to the area of special development and roles which include an illustration of home/school liaision at work and the development of a wider community role for schools. The section closes with extracts which make the issue of teacher attitudes more explicit, with a look at the multi-faceted notion of teacher professionalism and at some of the obstacles to change.

Although Gulzar Kanji's chapter is ostensibly a detailed account of how one school goes about its business, it raises a number of features of more general concern, by illustrating:

- the relationship between a thought-out rationale, based on general principles and a pattern of practice;

- a 'whole-school' approach in which the development of relationships and activities is seen to require organizational change;

- an approach in which emphasis is given to the laying-down of solid foundations for a long-term relationship between families and schools, so much a characteristic of education in the early years.

This is followed by the first termly report of a newly appointed home/school liaison teacher, in an LEA where this has been used as an important strategy of positive discrimination. It has a delightful clarity and down-to-earth enthusiasm. It is even more impressive as an example of what can be achieved, in a remarkably short time, by the addition of a specialist resource to a basic, general commitment.

It is also interesting as an 'official' view of effective home/school practice, since it was commended by the chief education officer, to members of his education committee, 'as a fine example of community education'.

In John Bird and Bob Croson's joint chapter, they refer to the pioneering work they have done, as heads of two designated community primary schools in a Midlands city. Whilst they share a broadly similar philosophy and commitment, there are significant differences in their style and approach and, above all, in the two communities in which they work and the respective needs, opportunities and problems that these embody.

Whilst they start by identifying a range of contacts with parents, they have both moved on to a wider commitment to community development. In their experience, positive attitudes and interpersonal skills are equally as important, if not more important than policies and organization.

Sheila Bainbridge's chapter is a short extract from a longer study, which was undertaken as part of an in-service course. It's main purpose was, in her own words, 'to spotlight issues, analyse implications and suggest strategies...' that enable parents 'to participate, with the teacher, in the educational advancement of their children'.

It serves as an illustration of the actual and potential value of study, through the release of teachers, to examine and reflect upon

their practical experience and to make plans for its further development. It also focuses attention upon teacher professionalism in
which conservatism and the defence of vested interests can be an
obstacle to the acquisition of the kinds of knowledge, skill and
experience that enable progress to be made. It seems characteristic
of both the rhetoric and the approaches of primary education that it
should give special emphasis to the welfare of, and benefits to
individual children.

In the final chapter of this section, the present author offers a
sanguine reminder of some of the obstacles to development and
change, particularly those that derive from unhelpful attitudes and
negative experience. In particular, it highlights the overlapping
areas of staffroom mythology about parents and teacher ignorance
of family and neighbourhood life, particularly as it concerns life in
working class and multicultural communities.

The extract tries to strike a balance between a strong commitment to the improvement of home/school relations and a healthy
scepticism about the extent to which this is being achieved, about
the distance that can exist between fine words and effective action
and the sheer difficulty of coping with the many, often overwhelm-
ing and contradictory demands that are made upon hard-pressed
teachers.

Partnership in Education

Gulzar Kanji

An enormous amount of learning has already taken place by the time a child of three enters school. She is not a blank copy-book to be written on but a thinking, feeling person who has formed ideas about how people behave, who has achieved an enormous feat of mastering her mother tongue and learnt a myriad of mental, physical and social skills. In short, a child comes to school with a view of the world. Any teacher who denies that view of the world does so at her peril and jeopardizes the very task she has set herself to do, i.e. to help children become successful learners. During the early years of growth and development, the parents have already played an important part in the process of the child's learning that starts perhaps in the womb and goes on throughout life. Teachers are not in competition with the parents but allies so that joint forces of adults work towards the benefit of the child.

Both the Plowden Report (GB. DES, 1967) and the Bullock Report (GB. DES, 1975) advocated parental involvement. The child development studies and language acquisition studies have highlighted the role of the parents in their childrens' lives. The rise of the playgroup movement and its rapid development proved beyond doubt that parents are able to organize successful pre-school education for their children without any professional help.

The Thomas Coram Research Programme carried out in Haringey from 1976 to 1979 under the aegis of the late Jack Tizard and conducted by Jenny Hewison and Bill Scofield showed that the reading attainment of children improved significantly *not* if a specialist teacher instructed the children in small groups but if the parents were directly involved in helping their children learn to read. The Belfield Project also proved conclusively that parental involvement in reading had a high degree of success. In *Learning to Read* Margaret Meek observes that a parent is 'the first person ever to help him (the child) make his way in the world and the most powerful model for what he wants to be able to do'.

The teacher's task is to facilitate access to the curriculum for both the parents and the child. Only then will there be optimum learning taking place in the child.

Barbara Tizard's research on parental involvement makes amply clear how concerned parents are about their children's success at school and that given support and guidance, they will join forces with teachers to help their children. No matter how hard a teacher works, there is never enough time to give children individual attention for a sustained dialogue or a discussion or skill learning. Now if a teacher spends say five minutes explaining to a parent a special task, those five minutes would not only multiply into several sessions of individual attention by the parent at home, but also forge a link between home and school and eliminate a dichotomy between the world of school and the world of home that is so confusing to both parents and children.

There are often areas of conflict because the interests of the parents do not always coincide with the values of the school. A parent may be over-anxious, over-ambitious, or the teacher may be unsympathetic and insecure, but in the final analysis it is communication and dialogue that help people understand and accept each other's point of view. Education of the young is too important to be left just to the experts. A young child needs all the resources he can draw from – the parents, family, neighbours, school, local community and any other facilities within his and his family's reach – in order to be a successful learner and a healthy, balanced human being with a lively sense of curiosity.

Partnership with parents does not mean that the professionals involve the parents in school on their terms, that is influence parents in their child-rearing patterns and impose a point of view that teachers are the givers and they the receivers. As professionals our first tenet should be to *listen* to our clients and modify our practice if necessary. Secondly we must make an effort to provide information to the parents about the school curriculum, administration, facilities and day-to-day running of the institution, and create time for parents to hold formal and informal dialogue with the staff. The third area of concern would be to create a sound theoretical and practical structure at school by our commitment to staff development through *regular* meetings, discussions and courses for all parties concerned. And fourthly through the provision of a parents' room, parents and toddlers club, classes for parents to keep fit or to learn English as a second language, craft or hairdressing sessions or informal meetings, an attempt should be made to create a network of parents helping each other at times of stress, ill-health, loneliness and other family crises, to give moral support to each other and above all to share their joys and sorrows and their resources for the benefit of the children and the community.

I set out below some practical suggestions which have helped us at Campsbourne to bring the community into the school.

(a) *New parents*. The school policy is to give time to the prospective parents, which consists of about an hour, to discuss the ethos of the school curriculum and the expectations of the school, and to answer questions. All parents are shown round the school and given information booklets.

(b) *A general meeting* with the new parents is held in the summer term before the start of the new school year. A panel of nursery and reception teachers and ancillary staff give brief talks on school routine, play activities, reading, mathematics and other topics. The parents are then invited into the classrooms to look around and ask questions about any areas of concern that they are preoccupied with.

(c) *Visits*. All nursery and new reception children are invited with their parents to visit their classrooms during the summer term in order to familiarize themselves with the teacher and the building.

(d) *Home visiting*. Home visits are organized in the first fortnight of the autumn term by the nursery teachers and the ancillary staff to establish good relationships with the parents.

(e) *Settling-in-period*. The school policy is to make the settling-in-time flexible. In Haringey all children start in the reception classes in the year they are five. Therefore in September of any school year, some children are just four. Those children who can do a full day without undue stress are encouraged to stay till 3.30 p.m. but others are allowed to attend the morning sessions and gradually build up to a full day. Each situation is discussed with the parents and a solution found to help the child as well as the parent.

(f) *Meet-the-teacher evening*. Once the children are settled in their new classrooms, we organize a meeting around the fifth week of the autumn term to socialize with parents, create opportunities to iron out small problems and also to elect parent representatives and teachers' representatives for the PTA.

(g)   *Parent Teacher Association.* The Association consists of a parent representative from each class, a member of the ancillary staff, a teacher, a parent co-chairperson, a treasurer, a secretary, the headteacher and the deputy head. The job of the class representative is to mediate between parents and teachers, to assess needs in their own classrooms, to organize coffee mornings or evening sessions and help with the parent rotas in the classroom. The PTA meets two or three times a term and is kept fully informed about the school programme and activities; help is sought from the PTA in terms of time, money and any expertise that parents are able to offer. For example parents have funded the school library, bought outdoor wendy houses and curtains, painted a miniature road system, built sandpits and helped with the playground equipment. Parents have occasionally helped with the school assemblies. Talks have included topics like the 'Plight of the American Indians in Brazil', craftwork, musical sessions and dressing a child's hair in an artistic fashion.

(h)   *After-school club*, from 3.30 to 5.30. This was originally set up for the children of working parents and was run by the parents but it has now been taken over by Community Development Division and run successfully in the nearby community centre. The playleaders are employed by the council and they also run a holiday play scheme from 9.30 to 4.00 in the school holidays.

(i)   *Letters.* Many members of staff write letters to parents describing some of the work that goes on in the classrooms, and invite parents to discuss some educational issues at coffee mornings.

(j)   *Coffee mornings* are held from 9.15 to 10.30 a.m. or afternoon sessions from 2.30 to 3.30 p.m. for parents to discuss specific topics such as reading, maths, play, etc. with the class teachers, who often demonstrate how a particular activity is organized by bringing in materials and leading discussions.

(k)   *Handouts*. Specially prepared handouts on reading, maths, handwriting skills and science are given out to the parents to forge links between the activities at home and the work that goes on in the school.

(l)   The headteacher and the staff meet regularly once a week to discuss various aspects of the curriculum and cross-curricular issues, and to plan parents' meetings and exhibitions or displays for the end of a school year. Outside speakers are occasionally invited to help teachers keep abreast with the research.

(m)   *Resource room*. All the resources in the school are centralized in a spare classroom which is the focus of the school and a central point from which the majority of the activities arise. It houses maths resources, reading books, language and phonic games, science equipment, classified non-reference books for topic work, some craft materials, fabrics, posters, story cassettes, picture books, paperbacks and new materials. There is a part-time teacher in charge who co-ordinates the work of the staff and the children.

(n)   *Parents and toddlers room*. This is essential for creating a secure territory for the parents in the school. As no room was available, the existing storeroom and a fiction library were combined to create a parents' room. One resourceful parent knocked down the partition between the two rooms to open the whole area to the toddlers as well as to the mothers and fathers!

(o)   *Parents' rota*. We heavily rely on our parents to come in regularly and help with cookery, language games, story-telling, craftwork, library and book-shop repairs, toy repairs, swimming and outings.

Help with reading activities

Besides giving handouts to the parents, the teachers organize frequent meetings with the parents. There is a colourful and well-equipped lending library in one corner of the school hall, where parents are invited once a week to select books with their children. In the past the money has been raised through fairs and sponsored word lists, and small grants from the advisers.

There is a flourishing school book-shop which opens once a month to sell a comprehensive selection of paperbacks which are acquired from an efficient firm called 'Books For Students' in Leamington Spa, Warwickshire, who provide books at a discount of 15 per cent, and also stamps, cards and wallets. The profit margin allows us to give books away to some who cannot afford to save. All children are encouraged to save 10p to 20p every week. One of our enthusiastic parents comes in every Tuesday to collect the money which ranges from £12 to £20.

The school provides all children with transparent zipped plastic wallets, for protecting books and other equipment.

The crucial document is the child's *reading card* which goes on regular journeys in the plastic wallets to and from school. The teacher writes down the name of the book, the number of pages a child is supposed to read and any other comments, and the parent is encouraged to do the same. The card often becomes the main means of communication if both parents are at work and unable to come into school during the day. The card is often used for other comments, suggestions and homework pertaining to other areas of the curriculum. But what about parents who cannot or will not write on the card? As we all know, not all parents are forthcoming. Verbal communication at the classroom door, a telephone call, a quick home visit or an organized meeting with the individual parent often clears up problems.

Parents are encouraged to make suggestions for buying books for the school library, and make comments about their likes and dislikes. Issues such as sexism, racism or children's fears and anxieties are brought to the forefront and discussed. We do not pretend to change society but at least we can make people aware of some of the issues that preoccupy us at the present moment.

The idea of our next project comes from the book of Tizard *et al.* (1981a) in which there is a succinct description of Heather Sutton's work in using parents as authors. We hope to encourage groups of parents to write illustrated stories with their children about their childhood experiences in English and other languages and use these as a part of our reading programme which has already been expanded to incorporate real books alongside the 'reading books' to help children learn to read.

Our roots in the school are inextricably intertwined with those of the parents. Our whole system would collapse if the parents withdrew their services. In fact we would not know how to work without them.

Home/School Liaison: A Community Teacher's First Report

Fiona Roy

Community teacher's report – Autumn Term

After having spent three years in Secondary and Junior schools, my first term in an Infants School has been a stimulating and educative experience. Never having had a great deal of contact with Infant School work, I have come to realize fully just how vital the early years are and the skill that is needed when dealing with the education of very young children.

My first task was to become acquainted with Infant School methods and during the first half of the term I have tried to spend as much time as possible in the classroom. The teachers in this school have been very cooperative and they have helped me a great deal in explaining apparatus and approaches dealing with the teaching of basic concepts.

When I took up my post here I found that the parents were involved, and encouraged to be so, in the everyday life of the school. Many of them helped individual teachers by taking baking and sewing groups. There are always a number of parents who come every week to help the children choose library books from the school library, and many mothers go swimming with the children during their weekly swimming lesson. I found this very encouraging.

As a Book Fair had been established the previous term and had been very successful, Mrs Clough suggested I might like to organize another Fair, leading to the introduction of a permanent Book Shop in school. This I did and we now have a continuing order of books for display and sale in the school. At the Book Fair I arranged a small exhibition of the methods used in the school in teaching reading, and I supplied parents with duplicated information sheets entitled, 'How you can help your child to read'. On display I had samples of the children's written work, the different stages of reading books, the Language Master and the Breakthrough Reading Scheme. Other equipment (audio-visual) was also shown for parents to look at and use.

During my first week at school Mrs Clough suggested I could run the library on Monday, Tuesday and Wednesday mornings. On these occasions books are available for the older children in school to take home. This activity is now run entirely by the mothers.

Fortunately, I have had some previous contact with Hucknall as I have been a member of the Holgate Players for some years. Our plays are performed in the Junior School close by and so I am not a complete stranger to the area. I have found the people welcoming, family orientated and very keen to be involved in community activities. Everyone I have met seems to have a number of uncles, cousins and other relations, living in this area. The 'extended family' is very evident. Hucknall is in a mining district and many of the fathers of the children attending this school are miners.

The school is served by two Council Estates and by private houses in Beauvale, Watnall Road, Shortwood, Polpero Way and Ascot Drive. However, many of the children from Ascot Drive are leaving at Christmas to go to the new Community School in Edgewood Drive. Many of our mothers work full or part-time, but I have found that their attitude towards school is on the whole quite positive. This was borne out this term when we had a series of Open Days in school.

We have been fortunate in having the staff of the new Nursery wing working in the school this term as their new building had not been completed in time. As a result members of the Infant School staff have had plenty of extra help and so were able to spend more time talking to the parents. Whilst the parents were in school during Open Day they were encouraged to take part in activities with the children. There was an impressive turn-out of parents, both fathers and mothers. Only fifteen parents out of the whole school failed to appear at these Open Days. I have since done a follow-up of the meetings and by Christmas every parent will have met their child's class teacher. This is where I feel I can be of benefit in promoting links between parent and teacher. In fact, since September, several mothers have come into school to help and in these cases a greater communication between teacher and parent has been established.

I have found that organization of time and priorities are very important areas of my post. Keeping in mind long-term aims, is,

I feel, essential. There are so many different facets to consider that a clear picture of my ultimate goal is vital. Mrs Clough has allowed me to organize my own day and this has demanded a self-discipline not experienced in the classroom where a working routine establishes the pattern of the week or term. There are many aspects of my work in which I feel I am a novice yet. An example was mentioned at the course I attended at Ollerton – being sensitive to signals and responses of parents and staff. This is an important skill to be developed.

I have been very fortunate in working with a Headmistress who is particularly keen that parents should participate in school life. Mrs Clough has been a great help to me during this first term and I have listened to and followed her advice and direction. I discovered from Mrs Clough and the staff that the main educational problem the children have is a lack of a rich language experience, so that when they come to school their speech is often restricted, colours are not known, and experience of numbers very limited. There seems to be reasonable playgroup provision in the area and I would have thought this would have helped. Our own Nursery is opening in January and will cater eventually for 120 children. Perhaps not enough time is spent at home playing with the children under school age because of working mothers, television or simply not being aware of the importance of talking with the children. I feel that much of my work can be done here both with children in our school and in the wider community.

Although I visited all the playgroups in Hucknall this term and found willing cooperation, I feel that an important contact has been made with the two playgroups that 'feed' our school. In fact, the two groups are run by mothers of children already at our school. The playgroup leaders expressed interest in the school, especially regarding the methods we employed in developing reading skills. I have been able to arrange for weekly visits of a playgroup leader to the school as a result. I have also taken books from our book shop to the playgroups and I hope that further contact will be made next term at the Mother and Toddler sessions held on Wednesday afternoons.

Being on a campus, our Junior and Secondary schools are within easy reach and some first steps have been made towards creating links with our children's future schools. We invited the Junior staff to a 'social' after school and found this successful and they intend to return our invitation. I assist the teacher of first year Juniors on a weekly basis, and I hope that this will soon include other members of our staff, as some have expressed interest in the follow-up work in the Junior School. The Junior staff have been most willing for us to spend time in their classrooms and therefore I feel that there are many possibilities for future cooperation here. I think the most important fact at the moment is that both sets of staff recognize the need for greater flexibility and interaction.

When I made contact with the Secondary School I found a willingness to communicate. The Senior Mistress came to visit, at her own request, our Deaf Unit and was shown over our school generally. The Headmaster also visited our school to discuss ways in which we could cooperate. One of his teachers is running a Home Craft course for school leavers and it was arranged that Mrs Clough would talk to the girls about language development in young children. Mrs Clough took as her starting point the making of scrap-books for talking experience and since her visit the girls have been making scrap-books which they hope to use with young children when they visit the play groups.

I called at the Secondary School the following week with some toys for children aged up to 3–4 years old. I arranged them for the girls to 'play' with first (as their teacher commented, this was probably the first time many of them would have played with toys themselves). Many of the toys were home-made – cotton reels on string, old containers filled with wooden blocks, etc. We discussed how such toys developed hand/eye control and were forerunners to counting, number concepts and writing. I duplicated a hand-out for the girls as a follow-up. Mrs Nurse (their teacher) and I discussed how the girls might like to visit playgroups and they are at present working towards this. Two of the girls have been to our school and perhaps more of this could be done next term. After all, many of them are our future parents.

Another contact I have made this term is with the Speech Therapist, as two of our children have speech defects. Most teachers seem to feel that more contact needs to be made with the Therapist so that they may have a better idea how to help a child with speech problems. As there was no regular contact with social workers, I invited several appropriate people to a meeting held in school. The following attended – Mrs Shelbourne and Miss Brackenbury (social workers), Mr Pilling (Methodist Minister),

PC Mullin (police/school liaison officer), Mr Liptrot (EWO), Mrs Nurse (Sec School), Miss Everett (Junior School), Nurse Wysokki (School Nurse); our Headmistress and her Deputy were also present. It was generally agreed that such gatherings could be useful and we have arranged to meet once a term. Our next meeting is on February 11th when Mrs Shelbourne will talk about her role in the community.

Resulting from the meeting I have discussed future contact with the Antenatal Clinic. Nurse Wysokki is keen for cooperation with school and visits us regularly. I have been to the clinic – again Mrs Clough and I visited with scrap-books, our book shop books, and pre-school books – and talked to the mothers generally. We are interested in developing this link next term. It is planned that the clinic will take place in the youth wing of the Secondary School in March – an ideal setting! I am sure that there are many possibilities here.

I felt it would be beneficial if a time was set aside each week for parents to come into school. This has taken shape in our 'Pop-Ins' which this term have been held on Thursday afternoons. These sessions have been valuable. Parents have met each other and pre-school children have been welcomed into school. We have had scrap-book-making sessions when children from school have joined their mothers for a session of picture sticking and choosing. Much of the time, however, has been taken up with coffee and chat. During the past few weeks we worked towards our Christmas Sale which we felt was a success, not only financially, but in the degree to which mothers felt involved. This was especially so in the making of things, exchanging patterns and ideas. Two or three of our mothers and I set up a 'Nearly New Stall' which operates on Thursdays and we have accumulated quite a lot of clothes and toys. We have had to have our 'Pop-Ins' in the school hall now as so many parents attend. I am inheriting a whole classes equipment next term and I hope to develop a properly organized area for pre-school children with this material.

Another contact that was made was with the local shops. Our first shop in this respect was the Cooperative on our estate. During the term, children's work was collected from the teachers and displayed in the shop in November. When I came to take down the exhibition the manager said how much the children had enjoyed seeing their own work, and that he would like us to do this sort of thing again.

Parents have also commented favourably at seeing the children's drawing, paintings and writing on display.

Hearing comments from parents and teachers who were worried about certain children's reading progress, I attempted, along with two mothers, to make some home/school kits. These kits are very basic as I am still learning myself about infant method. I intended them to be a means of involving parents with their children's difficulties at home. The kits consist of a fishing game related to the child's reading book and a Snap or Pairs card game, again many of the words being found in the child's reading book. At the moment I have loaned three kits. I think the children certainly receive a boost from this personal interest and being in game form they are willing to cooperate.

One very successful home/school link introduced by Mrs Clough this term has been the home/school books. These are continuing dialogues between teacher and parent. The teacher writes any comments on the week's progress and happenings and the parents reply during the weekend. It is a form of diary keeping and we all feel an invaluable form of liaison.

I have also had contact this term with the College of Further Education in Hucknall. I had hoped to begin some day classes in school for mothers. I contacted Mr Thomlinson and became aware that Adult Literacy Classes were held at the College and I have referred two mothers, at their own request, to him. I have also had contact with the playgroup for socially deprived families run in Hucknall by the College of Further Education. Again, I hope this contact will be developed next year.

Our children go swimming every Friday and a number of mothers also attend, some of whom go into the water with the children. Next term I hope to be able to begin an after-school swimming club for parents and children. Throughout the term I have felt the need for fathers to be more involved; naturally working hours are a stumbling block, but this is an area that needs attention.

All the teachers in our school are in a sense community teachers as all encourage parental interest and involvement. I think valuable communication can be seen in a written comment to one teacher in a home/school book viz: 'I don't get to school much so I think having this book is just great!'. This parent has five children.

During the last two weeks of the term I have been decorating part of the school foyer with a group of parents. We have all thoroughly enjoyed this venture, and produced an attractive illustration of the Sorcerer's Apprentice and Aladdin's Cave. We arranged an outing to Nottingham on 17th December to see the decorations and lights. Over fifty mothers and children took part and I gave each mother a duplicated list of suggestions for discussion with their children during our visit. The main purpose was for a talking experience between mother and child. Although for one mother it was the first time she had been to Nottingham in 16 years. These then have been the main events of the term. It has been a time of finding out, of getting to know people, existing organizations and the general neighbourhood of the school. I think that one of the most valuable assignments I carried out this term was when I visited the homes of pre-school children during my first week at school. This enabled me to meet all the new children and their parents and have a point of contact for them and me. Further contacts with the 'new' parents, I feel, have been more meaningful because of these initial visits.

There have been many small incidents throughout the term, such as when one parent would not allow his child to go swimming. He was gently persuaded first to come and watch and then gradually the parents allowed their child to go in the water. Now the child is swimming along with the rest each week.

As must be expected there have also been disappointments, but most of all there has been a richness and variety of experience. I have been made aware of the continuing process of education, seeing in fact the full span from pre-school to secondary. This to me as a teacher has been an experience of immense value.

Involving Parents and the Wider Community

John Bird and Bob Croson

Meadow Farm Primary School and Pear Tree Junior School have, since 1983, embarked upon a process of developing community education. Through our initiative as headteachers, and that of the governing bodies, both of the schools were selected as pilot schools by Derbyshire County Council, and have received support to facilitate their development.

Meadow Farm Primary School was opened in September 1968. It was built to serve the new community created by the building of a large number of council houses and flats. The new estate, known as the Albert Road Estate, was built behind a well-established area of private housing which also forms part of the schools community. This mixed community lies on the north-western edge of the city, and is clearly defined by four roads which contain it. There are very few facilities within the area, in fact the total provision comprises a pub, five shops, a residential home for the elderly, and the school. The community is virtually all white, with about average unemployment. In recent years the population has become more transient.

During its early years, the school population grew very rapidly to about 500 children. This has fallen now to around 260. The fall in numbers has made teaching spaces available for other use. The school now comprises a main clasp-type building containing three pairs of classrooms. Each pair of rooms share a practical area and can be open-plan or separate. Also in the main building is the family room, the school resource room, a maths resource room, and the hall which is used for dining. On the site are three terrapin blocks. One contains two classrooms, a second contains one classroom and the creative arts room, and the third is the community block containing a lounge or general purpose room, a pre-school room, storeroom or darkroom and toilets. A nursery is also currently being built on the site.

Pear Tree Junior School rises, a large, Victorian, 'Lowryesque' monument, amid a typical inner-city area. Due to fluctuations in the school population, which now stands at 310, there are a number of free areas available which have been adapted for different uses. The school now consists of one large two-storey building housing two halls, eleven classrooms, working bases, library, and admin. rooms; two single storey terrapin type blocks, one containing two classrooms and working bases, and the other converted into a community block with a lounge-cum-coffee bar, a workroom-cum-classroom, office, storerooms, and a toilet; a two-storey block housing dining and craft facilities, together with a dark room; two large playgrounds; and a sports field. Next door is a modern low-slung infant school, and close by is a nursery school.

The surrounding area is a mix of rented terraced housing, some owner-occupied terraced or small semis, factories (many now derelict), and a mix of shops and other services. To many people in the city, Pear Tree is an area 'gone down'. It used to contain many people from trades and lower to middle management in the local industries. As these people moved away to newer owner-occupied estates in other parts of the city, the housing gradually declined. At the time of large influxes of immigrant workers to work in local factories, it was to this area of the city that they came, finding cheap accommodation.

The school population to some extent now reflects the ethnic balance of the area. The ratio of the school families is approximately 70 per cent Sikh, 10 per cent Muslim, five per cent Afrocaribbean and other minorities, 15 per cent Indigenous white.

In recent years both City and County Councils have helped in the development of a variety of 'community facilities' in the Pear Tree area, including sports halls, a number of community centres, library, youth clubs, etc. Added to that there are other infant, junior, and nursery schools, local churches, etc., all of which are involved in some way with 'the local community', and led by both professional and voluntary groups. Finally, the area is blessed with the presence of Derby County Football Club!

It is very evident that in every respect the two situations are very different. The buildings, the children, the nature of the communities, and the community facilities available bear little resemblance to each other.

Community education is notoriously difficult to define in a few words. Eric Midwinter defines a community school as one which 'emphasises the differences rather than the similarities of schools precisely because it attempts to relate fluently and positively with the ethos, character, and values of the community it serves'. Community education is characterized by a variety of activities and structures which can be found in any genuine community school. One of these characteristics is the involvement of parents and the wider community.

In 1983, there was little parental involvement in Meadow Farm School. There was a Parent Teacher Association which raised money for the school, ran occasional events and was little involved in the school otherwise. The school had parent interviews each year. Home/school relationships were rather formal and could in no way be described as partnerships. The school is a primary school with children joining at rising five, but the opportunity which this presented for parental involvement had not generally been grasped.

Pear Tree Junior School also had little parental contact in 1983 apart from formal open evenings, and did not have a Parent Teacher Association. Other contacts with the parents were not encouraged apart from formal visits to the headteacher over areas of complaint. As the children do not start at the school until junior age there is also limited natural contact with parents who bring their children to school. The school was not used at all by the community apart from one football playing youth group who worked entirely independently of the school and local community.

Since school forms one part of the daily process of learning and an even smaller part of the lifelong process of learning, it is important that people other than schoolteachers, particularly parents, should play a part in childrens learning. Therefore, a fundamental part of the role of the school should be to develop educational partnership between teacher and parent, home and school. The attempt to develop this partnership has been one strand of the development of both schools since 1983.

At Meadow Farm we planned carefully what we sought to achieve, set ourselves termly objectives, and regularly reviewed them. We wanted to create an open school, as natural to its community as a pub, a launderette, a chip shop, or a library. In order to bring this about, we took several planned steps.

First, we created a Family Room. What had originally been changing rooms were carpeted and had fitted units put in. The room has outside access for prams etc. and the doors are labelled 'Family Room'. Refreshments are always available, and the room is close to the staffroom and office. It is now used more and more by parents informally and in small group meetings. Secondly, we made our reprographic facilities – which were quite good – available to the community. Thirdly, and most important, though most difficult, we began to develop a more open atmosphere. Anyone who comes into the building can always find someone to help and anyone is available at anytime, be it headteacher, classteacher, or whoever, and everyone is welcome in the staffroom. Added together these things are creating a more open school which the community increasingly sees as its own.

At the same time, similar beginnings were being made at Pear Tree. After initially persuading the local authority to redecorate and renovate the main school buildings we too began the process of 'opening up' the school. Community rooms were developed from a terrapin block, which included a lounge area with a snack and drinks area, a community workroom, and an office for the newly installed community teacher. Although Pear Tree seemed to be working from further back in community confidence than Meadow Farm, gradually more and more parents are using it as a drop-in area, and more recently as an advice centre. As with Meadow Farm, we at Pear Tree have made our reprographic facilities available to the community.

In our desire at Pear Tree to make a more open atmosphere the entrance area to the main school was redesigned to encourage a feeling of 'welcome'. This area is where the headteachers room is situated, and within that room the desk was moved to place me in direct line of vision to the entrance so that I should give a welcoming smile whenever possible to every visitor. This also necessitated removing the metal cover that had been placed over the glass of the door! Every effort is made to welcome any visitor, by whoever is available, an attitude which has spilled over to include the children. Parents are encouraged to wander freely around the school to help, look, or seek advice as required. Pear Tree has also opened up its staff room where parents, visitors, and staff are treated equally. This seems to have happened quite naturally and gradually, and is merely a reflection of 'open attitudes'. A fundamental aspect of the aims of both schools was the development of genuine educational partnership.

At Meadow Farm this meant taking a number of initiatives related to its community. It seemed important to develop pre-school activities on the site in order to begin to develop a partnership with parents as early as possible. Therefore we facilitated the establishment of a Parent and Toddler group and a Playgroup on the site. These groups are now very well established and successful.

We also felt that it was important to organize a procedure for familiarizing children and their families with the school, for helping parents understand the schools procedures for helping the children learn, and also learn their role in the learning process too. To this end we set up an induction procedure which provides opportunities for all children and their parents to become thoroughly conversant with these things. The procedure includes home visiting by the community co-ordinator and separately by the class teacher.

We established a home/school reading scheme in which parents have a role to play. Regular communication takes place between teacher and parent via a reading card. Parents have the opportunity to attend reading workshops to learn more about this role.

We have reorganized our parent/teacher discussion evenings to be more informal and equal. The purpose of the evening is explained beforehand and an open record is kept of points raised by the parent and the teacher. We also take every opportunity to involve parents in decisions about the child particularly concerning behaviour when parents are consulted at a very early stage. We have established 'Meadow Farm News', a community/school newspaper which is published once each month.

Also established is a school volunteers scheme. Many parents, other adults, students in training etc. come to school during the week to assist teachers in the classroom or help in a volunteers workshop. The whole group from time to time then convenes to give feedback about the schools curriculum and organization. This scheme is organized by the deputy-head. Pear Tree, of course, did not have the same involvement with pre-school and infant children. The infant school next door was supported in its development of a Parent and Toddler Group. Close by are nursery schools and community centres all running similar things with the same pool of parents, so this issue became one of support and encouragement, rather than setting up another of the same.

It was of course an important part of the development at Pear Tree to improve the induction procedure in the school as well as the information to parents. Serious thought had to be given to suitable consideration for language and culture in the development of materials and meetings, but the fundamental principles were the same as those followed at Meadow Farm.

One of the key areas of development at Pear Tree has been that of 'links with parents'. There is now an ever-growing variety of involvement. A great deal of time and effort has gone into the development of home reading and home maths work. With both the schemes explanatory videos have been developed using children and staff, which have been supported by meetings, visits, publicity etc. This work was built on a sound base of home-links. The principal developed has been one where each class teacher visits the homes of the children in his or her class, whilst the community teacher takes the class. This was developed through an observation of the great lack of confidence obvious in many parents coming into school, and a desire by the staff to be more practically aware of the home and individual culture of the children. Whilst staff gained confidence, the initial visits were by the home/school/community teacher, but soon the obvious benefits of visits by the class teacher led the development on. The school has now moved far away from the 'visits to tackle problems' situation, and into the area of positive sharing and mutual encouragement. Allied to this Pear Tree has worked hard at improving communications with home, and encouraging parents confidence to use the school as a resource for advice or to give directions towards where advice can be given.

Some parents at Pear Tree have also helped form a local group called Pear Tree Project Group, which links with the school, social services, and a local community centre, to provide and encourage the development of a variety of community action programmes such as summer and easter playschemes, discos, youth clubs, etc. This is a developing group which has moved into the area of such things as arranging training for volunteer workers, 'roping in' other local agencies, raising funds for charity, supporting other local need groups like senior citizens, etc.

Much of the increase in confidence, which has led to a variety of ways in which parents and members of the local community have become involved in Pear Tree has come from a development of the ethos and atmosphere generated within the school. There is a drop-in centre located in the community lounge where adults can call for a chat, a drink, a place to relax or escape for a while. However parents can and do wander into school for a chat at any time.

The school also encouraged the start of a local community

newspaper, which is delivered about three times a year to every local house, and contains articles and information for and by local people. At the same time, we at Pear Tree have been looking at ways that the school can be involved as a resource for the community outside of parents and children alone. Clearly, for Pear Tree to become yet another provider in an already crowded area, in competition with other groups would be a mistake. The direction that community education took in the wider community therefore meant first looking at the many 'communities' involved around the area, then seeing how through cooperation, education, confidence building, and an open attitude, the communities and providing agencies could be intertwined.

The local Gurdwara has used the premises for community language classes for children in Punjabi. This has now developed into over 200 children each night coming back for supplementary schooling in Punjabi. The school has sought to help in any way possible and from that group initiatives in youth activities have developed.

The facilities are also used by a number of local youth and adult sports clubs. A number of local community groups use the premises for all sorts of functions, both religious and secular, normally opposing groups sharing the site with little trouble. Many of these activities are becoming more and more open and supportive of and towards the local community, rather than exclusive to a particular interest group. These activities, which cover a wide variety of events, have grown so much that the caretaking staff has had to be enlarged to allow for almost seven day, all-day usage.

At Meadow Farm the community around the school is within a clearly defined area, and does not have a confusion of agencies, which has required a different approach to the same fundamental notion of cooperative community involvement. There, community education has involved many parents and other adults from the community. Involvement has helped to build individual and collective confidence. This in turn has led to the establishment of Women And Health Groups, several self-help groups, 'O' Level English and Basic Maths groups, a Luncheon Club for the elderly, a Youth Activities club, etc. The premises are in use for five to six nights each week. Increasingly the impetus for the creation of new groups and activities is coming from the community.

More recently a Management Committee has been established to co-ordinate the activities of the many community groups now active on the site at Meadow Farm. So, parents and other adults are actively involved as helpers, educators, community providers, and learners at both schools, thus bringing about a considerable degree of personal growth and community confidence, even though the actual outworking of the principles is different in each establishment.

Community education is about the individual of whatever age learning to contribute to and be a part of, his or her community. It encompasses racism, sexism, and all the other isms of society. It is also about the process of learning. It is about self-awareness, self-direction, and self-expression. This may range from mastering a language which can provide the power to communicate, to gaining confidence in relationships which will enable the learner to discover new knowledge and enjoy new experiences. Community education is about learning together, caring and sharing, a partnership, giving and receiving. It involves the sharing of power – there can be no education for community where control remains largely in the hands of the professional and the privileged, expertise (the professional) being used to free people in their minds and actions rather than entrap them in institutionalism. Community education is about justice. It is about the fairer distribution of resources so that all can give as well as receive. In community education any activity which enhances learning as living, for freedom, wholeness and fulfilment, is an integral part of the process. It is about turning the education process on its head. It is about discovering the immense resources available, and by encouragement, facilitative support, and networking, liberating these and their possessors to be educational resources for others. It is about the teacher being a facilitator, using discernment and sensitivity.

In all these directions the two schools have moved a little way down the road. The main achievements can be seen in a variety of obvious ways:

1. the atmosphere and relationships that permeate the schools, which has led to an enhancement of the learning process;

2. the way the schools have become more 'open' and 'owned' by the community;

3. the developing growth in educational partnership;

4. the way that the children's 'education' is benefiting from a community-conscious curriculum;

5.   the schools are becoming successful as a focal point for community activity and development;

6.   the considerable amount of personal growth taking place in adults involved with the schools.

Yet there is still a long way to go and considerable difficulties, confusions, discouragements and irritations have been experienced. Some of the main ones are listed below.

- The two schools constantly try to avoid being classed as schools that 'get their premises used', yet this is so often seen by outsiders as the measure of success. Schools must beware that the tremendously valid experiences of multi-used premises and involvement in the learning of non-school-age people that seem to happen in a more open environment do not beguile them into thinking that is the sole or even major objective of community education in the primary school.

- Some degree of lateral thinking and ingenuity has had to be used in the way the two schools have been organized. Priorities have had to be rethought. The schools have found it important to order priorities, deciding on specific, manageable courses of action, establish them, seeing others (i.e. parents) take responsibility if appropriate before moving on – always remembering that each school and community is unique, can only progress successfully at its own unique rate, and should not be compared with another.

- It has been both schools experience that if one is in the business of giving confidence to communities (parents, staff, etc.) the first thing they criticize with their new found confidence will be the perpetrator of that confidence booster. It is also true that in order to develop initiatives risks have to be taken in all sorts of areas, particularly when responsibility is handed over to 'non-professionals'. Sometimes things have gone wrong, and some form of safety net is vital, but at the end of the day risks have to be taken, and that requires courage: personal, corporate, and professional.

- One of the real keys to the process of open schools is 'good communications'. It has proved important to work hard as a community in the school on improving verbal, visual, and written forms of communication. It is so easy to relate the message to the experiences of the staff sending that message, rather than understanding the experience of the receiver. The images and messages that are presented are important in encouraging openness.

- A continuing headache in schools is that bureaucracy rarely keeps pace with progress. It tends to run along behind where it is safe. This has obviously been the case during the 'piloting' period, the existing administrative structures were not designed to cope with community education and what it implies. However it is vital that eventually administration is redesigned. Administration and bureaucracy must reflect the philosophy of community education being developed in schools before there is any hope of a successful relationship between the two!

- Time is, of course, always short in schools. In developing community schools when staff or curriculum development is vital, particularly in the area of human relations, the lack of time in which staff can meet to learn, plan, and visit becomes acute. Development would benefit from an increase in the availability of such time.

- There are many occasions when, faced with the considerable demands as the leader of such developments, one questions one's own philosophy. In working it out in practice there are many disappointments, failures, regrets and hurtful experiences. It is vital at these times to cling on to the vision and find support in others who share it.

For schools, the implications are that we must hold fast to our task of serving the community by helping them to bring up their children to be fulfilled within the communities of which they choose to be a part, and to learn to be caring and sharing partners in those communities. This involves not just looking at things the schools provide for the community, but also how the schools as communities address the issues involved, those of curriculum, attitudes, relationships, etc. Schools must live what they preach!

Schools must work hard at establishing true partnership with parents and not seek to become providers of activities for those that like them alone. We must continually be looking at how we teach children to see whether we use methods appropriate to our aims. And, most important of all, we must ensure that we are consistent ourselves with the attitudes and relationships that we are attempting to encourage.

It would be wrong to say that taking on board 'community education' is easy. Bridging the gap can involve challenging pre-formed attitudes, becoming involved in relationships that would normally be avoided or carefully controlled, and accepting new ways of democratic choice. Cooperating with other groups, agencies and individuals in the development of children within the community is a process fraught with misunderstanding and 'collisions of interest'.

However, in schools which are committed to 'relevant' education, these issues have to be faced. Without a holistic approach, involving as many influences on a child as possible, the process of educating in school is like trying to paint a picture deliberately not using half the colours on the palette. The painting can be done, but it is not half as good as it could have been.

Teacher Attitudes and the Involvement of Parents

Sheila Bainbridge

In an attempt to shape positive attitudes the school may decide to take steps to provide an opportunity for parents to involve themselves in the life of the school and in their child's education. Important issues and implications thus arise and which need to be taken into account by the school. Four main areas of parental involvement can be identified, and are identified in Table 7 as Levels 1–4. In practice these are likely to overlap to some extent: the diagram is intended only to provide a framework for discussion. The activities identified in the boxes are not exhaustive: neither are they meant to be so. The reader may consider other activities of equal or of more importance than those cited but it is hoped that the matrix as it stands will serve its intended purpose.

The implications for the involvement of parents and other agencies with the school may have far-reaching consequences. Therefore, although this chapter will focus upon Level 2, it is necessary to consider briefly the other levels as none can operate in total isolation from the other three.

Fundamental questions immediately arise:

1. Who decides and controls the degree of involvement?
2. What are the implications for the teacher?
3. What are the implications for the parent?
4. What are the criteria for evaluation and assessment that the child benefits from such involvement?

If the school takes the initiative for a parental involvement programme, it is likely that those professionally involved are likely to feel that they ought to have overall control. If the school sets the rules, how far may they be kept by the other agencies concerned?

Table 7: School and community: participants and levels of involvement

Level of Involvement

		LEVEL 1	LEVEL 2	LEVEL 3	LEVEL 4
		Parent as Practical Helper	Individual Child	Classroom Involvement	Policy
Participants	Teachers	Teacher directed e.g. making equipment, mounting pictures, covering books, taking place outside the classroom	Professional expertise	Professional expertise	Professional expertise
			Curriculum planning, content and emphasis Evaluation and assessment		
	Parents	Parent Groups e.g. PTA, Parent Association, Friends of the School (Family circle). Fund Raising events. Educational programmes – teacher initiated	Teacher initiated and directed programme to involve parent and child together in an educational activity	Parental assistance on educational visits Group work in curriculum activities – teacher directed	Individual/ Group parental intervention in curriculum and/or school organization pressure groups support groups
	Partnership	Parent groups e.g. equal decision with school on spending money raised; on educa- tional projects	Parent having equal voice with teacher relating to educational needs of the individual child	Discussion, negotiated agreement of what and how educational activities may be undertaken	Negotiated consensus
	Community	Friends of the School to include others as well as parents – under school control		With community services With members of community e.g. OAPs business church college	Political religious action groups. Governors negotiated consensus of community involvement. Imposed Community involvement

Level 1 is often the first step in introducing the parent to participate in the life of the school within the building itself. 'Parent as Helper' outside the classroom is the level at which teachers and parents are likely to feel least threat to their autonomy and self-esteem. The work, such as making apparatus, or covering books, is teacher directed. Helpful parents who do not intrude upon the teacher's time or classroom are likely to be looked upon favourably by most teachers. Little contact may result except in discussing the task and appreciation of the help received acknowledged. It is unlikely that education itself will be discussed in any great depth. Resentment of parents working as unpaid teacher's aid may be manifested in some quarters. According to the manner in which the parents perceive themselves to be received by the school, adverse or positive attitudes of one group towards the other may be reinforced or modified.

Still at Level 1, PTAs and other associations are mainly involved in social activities and fund raising. Programmes to explain educational methods are initiated. These activities provide a controlled social outlet for teachers and parents to meet. Such organizations are essentially teacher controlled but demonstrate a degree of democracy within their structure.

It is when such associations step beyond the boundary of acquiescent provider and listener and, for example, wish to direct how money raised ought to be spent or wish for a voice in curriculum development that problems can arise. If ideas of parents and teachers coincide, equilibrium is preserved. If parents perceive the educational needs of their children as different from those perceived by the teachers, books for the library versus a computer for example, then conflict is sparked, the 'professionalism' of the teacher is evoked and communication soured.

On the other hand, if parental involvement is to mean shared experiences and ideas of equal weight with teachers, then logically a move across the levels of involvement to Level 4 must be taken into account. Close involvement with outside agencies occurs. With parents, school and community in partnership, negotiated consensus may be reached; this may be at the social level or, for extended educational activities, include the community and be centred upon the school. If this concept can be accommodated and accepted as reasonable by all concerned, an environment is created which will enrich the education of children and adults alike. The school becomes part of the community and not simply located within it. This is a real community school.

However, it must be taken into account that fringe pressure groups or individuals, whose thinking is not in line with the majority, can develop. Or a ground swell of opposition may occur. Attempts may be made to influence educational or organizational policy and there is strong leverage if such stirrings for change come from those with a firm foothold in the organization. Ideas of people seeking policy change may not coincide with the professional philosophy of the school. The Head may then find him or herself at the centre of a power struggle. The school and others will need to be aware of and understand the agreed policy of the LEA and Governors in such an event.

The ramifications (political, social and educational) of such situations do not fall into the brief of this study. Suffice it to say that it is important to be aware of the possibly adverse, as well as advantageous, developments which may arise if the school adopts a policy to invite outside agencies to become involved with it and in it. It appears then that although the school initially felt itself to be in charge of the situation, others may have a different perspective. The school feels its autonomy eroded. Time is taken to engage in boundary disputes and the children's education is in no way enhanced. Conversely, conflict can arise if the school seeks to alienate itself from the community.

Leaving aside these issues but not ignoring them, the level of involvement to be considered here concerns teacher and parent liaison aimed at improving the educational attainment of the individual child. What are the implications for the teacher and parent? Teachers often believe that a more enabling parental attitude towards education and school would help the child to achieve more. The onus is upon the school to communicate to parents its aims and methods as they affect the individual child in such a way as to be understood by people outside the education profession. To help parents to understand that they have an important influence and do have a role to play in the education of their children is the major problem for the inner-city or urban school.

Goodwill is an important factor in parent/teacher contact and needs to be nurtured. Mutual feelings of regard will help the teacher to initiate dialogue with groups or individuals, leading to activities involving the parent in the child's learning process. Such activities may be teacher initiated or result from negotiation between teacher and parent.

At this stage, teachers are likely to ask questions about the nature of their professionalism, the degree of commitment required and the demands upon their time. Activities which are perceived as challenging the professional status of the teacher are viewed with suspicion and sometimes with hostility by many in the profession. If the teacher initiates the learning programme, monitors and evaluates it with the parent as acquiescent onlooker, the professionalism of the teacher is unlikely to be felt to be challenged. If the involvement of the parents moves towards consultation with the teacher where equal consideration and importance is attached to the views of both groups, the teacher may feel less secure. Reservations about the initiative may arise and the teacher wish to withdraw.

However, most people can recognize the value of specialist professional training. The professionalism of the teacher lies in the decision making role. A communications gap between lay persons and professionals is unavoidable and not easily overcome by brief verbal explanations and exchanges. A comparison may be made with the situation of the doctor. Successful communication needs time and thought. Teachers are not used to asking for ideas, suggestions and opinions from lay persons. It is the very belief of parents in the professionalism of teachers which makes them reluctant to ask, to offer opinion on educational matters, or sometimes to help. It does not deter some, however, from challenging the values of the school, either by face to face confrontation or by staying away. Goble (1977) cautions that

> If the school seems to be in any way scornful of the home, or the home scornful of the school, or if either feels threatened by the other, the alliance between them will not operate, and neither encouragement nor coercion can be very hopefully attempted.

Unproductive contact and alienation is better diffused. Therefore, sharing, explaining, working towards an understanding of the teacher's aspirations for the child may strengthen the professionalism of the teacher in the eyes of the parents. The spirit in which dialogue takes place is central to effective communication. It must be freed from an attitude of patronage. It must not be seen as a means of manipulation to gain more control and power over people's lives. If there are entrenched positions of one group threatening another it is unlikely that progress towards worthwhile contact can be made.

There are other considerations needing attention. Teachers may well feel that they are not employed to embark upon public relations exercises, but to teach. It may be that this, in their view, means little contact is necessary with non-professionals other than those under their control as invited visitors to participate in a one-off situation, Parents' Evenings, Open Days. For others, recognizing the value to the child of time consuming dialogue with parents, the aims regarding parent/teacher involvement ought to be clearly defined. They may be arranged under three headings:

For the child: improved educational attainment; improved motivation; greater self-esteem; positive attitudes towards school; recognizing the value and worth of parent as educator with the teacher; the beginnings of social awareness reinforced.

For the parent: recognition of self worth in contributing with the teacher in the education of their children; an understanding of the school's aims and methods; modification of inhibiting attitudes towards education and school; reinforced social awareness of their role in the community.

For the teacher: improved communication with parents; knowledge of parental expectations and aspirations; some knowledge of the child's home circumstances, information about the locality and community; opportunities to work in harmony with parents and reduce tensions and conflict.

It is within these areas that evaluation and assessment of the initiative needs to take place. However, few of these important aims are quantifiable by measurable results. Nevertheless a professional judgement is necessary to serve as an indicator for future action. It is important that the parent/teacher involvement be recognized as educationally worthwhile for the child, by all participating groups. Otherwise, the teacher may feel to be in an invidious position. That is, the idea of parent/teacher partnership may be approved of in principle but its implementation and development may be disagreed with as regards individual participation.

Staffroom Mythology and Teacher Ignorance – concerning parents and family life

John Bastiani

Teacher lore and staffroom mythology

Even when they are not directly involved in the life and work of the school, parents operate as an unseen presence. Talk about 'pushy', 'over-protective' or 'uncooperative' parents is rife in most staffrooms. Such generalizations are often based upon very limited contact with families, particularly on their own home ground and upon hearsay and circumstantial evidence.

There are two parent stereotypes in particular, which are used to buttress strongly held and widespread beliefs about parents in general and which are also used as a point of reference in home/ school matters. These two are loudly voiced in staffrooms of every conceivable type throughout the country.

The 'interfering' parent – 'before you know it, they'll be taking over!'

The best way of coming to terms with such a view, is to recognize that it is readily contradicted by the extensive experience we have of parental involvement in schools, especially where this involves working alongside teachers in classrooms. Such contact appears almost always to increase parents' awareness of the difficulties of organizing and managing classrooms effectively. Typical reactions are:

> I don't know how they do it. It's bad enough with my two.
> I don't know how she copes with all those different things going on at once.

In my experience such a stereotype can be traced to a misinterpretation of the efforts parents make to find out more about their children's schooling, so that they can help them more effectively. This seems light years away from wanting to take over the running of the school, which is the last thing that most parents want!

The disinterested parent – 'you never see the parents you really want to see'

This is the most deep-rooted and widespread parent stereotype of all, used to account for an enormous range of parental inadequacies ranging from non-attendance at school events to the failings of their children in class. Don't jump to simplistic or over-hasty conclusions. They may well be wide of the mark, for there are a number of important and legitimate explanations for such behaviour, which need an airing.

In the first place, there are a number of *practical difficulties*, which can prevent many parents from attending school events, or taking as active an interest in their children's schooling as they would like. Patterns of shiftwork, care arrangements for small children (especially for single parents) and problems of culture and language, vividly illustrate the range of intractable and continuing obstacles that many families face.

Does *your* school recognize such difficulties? Even more to the point, does it make practical arrangements to tackle such problems constructively?

Secondly, there are a significant number of parents who do not see the need for cosy partnership with schools or active involvement with their children's teachers. For, although they are concerned and effective parents, they regard home and school as separate domains, each with its characteristic and important job to do. 'You do your job and I'll do mine' is a view in which contact is really only needed as and when problems arise. Many teachers find this stance very difficult to understand.

Thirdly, there are parents whose previous contact with schools has made them suspicious, or even hostile. Their previous experience, as pupils themselves, may have been negative and associated with failure; many things that schools do are also culturally alien to many parents. Above all, schools that divide children clearly into sheep and goats, are inevitably going to alienate many parents. This is established long before children go to secondary school.

So it's worth taking a second, more critical look at the idea of 'non-attending parents'. Who are they? What explanations are there for such a picture? What can, and should, we be doing as a response to their wishes, needs and experience? Above all, is it really *their* problem?

Just as teacher lore and staffroom mythology contain deep-seated stereotypes about what parents are like so, too, parents harbour stereotypes of teachers and school life. In the same way, too, such views flourish in the absence of opportunities for genuine communication and contact. Currently, reinforced by media images and treatment of educational issues, many parents are encouraged to believe that:

- school is all play and no work
- pupils can largely please themselves when they work and what they do
- teachers have lost control: teachers are too friendly with their pupils
- schools are large, blackboard jungles in which there's no place for the individual
- there has been too much emphasis upon new-fangled ideas at the expense of basic skills and knowledge
- educational 'standards' aren't what they used to be.

...Or are *your* parents different? And what are you going to do about it?

Some cunning ploys for avoiding and resisting change

Books about social and educational change tend to imply that we would all go along with proposed changes, as long as there are convincing reasons for doing so. In the everyday life of schools, however, teachers are no different from anyone else in wanting to avoid changes that are likely to bring threat and anxiety and which will almost certainly make further demands and involve extra effort.

Here are some of the commonest ploys used to deflect proposals that involve changes of attitude and behaviours:

'We're already doing it!'

Of course, this *may* be true! Quite often, however, such a ploy works by drawing attention to a few superficial similarities between what is being proposed and what is already done, conveniently ignoring deeper differences. Or it may be that the *form* of the activity is similar but the spirit is very different, half-hearted or lacking in conviction, so limiting its effectiveness. For example, the occasional home visit as a last resort, hardly constitutes a firm commitment to the value of listening to parents in their own homes.

'The Head won't let me' 'my staff aren't interested...'

Again, this may be true. But it often sounds rather like scapegoating as a way of deflecting responsibility or blame for failure to change. Whilst the personal support of headteachers in British schools, particularly in the primary sector, is clearly important, I do feel that it has sometimes been over-stated. Either way, such a view understates the extent to which the teaching profession, given the right kinds of incentive and support, have shown their willingness to change in recent years, particularly when they have seen the benefits of doing so.

'The parents wouldn't stand for it'

Another case of scapegoating? The real problem here is that many teachers are simply ignorant of what real parents actually do want for their children. There is now plenty of evidence that many parents do not have Gradgrind-like views of the curriculum or Judge Jeffries-type views about discipline. But there is always a danger of replacing one stereotype with another, particularly if it is more acceptable. Parents have widely-differing views and expectations of the education system for their children and there is no substitute for a first-hand knowledge of what these are, which grows out of your situation and experience.

'Research shows that...'

Considering the low regard that most teachers have for educational research, it is intriguing how often it is used in discussion as a point of reference. Upon closer inspection, however, such reference is always used to support preconceived ideas and prejudices and hardly ever quotes actual or particular researchers. The brutal truth is that home/school research can be as inconclusive and contradictory as that in other educational areas. But there are conclusions that can be drawn, which are useful as a general orientation to the discussion of home/school issues. Here are three to be going on with:

- parents *are* crucially important in terms of their effect upon their children's educational achievement

- parents draw upon widely-differing attitudes and experience in their dealings with their children's schools

- there are inevitable tensions in the relationships between families and schools – for *all* parents regardless of background and experience.

'After all we've done for them!'

Here, lurid illustrations are used to contrast the inspired and ulcer-inducing efforts of teachers with the lack of response and ingratitude of parents. Against the background of such negative experience, new developments seem a very poor risk. A useful response here revolves around patient and honest evaluation. Are we on the same wavelength as our parents? Are our efforts appropriate? Exactly *how* do we decide whether a home/school activity has been successful or not?

At the root of this problem, poor communication or 'cultural dissonance' can often be found. Many teachers do not seem to appreciate that cheese and wine do's, barn-dancing and parent–staff tennis tournaments are not necessarily everyone's natural or favourite pastimes!

'Where can I find the time?'

In many ways such a ploy, where it is genuinely believed or where it has some substance, has some claim to be taken seriously. But it may also be due to a distortion of the problems presented by the improvement of home/school relationships or the deliberate exaggeration of the very real pressures upon hard-pressed teachers. The best corrective to such a ploy, is to recognize that parents have much to offer, through their practical help and support, in return for the new demands that increased involvement brings. Much can be done, from the earliest stages of a proposal, to build in the conditions for its continuing development and for parents to take over the responsibility for some activities themselves.

In this section, attention has been given to some of the deliberate and unofficial strategies that teachers can adopt to fend off unwelcome pressures for change or threats to established ways of doing things. The emphasis, however, is upon the wholesale rejection of ideas, without reasonable consideration. This is *not* the same as recognizing the genuine obstacles and practical problems in the area, which are dealt with throughout this account.

Special needs

Our main concern in the following section is the special needs of individuals and groups within the wider parent body. This is done through the brief use of two illustrations:

Neighbourhood differences and social divisions within the school catchment area

Despite the 'Coronation Street' view of community life, most real communities are characterized at least as much by deep-seated tensions and conflicts, as by cosy solidarity. This is particularly reinforced by differences of class and race, by migration and changing patterns of settlement. There is an important and difficult role here for schools in relation to the communities in which they are located. For schools are often expected to act as a unifying influence, creating a consensus between conflicting attitudes and widely-differing experience.

On the other hand, schools with a concern for their children's families and who have a well-developed programme of home/school links, generally come to identify special needs, of both individuals and groups, which are unlikely to be met by the existing arrangements, at least without special modification. A good illustration of such a concern at the present time is the need to develop appropriate forms of communication and contact in multicultural settings. So often, the needs are dismissed as 'simply' those of language. Events of recent years have shown that racial divisions in our society are far more complex and intractable than that.

Responding to the widening range of family needs, patterns of organization and lifestyles

It often comes as a shock for teachers to realize that the 'cereal packet norm' family, within which most of us grew up, is now in a minority. Some of the features of contemporary family life, whose implications for home/school links have yet to be worked out, would include:

- the special needs and problems that stem from family breakdown, separation and divorce; problems of communication and contact that relate to custody and access; the issues raised by re-marriage in 'reconstituted' families etc.;

- the variety of parenting arrangements and styles, which are altering the patterns of breadwinning and caring, conjugal and family relationships and, of course, attitudes towards child-rearing;

- the problem and, occasionally, opportunities, created by the effects of long-term unemployment upon family life. A number of these issues, as they might concern schools, for example, were raised in a heightened way during the miners' strike; others are raised by the slow but steady increase in the involvement of fathers in their children's early education.

The diagnosis of special needs amongst parents and families, together with the development of appropriate forms of action, can only be really effective as the by-product of an increasing familiarity with the catchment area, and with the winning of trust by the school. Many schools, particularly those situated in areas where family problems are widespread, find it increasingly necessary to develop practical arrangements that offer considerable support, or forms of communication and contact that acknowledge difference of culture, background and expectation.

Part Four

The Evaluation of Home/School Practice

Editorial Preview

The two contributions in this section have been deliberately written to complement each other. The first explores the evaluation of home/school relations from the perspective of a large LEA-sponsored project, involving a range of schools in different settings. The second focuses upon the planning, organization and evaluation of home/school links within individual schools, using teacher–parent interviews to provide a series of illustrations of the links between evaluation principles and procedures.

What is more marked than the differences between the two accounts, however, is the common ground they share, in terms of both values and approach. Both stress the need for evaluation to relate to the original intentions and goals of those involved, to acknowledge the spirit of the enterprise and the ability to offer sympathetic, although critical, judgement.

Both accounts stress the similarity and overlap between useful evaluation, inset and educational development. They offer a view in which professional development has a central place, built upon the acquisition of the kinds of knowledge and skills that are required for the emergence of more responsive institutions and more thoughtful work with parents. Finally, both eschew a technical or narrowly specialist approach to evaluation, seeing instead its major contribution to the development and consolidation of more effective practice.

John Davis, writing about the well-known Parent Support Programme in Liverpool, picks up and amplifies a number of problems that emerge from his experience of evaluation and change, which most of us will recognize. He writes vividly about the problems of legitimizing new developments and seeking wider support, both at the political level and within the education service. His account acknowledges both the achievements of the scheme and also the problems of insecurity and risk-taking that change brings, together with the need for continuing support and encouragement from within and without.

Above all, the account explores the ambivalence and role tension that are an intrinsic part of educational evaluation. The author describes some of the difficulties in walking on a thin line between being on the inside and achieving the degree of critical detachment that enables a wider view, between making things happen and responding to expressed needs and between the claims of the ideal and the problems of living in the real world.

John Bastiani's contribution picks up a number of these themes and concerns and reformulates them. He is particularly concerned to continuously relate ends and means to each other, so that evaluation does not become a technical exercise carried out in an ethical vacuum. His account attaches great emphasis to the need, on many grounds, to involve parents themselves in home/school evaluation – as both subject and object of the inquiry. Finally, whilst recognizing the special features and claims of home/school relations as an area, his account locates such evaluation in the light of and as part of, a school's continuing and general development.

Evaluating an LEA Approach: the Liverpool Parent Support Programme

John Davis

Liverpool now has Parent Centres in 30 of its primary schools, the outcome of a scheme, initiated with the help of Inner City Partnership funding in 1979, that was originally intended to provide such Centres in all inner city primary schools. While many people will remember Midwinter's E.P.A. Project in Liverpool (1968–71) the tradition here extends at least as far back as Jessie Reid Crosby, who started her Mothers' Fellowship some eighty years ago with the words:

> You are all wondering why we have invited you to school today. Well, I want you, at these meetings, to tell me what you are trying to teach your children at home, and then to listen whilst we tell you what we are trying to teach them in school.

The problem for the school remains essentially the same: the under-achievement of children from areas of social deprivation. In EPA work the additional resources, and by implication the responsibility, were given to schools. In the Parent Support Programme (PSP) resources are made available to the parents, in an attempt to support and reinforce their responsibility as partners in the education of their children. The original bid for Partnership funding also includes a wider set of aims: to 'identify and react to the educational needs of the community', to 'develop a preventative response to social problems' and to 'nurture local community spirit'.

Each Parents' Centre has been developed from a surplus classroom, sometimes two, which have been furnished, decorated and equipped for activities for parents and pre-school children. Each Centre is staffed by a Teacher Keyworker and an Outreach Worker, both of whom are permanently appointed to the school by the Governors and are responsible to the Headteacher. Each Centre has an allocation of five hours paid adult tutor time per week, also funded with Partnership support.

After a year of planning, led by an Advisory Committee, the first phase (17 schools) began operation from September 1979. Subsequent second (1982: ten schools) and third (1984: four schools) phases inevitably suffered from the prevailing economic stringencies.

The evaluation

As an evaluator permanently appointed to the Authority I had been working with other projects and was asked to become involved with PSP in June 1979, and have remained so until recently, although it has not been the only development to which I am attached. The trouble with looking back, particularly with an exploratory project in which the evaluative role is inevitably bound up with the development process, is that it is easier to rationalize after the event when in practice no such rationale existed at the time – things have become apparent to us as time went on. Inevitably this retrospective rationalization tends to be dominated by my own perspective and suffers from underplaying the role and influence of others. The evaluation also looks, from where I stand now, to have had great gaps in it.

The scheme began with the intention, expressed in proposals to the Partnership and letters to School Managers, that the Parent Centres should respond flexibly to local needs. No guidelines were produced, other than the very general, all embracing (and essentially identical) job specifications for the two workers, and responsibility was firmly in the hands of the Headteacher – there was no project team to whom the workers were accountable. My intention with the evaluation too, was not to channel and constrain: I set out as a critical sensemaker to understand and provide formative support to the development processes, whatever and wherever these might be. I had no brief, indeed have never had a job description: Liverpool is not unused to operating with such 'creative ambiguity' and it can be both a strength and a weakness. This lack of an initial 'contract' means for me that negotiation about my role is inherently a continuing process, focused around what is to be done about matters raised in the evaluation.

Initial concerns

I was able, then, to provide my own answers to the first two major issues: who is the evaluation for? What is the evaluation for? It was to support development, and it was for everybody who had a part to play in development.

In going round schools talking to workers and Headteachers in those first weeks it was apparent that in a number of instances the Heads were not entirely sure how they came to be involved in the PSP scheme, and did not necessarily regard their involvement favourably. Despite a conference organized by the Advisory Committee many Heads were hazy about the aims of the scheme and hesitant about the prospect of parents in school. Some had been trying to get Nursery provision, but had been given PSP and viewed the scheme as an opportunity to create a nursery class. We were surprised, too, by the strength with which some staff expressed their reservations. In some Parent Centres thriving groups of mums were soon producing soft toys and pinafores, in others, workers had great difficulty in enticing parents through the door. An induction course for workers, organized by an Adult Education Adviser, had begun the process of clarifying roles and had generated group coherence and the beginnings of networking. Eleanor Connor, pre-school organizer and one of the few remaining links with EPA, played a vital anchor role in providing workers with information and a sympathetic ear. Heads and workers from various schools began to meet at lunchtimes, and a group of workers met regularly for mutual support in a theatre coffee-bar. One worker was not allowed to contact other workers, and her contacts with outside agencies were also being restricted. Another worker was pursuing such contacts without keeping the Head informed.

Very rapidly, then, a number of fundamental concerns became evident: there was a need for Heads and workers to meet to exchange ideas and come to terms with their experiences; for training to extend perceptions and clarify roles, they needed mutual therapy and support, although clearly not all Headteachers had the same views about the need for workers to meet together. This no doubt reflected a range of understandings about the nature of development and concerns about who would control PSP activities: schools were learning individually about administrative procedures, and new routines needed to be established in the office. The first evaluation reports were directed at Officers, expressing such needs 'for their eyes only' and raising questions about mechanisms for response. Suggestions, not from me but from various people I talked to, included the need for regular liaison meetings between Heads, workers and 'The Office'; legitimization for regular meetings for PSP workers to be timetabled out; for training for Heads and workers; for the circulation of information; for some overall coordination; and for some designated person who would take responsibility for promoting PSP concerns within the Education office.

With hindsight the fact that 'The Office' intended to disband the Advisory Committee because the PSP scheme was not considered to be operational, was a signal I should have given more attention to. Also the rejection of a suggestion that an Adviser should be given oversight of the scheme. Some years later I inclined to the view that Office Administrators had a substantially different notion of how development should be handled than had Advisers, or indeed myself. So we didn't get a co-ordinator but we did get a Liaison Committee and, for a time, a Steering Committee. Through these we got agreement that Eleanor Connor would be attached to PSP, though her job description was not changed and she never felt she had any 'authority' in that attachment. We also had Tuesday mornings set aside for workers to meet. The AEO Primary Schools, through whom all administrative matters for the scheme were channelled, was the nearest we had to someone with responsibility for PSP within the Office. He convened and chaired the Liaison Committee and Steering Group and, from time to time, meetings for Heads. We also set up meetings for Heads and workers in four Area Groups, from which representatives to the Liaison Committee were elected.

'Preserving the bubble'

So on Tuesday mornings the workers met to exchange information and for mutual support and training. In a series of evaluation workshops we clarified aims, roles, ways of involving and working with adults, links with other professionals and community agencies and, in time we tiptoed into such tendentious areas as teacher attitudes and parents as educators. We videotaped good practice, wrote a Handbook and visited other parts of the country to see how they did things.

I say 'we' because I took part in all of that, as one of the group, and also because much of the actual organization and leadership fell to Eleanor and me. For quite some time I was bothered that an 'evaluator' should in practice become so involved in helping to lead and develop. I certainly felt part of the 'we' rather than a neutral, independent observer, and not least in confronting the basic problem of survival which we all thought the scheme faced. People saw PSP in terms of a project or an Urban Aid scheme, and since these generally had a specific duration they naturally had worries about their jobs. While evaluation could be construed as providing information to help decision makers to judge whether the scheme was value for money or not, it was also in the business of management of change and for that the 'bubble' needed to be preserved long enough for developments to become consolidated and institutionalized. Inherently the formative role is a proactive one, the evaluator is part of the development process and the worth of the evaluation must be judged in terms of its impact; and if things are going to take time to develop then various target audiences need to be clear about that, and other target audiences must be drawn into the development process because their roles are influential ones.

So in the early years, apart from a baseline survey of parent involvement in schools and written accounts of evaluation workshops, we circulated transcripts of discussions with groups of parents because of the power of the messages these conveyed. We also deliberately collected information about the burgeoning adult classes in schools that we knew would interest officers and those in the Treasury Department who we felt were closest to Partnership decision making. Apart from the adult tutor sessions many of the activities in the Parent Centres were run by the workers themselves, or by invited outsiders and by teachers, and of course there was work with toddlers and contact with agencies as well as developments involving school and curriculum. To understand what the workers and the schools were doing and to clarify what could be included in annual returns, I went round the schools to help fill in my forms and came to realize the significance of questioning and discussion in helping them, as well as me, to clarify and develop a rationale for the various aspects of the work. Very probably these verbal, interactional aspects of evaluation were more 'formative' than my reports, and a much sounder and probably quicker way to disseminate 'good practice'. Which meant that Eleanor, in her visits to schools, was also doing 'formative' evaluation as well, indeed weren't many people? Who then is the evaluator? What then is my role? Perhaps to write it up for them, although I rather hoped they would help with that too! Partly to encourage and develop the evaluation role that these other people had. Certainly to hold various matters in front of people long enough for them to be considered and dealt with: I was a dealer in the communications that were necessary if developments were to be facilitated.

Evaluation and response

The data on courses, adult student numbers and toddler work undertaken, aimed at officers and treasury, seemed to produce what we hoped for: phrases like 'embarrassingly successful' were circulating round the office. But the workers felt threatened by what they took to be comparisons between schools, and after we had done that exercise twice it was dropped.

More difficult to respond to were the sensitive and difficult matters that people wanted to discuss when we went round the Parent Centres: about Heads, individual staff, particular parents, the Office. How does a PSP worker approach her Headteacher to discuss the attitudes and behaviour of colleagues towards the parents? What do we do about the apparent lack of action by the Office on matters raised in Liaison Committee? Inevitably in such discussions the evaluator is faced with adopting a counselling role. Frankness depends on trust: the evaluator can ill afford to appear remote, indeed there is a trade-off aspect to gathering information. But evaluation is more than just the collection of information: impact is what matters. Solutions need to be sought collectively but also at this individual level too, particularly where information is too sensitive to make public – as much of it is. But often the sensitive matters are common to many of the PSP Centres, and the problem for the evaluator is to find ways of raising and getting them addressed openly.

So at one of the Tuesday morning meetings we discussed how to strengthen committee procedures, which resulted in a series of recommendations – including the election of a PSP Head as Chairman of Liaision Committee – that were subsequently put into effect, and still obtain. Yet the major problem, and the one that is most difficult to express openly, was and still is that of Head and teacher attitudes and practices. Although it was not and probably could not be expressed in the original bid, teachers are as much a key target of this scheme as are the parents. By and large we have made less progress with the teachers – a slow business that depends substantially on climate within an individual school and within the LEA. Responsibility for progress in developing new attitudes and practices cannot be effectively delegated to a Project such as this, active support is needed from other parts of the system, and particularly from Senior Officers and Advisers. Part of the function of Projects is to validate and generate greater currency and acceptance of these new attitudes and practices, and one of the problems facing me as evaluator has been to find out sufficient about the procedures and plans within the Authority in order to facilitate links for PSP that give the scheme a reasonable chance of becoming institutionalized, of being included rather than overlooked. This involves developments like TRIST and GRIST, as well as existing procedures such as Headteacher appointments and school monitoring, but it is also about raising the visibility of PSP activities. Such is also the case for other current educational concerns, in working for a response the evaluator here is intervening in the processes by which the Education Office develops and implements its strategies. Ideally the evaluator should relate to the key people driving such processes, but in our case this was by default – PSP has no Project Co-ordinator or other voice to make such links. What is at stake here is the inherent conflict between the strategy of giving individual schools control in the interests of flexibility and professionalism and the need to develop coherence within the Authority. I am not at all clear how far along such paths I am expected to travel, but in my experience any evaluation ends up in management issues.

Transmitted roles

Evaluation products will naturally raise the profile, the visibility, of an activity, and most of the written reports were distributed widely within the Education Office. There is then the tendency for the evaluator to be seen as a voice, and here in the absence of a Project Co-ordinator perhaps as 'The Voice', for the scheme. As Eleanor and I have assumed organizational roles, and been cast by the office in the role of 'experts' who would lecture and meet visitors, and 'managers' who could cope with day to day running of the scheme, so we have usurped some of the potential commitment and learning that active involvement of officers and Advisers could provide. They had distractions of their own, and we needed to consider how to ensure that PSP remained a practical concern in their deliberations. Part of the problem, too, was that we and the PSP workers knew rather more than they did, and it was important that they weren't making decisions on the basis of partial understanding. We needed to keep them up to date.

But for the PSP workers the perspective at this time was, perhaps also inevitably, one of apparent isolation, of omissions, of an apparent lack of approval and support from 'The Office'. New developments have to pioneer new attitudes and administrative routines within the office, and these, naturally, can take some time to become established. The evaluator needed to ensure that PSP workers, and some Heads, had a realistic perception of how the office works and what may be expected of it. Actually the Office did approve and was very supportive – doubtless all bureaucracies present such outward faces and Liverpool's politics have compounded the complications – but for the PSP scheme, morale was a need and Eleanor and myself were being cast by Heads and workers in the role of 'leaders' and 'main points of contact' with the Office.

What data is needed?

A major difficulty that any evaluator has to resolve is that of how much data to collect. It is easy to become submerged in processing information, for much of which there may seem little direct use, and I was faced with the problem of doing justice to an extremely broad range of activities. Several kinds of work were developing in all the PSP schools: drop-in, parent–toddler, inter-agency collaboration, adult education very broadly interpreted and, lagging somewhat behind, links between the parents and the work of the school. But

in addition the adult education was generating productive collaboration with further education, there was the matter of how PSP was
being 'managed' in the LEA and growing interest from other
schools was giving point to considerations of how the LEA would
build on PSP experience to develop parent involvement throughout
the Authority. For that matter PSP was in reality 'community
education' and I was developing a personal interest and commitment to the field.

There is a pressure to be 'seen' to be evaluating, and visibility
tends to mean written reports, but I couldn't possibly cover everything myself nor did I have much faith in the impact of written
reports. I set out to maintain a flow of short working documents and
to produce a series of descriptions of developing 'good practice',
hopefully involving the PSP workers in doing some of the writing,
which would identify and illuminate the significance of what people
were doing. I produced a regular Newsletter and I also did some of
the more usual things like asking teachers to record contacts with
parents, asking schools to formulate projected developments,
checking on how many and how often adults attended the Centres,
and attempting to establish whether teacher attitudes were changing. I was dissatisfied with the information a questionnaire on the
latter had produced: the attitude scale completed by the teachers
indicated a definite change, but I knew very well that little real
collaboration was occurring between teachers and parents and the
PSP units were, in many cases, still largely working in isolation from
the rest of the school. Key changes were still largely to be achieved.
I forebore to survey the parents and other adults, grasping at the
straw of the workers' apprehension that searching questions would
undermine the often delicate relationships they had laboured long
to construct, and instead interviewed groups of them about how
they felt about the activities they were engaging in. I tend to think
that direct quotes from the participants give a descriptive account of
an activity much more impact, but perhaps more importantly we
were learning to listen and we were finding out about the significance
of the scheme for the parents and other adults.

When the parents wrote for their magazine, for instance, about
how they felt about taking part in a pantomime they had put on for
the school, we began to understand the series of practical and
emotional hurdles they had had to overcome:

I woke up that morning and I thought what the hell am I doing, I don't even want to go in there. But when I did I didn't want it to end.

We began to realize, too, the role that the pantomime was playing in building not just individual confidence but group coherence and valuing others. We began to appreciate the power of a collective rather than an individual success. We saw that activities like the pantomime and producing the magazine made them feel special, and we came to understand that if teachers had been more involved in them the value of these activities for the parents would probably have been diminished. We began to see our own agendas from a different perspective:

What I mean to say is, as well as the skills that you pick up here, like how to paint with your child, how to make play-dough, and so on, that's not the most important thing. The most important thing is gabbing to Linda, or whoever's in, you know what I mean.

The skills of painting and using play-dough are the teachers' agenda, and the adults have different needs. But to a teacher 'gabbing' is not work, and the PSP staff have a cushy number. Until you begin to realize the range of things the parents are 'gabbing' about: problems with children, and husbands, and the house, and health, and the DHSS – a real curriculum. We began to understand what they're learning and who they're learning from; and what skills the PSP workers are using to build this 'gabbing' into activities around which groups cohere. How they facilitate, how they encourage the adults to manage and control the pace and direction of their own learning – quite probably for the first time in their lives.

Impact

In choosing to concentrate on qualitative, illuminative material I have tended to duck the question of how much benefit is being derived by how many although, in preparing for an exhibition and conference which they mounted, the workers themselves generated information on numbers of adults from PSP who were attending activities run by FE College staff. It was clear that, in dealing with a clientele who had left the education system with virtually no formal qualifications and who would not normally contemplate returning for FE or adult evening classes, PSP was increasingly affecting college intake and was beginning to influence the kind of responses the colleges were making.

Apart from seeking the professional opinion of the teachers I also ducked the question of benefit to the children, not least because any direct relationship between the child and much of what the parent was doing in the Centre is hard to sort out, also because I hadn't the energy or inclination to follow cohorts through the vicissitudes of the education system when any conclusions looked like being easily challenged on a host of dependent and independent variables. I suspect, nevertheless, that this disappointed various expectations in Liverpool and elsewhere, because people wanted 'proof' that could be used to support arguments for more provision. There are inevitable tensions here: researchers have norms and outsiders have expectations about what evaluation is and about the kind of evidence that is needed for them to use. I still feel that PSP's local battle was won quite early on as a result of favourable reports in the national press by visiting journalists, and in terms of success with adult education in the minds of Officers. I also believe that much of the favour the scheme found with journalists depended on the vigorous advocacy they encountered when they talked to the parents themselves.

Concern about the impact of research on decision making is by no means new, and there are lessons for evaluators. If the worth of evaluation lies in its impact then we may need to reflect on how people learn and how decision makers' minds are made up. Not only may it be unnecessary to generate much quantitative data it may be important to reinforce more basic considerations, like interpersonal contacts and discussing the significance of findings, rather than relying on an impersonal external validity from 'damned statistics'. Yet the Tizard research on parent involvement in home reading schemes (1981b) has had a powerful impact on schools, and from time to time I tend to feel guilty about the decisions I have taken. Should evaluation be more like research?

Development processes

The PSP scheme was having some impact within the LEA: when the
County Secondary Schools were reorganized four additional posts
were created in each school, including a Parent Support Co-ordinator.
The Advisers' Primary School monitoring schedule included two
questions on relationships with parents and community, and the
council's Preschool Subcommittee saw fit to endorse one PSP Nursery
school's policy statement as guidelines for all nursery provision. Yet
we still encountered Heads who were appointed to PSP schools
without a question being asked concerning parent involvement and
there were Adviser Teams that carried out school inspections without
including PSP Centres on their schedules. Fundamental development needs were still very evident: in a Review that we held in the
fifth year, workers talked about lack of active support from their
Heads, lack of policy in school and from the LEA, lack of support
from the LEA in terms of INSET for Heads and staff, lack of accountability at all levels, lack of strategy for developing their work and for
linking it to other parts of the education system. It is not enough for
the evaluation to generate such information, matters need to be
addressed and the information fed into the existing processes by
which development occurred. What were they? In the absence of a
Project Co-ordinator, who was responsible for making progress?

I suppose there is a tendency for evaluators to look for people
who might have, or might be expected to assume, such responsibilities and, in effect, to pin the responsibility on them. It shames
me to admit that at first I turned to Eleanor with my 'Why don't
you...?' questions and I undoubtedly worried her considerably. I
learnt my lesson and am grateful to her for the manner in which she
dealt with me. Thereafter we worked together.

The Review sessions had been attended by the new Chief Inspector,
certain of his team of Advisers, and by several Administrators, and
a report was circulated widely within the Education Office. Nothing
happened. Eleanor and I arranged to speak at an Advisers' meeting
about the progress of PSP school by school, but little discussion
occurred and no plan of action emerged. If any in-service training
was to be undertaken then clearly the 'experts' were to be found
within the PSP schemes. Should we fill the vacuum by picking up the
development responsibility ourselves?

The Steering group had long since ceased to meet, indeed the liaison group had been ineffectual and had become perfunctory, but meeting regularly on Tuesdays over some six years had made PSP a close-knit group and, largely due to the drive of the PSP Head then Chairing Liaison Committee, we decided to mount an Exhibition and Conference. Various groups did a great deal of work in sharing information, in deciding who the target audiences were and what we should try to convey to them and in preparing materials. I underpinned this eminently valuable evaluation activity by taking notes and drawing up briefing documents. In the event we attracted a wide local and national audience, the thing had been very well done and we felt we had a great deal of support. More, the common purpose had given people motivation and it had pulled them together. It had been a very effective development process. How could we sustain that?

At about this time Eleanor announced her intention to retire. When the bid for Phase 3 extension of the scheme was being prepared PSP had developed a job description for a Project Co-ordinator which it was hoped might be included, though none materialized – perhaps because 'The Office' felt the attachment of Eleanor and myself was enough. We pressed for Eleanor's vacancy to be redefined as a Project Co-ordinator, including responsibility for work with Secondary Parent Support Co-ordinators and with the increasing number of schools we knew were developing work with parents without PSP resources. But Liverpool was experiencing particular political and financial difficulties – it still is – and no co-ordinator has been forthcoming. It looked as though I would be on my own, I needed to take stock.

Being sanguine about the evaluation, it was clear that being sucked into the admin/organization role had diminished the range of contacts with PSP schools that I was making and, although there was no difficulty in identifying issues that needed to be addressed, the breadth of activity 'out there' was burgeoning – and only parts of it being 'captured' in evaluation (or other) products. In practice development depended on the workers and the links they were establishing, and this was happening without any facilitation from the Office or elsewhere – it depended on individual workers' ideas and energy, and on the opportunities and support they could find or generate. The evaluation was catching up with some of that, and helping to clarify outcomes and potentials.

Work in schools was decidedly patchy: some had made little apparent progress in seven years, few were encouraging staff to work with parents on curriculum matters. The evaluation supported such processes by interviewing staff and parents concerned, and making videos as a basis for discussing the work with Head and the whole staff. In general we were finding the teachers' rationales still pretty basic. Advances in PSP were essentially people-based, and evaluation had had scant impact where people were not already sympathetic and interested to make progress.

Despite the infusion of substantial resources – the Authority was now wholly funding part of the scheme from mainstream budget (without apparent reference to any evaluation) – major deficiencies were still evident and they were not getting tackled. No obligation was placed on schools concerning parent involvement and support, including those in the PSP scheme, either formally through an LEA policy statement or informally through Adviser monitoring procedures. No INSET resources were allocated to such work in schools and parent involvement did not figure in Curriculum Leadership or School Management courses. LEA strategy for the development of parent involvement seemed to consist of a view among senior officers that the present PSP model would be extended to more schools if and when the resources became available, but that rate-capping was resulting in pressure to cut staffing to the bone.

It has become apparent that the appointment of staff to run TVEI, SCIP, Low Attainers, ESG Maths, Science and Urban Primary and numerous other projects has created a cadre of experts that many LEAs don't have the mechanisms to support. While it may perhaps be true that advisers and administrators have rather different notions of how change should be managed, this certainly seems the case with a number of projects with which I am associated in Liverpool. Project staff, and indeed others in Remedial Teams, Multicultural Team and Language Development units, are all dealing with school management and staff development concerns – which overlap with Adviser's functions and require resources which are administered by Officers. Some LEAs, like Manchester and Birmingham, have undertaken substantial management reorganization within 'The Office', resulting in large new Development Service empires. Is the evaluation of PSP leading me in that direction?

Coming to terms with realities

If the LEA wasn't good at planning and structuring support for development, and if PSP gained strength from pursuing tasks collectively, then one solution might be to 'encourage' PSP to take charge of its own destiny. That could also resolve some of my own concerns about my role, not least of which was the feeling that consultancy aspects of the role imply that the client's capacity for self-determination should be increased and the consultant should eventually withdraw. How could they be encouraged to pick up organization and leadership of the scheme?

The loss of Eleanor meant that I could lay the organizational problem before them, although the response varied from 'we're already too busy' to 'If we do it ourselves they'll never give us a Coordinator'. The organizational problem could also be laid before 'The Office', but backing would be needed and in any case PSP could do with the support of a Steering Committee again. The workers needed little persuasion about that, and it was agreed that the worker reps. would meet as a 'Core Group' on Monday afternoons to plan and cope with routine administration. When GRIST came over the horizon, the Steering Group agreed that we should generate a bid concerned specifically with parent involvement and based on requests invited from PSP and other schools. I persuaded three advisers to include PSP workers on their curriculum leadership courses, both to offer some answer to workers' legitimate concerns about limited career opportunities and with the intention of encouraging Heads to treat PSP as a 'subject area' for which the Teacher Keyworker could act as curriculum leader, with responsibility for preparing a scheme of work and for developing the work with colleagues. Through Steering Group it is also possible to make progress on longer term strategies for development, particularly as Primary reorganization is yet again being contemplated. Workers and Heads were informed that senior Officers would be interested to receive their views on possible modifications to the structure of PSP, and a draft policy document on parent involvement for schools. We got our INSET money and there are sessions to organize.

The Core Group has plenty to contend with but, PSP being essentially close-knit, democracy has to prevail and everybody wants to participate in all decisions. Procedures for groups to work on tasks and then report back for decisions are in the process of being hammered out, but there are skills and tolerances to be learnt and progress is inevitably slow. As part of the process of 'handing over' I had asked them to select their own Chairperson to run Tuesday meetings, and people volunteered to do this on a termly rotational basis. Workers who already have the skills are beginning to realize that it is better in the long run if they do pick up the responsibility and volunteer.

With perfect timing I was recently asked by my Chief Education Officer (CEO) to become involved in the evaluation of INSET under GRIST, which will mean that I must spend much less time with PSP. One door opens as another closes: if INSET is about development then I can legitimately tackle issues about supporting developments, and I have a watertight reason for wishing to redefine my involvement in PSP. Not that I wish to withdraw entirely – part of my career is invested in parent support now and there are connections in progress with other things I am involved with, like links between modular accreditation for adults, open learning and an Open College movement in Liverpool. Also they need someone to front for them from time to time, as in running sessions for headteachers. Frankly, too, I like working with these people, I am committed to them and to this work and I would not like them to think I am letting them down. Evaluators have emotional investments.

Of course, PSP is maintaining its pressure on 'The Office' for a Co-ordinator appointment but, while I firmly believe the CEO will get around to it, I rather hope he won't hurry. Of course I could be accused of having a naive and romantic view of the practicability of self actualization, especially for a group like PSP. But then the PSP workers themselves talk about being concerned 'that people should value each others' ideas and experience and should learn to collaborate...use individual talents to solve a range of practical problems, dealing with real issues...and, through the experience, being welded into a closely knit and purposeful team'. In an evaluation report about one such parent group a worker comments:

What amazes me is the way it keeps going, with that kind of intensity. Even if not many people turn up one week it still seems to start up again. I don't really know why. But this kind of structure allows lulls, while a normal course would evaluate that rather differently. And while some groups do tend to go over the same ground again and again this seems much more authoritative somehow. What impresses me is that they know such a lot, and they've learnt how to find things out, too.

We shall see. Self determination as a strategy is more or less thrust upon us by the absence of (or PSP's isolation from) other mechanisms that support development in this LEA, but current emphases on school focused INSET imply that it may be the most efficient way. As an evaluator I have the feeling that I have known that for some time, and that I should have been more forceful about defining the issues and putting them in front of people for action. I think I've become more experienced in how to do that, and I'm also clearer about the kind of definition I need for my role as evaluator, but the basic problem for any evaluator is to identify the processes to which he can work. Evaluation is not an independent activity – evaluations are only as effective as the mechanisms they serve.

'How Many Parents Did You See Last Night?' A critical look at some of the problems of evaluating home/school practice

John Bastiani

In recent years, educational evaluation has come to be seen less as an externally imposed interference in the work of schools and teachers and rather more as a source of ideas for their development. For, whilst there is still a long way to go before its achievements match its promise, evaluation has the potential to offer much that is valuable and useful to the development of more effective home/school relations, as elsewhere.

In this short account, I am attempting to demonstrate its usefulness

- as an applied activity which requires the integration of thinking and practice

- as a cornerstone of an approach to professional development which is based upon the critical examination by teachers of their work

- as a key element in a process of educational development which links planning, implementation and evaluation.

In order to bring such general themes and concerns more sharply into focus, I shall be using previous work undertaken in Nottingham as a point of reference. This examines teacher–parent interviews and the arrangements that are made for teachers and parents to review the progress of individual pupils, as an activity that lies at the heart of home/school relations. It also provides a series of grounded illustrations of the views and experience of teachers and parents alike and a source of practical ideas for their evaluation (Community Education Working Party, 1982).

Why is evaluation important?

The evaluation of home/school relations by teachers shows the education service and the general public that it is taking this area of its work seriously, by subjecting it to careful scrutiny and critical examination. When this is made public it indicates both acceptance of professional responsibility in home/school matters and of the right of parents and others to know what is going on.

The activity of evaluation provides the basis upon which reasonable, informed judgements can be made and a value placed upon the work that is being done. This makes most sense when carried out in relation to its declared aims and intentions. It goes without saying that in the home/school field this can be complicated by important differences between and amongst parents and teachers.

Evaluation can provide a means of bringing ideals and realities into a critical but productive relationship, by matching up claims and actual experience, exposing inconsistencies, discrepancies and contradictions between the two. In the field of home/school relations, fine rhetoric is not always matched by effective practice – to put it mildly!

At the heart of evaluation lies the relationship between ends and means. For judgements, about the *effectiveness* of home/school programmes and practices must always be related to questions about their *value*.

The discussion of purposes, followed by the collection and interpretation of appropriate information and evidence, provides the basis for making more reasonable decisions about policy and practice and for judgements about its quality. This applies both to the programme as a whole, and to the examination of particular practices and developments.

Evaluation activities have considerable diagnostic potential. They can, for example, identify special needs and the extent to which these are being met, in relation to:

- the needs and wishes of parents and pupils, as opposed to teachers;

- the special needs of particular groups of parents (e.g. ethnic minorities, one-parent families, families containing children with disabilities).

Evaluation can often offer a guide to more effective action in the home/school field by revealing shared purposes and common concerns, as well as pinpointing areas of difference and disagreement more accurately.

Evaluation can help to identify and provide pointers to:

- ideas for improvement within the present arrangements and circumstances;

- gaps in both thinking and practice;

- areas of potential growth and development.

Evaluation can be a risky business!

Clearly, evaluation has a great deal to offer. There must be a catch somewhere – and there is! Whilst some forms of evaluation can be carried out in a relatively private and personal way by concerned individuals, much of the effective evaluation in the home/school field is likely to be part of a 'whole-school approach', involving colleagues and also parents themselves.

So it is not helpful to see evaluation as either a blank cheque or the lofty and disinterested pursuit of truth! For evaluation taps straight into the heart of institutional life and challenges our notions of professionalism.

In the first place, the impetus to look critically at our work does not come out of thin air. It usually comes from external pressures (and the need to react to them) from the DES, 'the office', or from the head or from a growing realization that there are gaps in what we do (that maybe the school down the road is filling) or that certain things that we *are* doing aren't working as they should be.

There is also an element of 'Heads you win. Tails I lose!' about the carrying out of evaluative activities in the home/school field, as elsewhere in education. For they are rooted deep in the midst of educational politics and institutional life where perfect solutions exist only as thinly disguised fantasies. For what we choose to examine critically means ignoring something else; what we discover may serve to reinforce the existing pattern of power and influence involving the head, or particular groups of teachers or parents – or threaten it. Either way brings problems!

Similarly, the evaluation of home/school matters, as well as confirming some of our intentions and supporting some of our achievements, will also tell us some things that we would rather not know, or that some of our most cherished ideas and practices just aren't working.

So, regardless of the particular approaches that are developed, evaluation needs to be a rather hard-edged, unsentimental business which, as far as possible, is located against a wider background than the parochialism of staffroom politics and the personality clashes that are an enduring feature of institutional life.

Evaluation as a professional activity

In addition to the problems of purpose and approach that have already been sketched in, there are perhaps two other issues that might be referred to here which concern problems of role and problems of technique respectively. They are both concerned with the issue of just *how* evaluation might be carried out.

There is a wide spectrum of viewpoint about the relationship between evaluation and the teacher's role. At one end is the view that only those who are involved directly in educational processes, who are 'in the know' or 'on the inside', can possibly have the necessary knowledge and understanding to examine the work of schools and teachers. At the other end of the spectrum, for almost exactly opposite reasons, is the view that teachers are the *last* people to do this – or at least to be left to do it alone. This is clearly a matter which needs further discussion. It is raised here because of its particular relevance to family–school relations and the importance that needs to be attached to parental perspectives and experience.

Evaluation, as a sphere of activity, could sometimes be said to be guilty of projecting itself as a rather specialized area, dependent upon technical knowledge and specially learned techniques. The stance taken here is one that sees the need to de-mythologize and de-mystify, if evaluation is ever to become a natural and effective part of the repertoire of schools, teachers and parents. Within such a view, evaluation techniques grow out of the development of social and occupational skills, sharpened through practice and more systematically applied, such as:

- the skills of gathering and recording information;
- the ability to listen to other people and see things from their point of view;
- the skills of critical analysis and comparison, and so on.

The evaluation of home/school practice: some illustrations

The following example is intended to illustrate both the possibilities and the problems of evaluating home/school practice, particularly at the point where thinking and practice meet. The area from which most of the illustrations are drawn is the teacher–parent interview, chosen for the following reasons

(i)   The practice of periodically arranging a meeting for teachers and parents to review the progress of individual pupils is widespread, almost universal, in schools of all kinds. Whilst in the past it has often been regarded as a voluntary activity deriving from 'custom and practice', it is rapidly acquiring the status of a legal, contractual obligation.

(ii)   The very familiarity of teacher–parent interviews constitutes an important part of its value as an example of evaluation issues and problems. For thinking and practice consist of a densely-woven set of assumptions and values which constitute a taken-for-grantedness about such arrangements. So matters of conceptualization and definition have an important impact upon the design of any work in this area.

(iii)   The task of evaluating the operation and the effectiveness of teacher–parent consultations embodies many, though not all, of the characteristic problems of evaluation in the home/school field as a whole. Typically, these concern problems of perspective and purpose, of approach and method, and of organization.

(iv)   The choice of teacher–parent interviews as an extended example also illustrates a number of the special issues and problems that can be found in both the study and practice of home/school relations. These are often attributable to the existence of wide-ranging parental perspectives and experience and to the conceptual and practical difficulties of taking these adequately into account.

(v) Above all, such a choice points to an important paradox at the heart of home/school relations. For most parents and teachers (and pupils for that matter) regular contact to review educational progress, based upon a semi-formal interview, is thought to be important, necessary and valuable and is approached with those expectations.

The actual experience of such encounters, however, is quite different. For invariably such meetings are, at best, disappointing, and frequently, deeply frustrating. Moreover, such a paradox provides a puzzle to which no amount of armchair theorizing can provide any adequate answers and to which inquiry-based evaluation has much to offer.

Two recurring themes

'Never mind the quality, feel the width'

(i) 'We think our Parents' Evenings work very well. We generally get an 85% turnout...' (Headteacher).

'A load of rubbish...a total waste of time.' (A Parent. One of the 85 per cent!)

(ii) 'I just don't understand it. We spent absolutely *hours* planning it [a maths workshop] designing group tasks, making equipment and trying to anticipate every conceivable problem. We promoted it as hard as we could, with written invitations, posters, nagging the kids and guess what...after all that only thirty parents came! Where did we go wrong?' (Maths Teacher)

Both of these examples, drawn from different settings and activities draw attention to an important problem at the heart of evaluation activity. In making judgements about our work:

– What kinds of information and evidence do we need to seek out?

– How can we interpret it?

In this respect, it must be quite clear that there is an important role for quantitative information in the home/school field. For information about the patterns of participation in different aspects of a home/school programme or of the involvement of parents in activities that directly concern their own children, is very revealing and of practical value. More recently, too, many schools have found it useful to keep records and employ formal measures in schemes that involve parents in their children's reading, as an important means of assessing their effectiveness.

But the counting of heads, whilst useful, cannot provide the sole basis of judgements of value. For statistics cannot, in themselves, constitute a judgement about the quality of parental experience. Let us return to the examples.

(i)   Attendance at parents' evenings

A series of studies have shown vividly that there can be great discrepancies between the 'facts' of parental attendance at parents' evenings and their interpretation. For there are many reasons why parents attend such events. A common link, for teachers and parents alike, is the way the presence of parents is seen as symbolic of their active interest in their children's schooling.

Equally, there are many compelling reasons why parents do *not* attend (see pp. 180–1) including practical expediency and both ideologically and educationally respectable grounds. However these are *not* officially recognized. Despite the flimsiness of the claim, 'You never see the parents you really want to see' remains one of the most enduring teacher myths about parents' evenings. It requires both investigation and explanation.

(ii)   Running a maths workshop

Was this event necessarily the disaster that is claimed?

On what grounds?

Where does this school go from here?

We clearly need to find out more – both in terms of the experience of those who *did* come, as well as the perceptions of those who didn't. Again, there are studies which suggest a range of reasons for non-attendance, which concern timing and organization, previous experience of school events but, above all, the anxiety that maths (especially 'modern maths') engenders amongst parents from all back-grounds. And what about those who came? What kinds of impressions and experience did they take away? In a practical and obvious sense, you never know until you ask! Until the evaluation of relationships between families and schools becomes a matter of course, this will need to be done more deliberately using more formal techniques.

In a less obvious sense, thirty sets of positive responses, developed during a lively and enjoyable curriculum evening and subsequently fed into the parental grapevine, are an indication of a successful and effective evening and a basis for subsequent development.

'Living in different worlds?'

...all the children's books would be out and the place would be milling with parents and there was no sort of, erm, privacy. The teacher sort of looked around and thought, 'Are you next? Or you?!' and you'd sit around saying, 'After you' and getting more and more furious. And if you had three children, you were there most of the night!...By the time you got to your third teacher, at nine thirty, you were worn to a frazzle... (Parent)

I do occasionally see the teacher, but only if I've got a problem, I don't like to be running up to the school every five minutes sort of thing. Because, well, the teachers do know roughly what they're doing, don't they? (Parent)

Personally, I don't think that a school presenting itself to you gives you that true a picture. I think the way to find out about a school is to go down and see and then maybe look around the school and talk to the teacher, your child's teacher... (Parent)

You get to know some things that really help. I had one boy, he was fascinated by birds and really knowledgeable about them – I never knew that until his mum told me at a parents' evening. (Teacher)

It's lip-service really, isn't it? You can't get anything meaningful said in that short time, but I suppose you have to do it. It's really accountability isn't it? (Teacher)

A close study of actual teacher–parent interviews (as opposed to some of the claims that are made about them) reveals, to a remarkable degree, a process which is characterized by mismatching expectations and mutual incomprehension; teachers and parents often appear to be on different wavelengths, talking at cross purposes – living in different worlds.

What is more, there appears to be a conspiracy of silence about such events. Invitations sent out to parents, for example, almost invariably say nothing about the specific purposes of such a meeting. Parents, for their part, do not feel able to ask about such matters or seek clarification. The difficulties are also compounded by the powerful hidden agendas that operate, in which parents' evenings are the exercise of professional authority and of client management and control.

Any evaluation of teacher–parent consultation will need to locate itself in relation to a wide range of purposes, both explicit and hidden, with some attempt to analyse their consequences for communication and contact between families and schools. Such an approach will also need to take into account the wide range of parental attitudes and expectations, shaped as they are by general considerations of perspective and experience.

This adds up to a complex task, which stands in stark contrast to the neat, but entirely false, view which characterizes parents (or teachers, for that matter) as a homogeneous, undifferentiated mass, with common attitudes and expectations, as the Sussex Accountability Study found:

It is clear that parents approach all school events – both the educational and the social – with different attitudes and expectations, that teachers handle parents in different ways and that the child's progress, behaviour and relationships in school also influence the tone of the proceedings. Neither the transactions between teacher and parent, nor the criteria by which these transactions are judged to be useful, satisfactory or insufficient are common to all teachers or to all parents. (East Sussex LEA/University of Sussex, 1979)

A general view

Close study of both the observed and reported experience of teacher–parent consultation reveals a general obsessiveness, reflected in the title of this article and in the quotations it incorporates, with numbers – the number of teachers and parents to see, the length of time each interview requires or is given, the number and proportion of parents attending and so on.

This gives us important clues to a number of issues and problems associated with the practical arrangements that shape teacher–parent contact and influence its outcomes. Teacher–parent interviews, perhaps more than any other aspect of home/school thinking and practice, seem trapped in a suffocating network of unexamined assumptions and conventions, which effective evaluation would need to recognize and clarify.

A second, equally obvious, feature of evaluation in this area is the enormous range of parental ideology, personality and experience, (of which only a small proportion is represented here). Such wide-ranging variations contribute significantly to differences concerning:

- the purposes of teacher–parent contact
- views about what is appropriate to family–school relationships
- stances towards the forms in which information and experience should be made available, to enable parents to formulate judgements about their children's schooling.

Some practical suggestions for evaluating home/school activity

A. *Develop a 'whole-school' strategy and approach* – which draws upon the school's growing experience of working collaboratively in pursuit of planned development and change.

In any area like home/school relations, where strong prejudices and contradictory attitudes are rife, it might be useful to distinguish between:

Phase 1: initial discussion of aims; opening-up the area and freeing attitudes in the early stages of a review; acknowledgement of wide-ranging differences of philosophy and experience;

Phase 2: The need for more orderly, more or less systematic examination of the area via:

- The analysis of existing aims and intentions
  - ends/means analysis
  - different perceptions analysis

- Development of appropriate 'tools for the job'
  - identify a set of key questions, which define the range and scope of both planning and evaluation and provide points of reference, against which activity can be organized
  - identify frameworks, with which to examine whole programme/key features e.g. Development Process: Planning – Implementation – Evaluation; Key Features – Teacher–Parent Interview – Preparations – Encounter – Follow-up
  - tackle issues, not only in relation to what is needed, but about the best ways of doing things, by comparing different version/'old' and 'new' ways of doing things etc.
  - collect information and evidence, with which to examine the relationship between what parents seek and what the school provides e.g. collect 'Questions parents ask'
  - above all, seek critical feedback from parents as a matter of course. This suggests a role for evaluation that is continuous, long-term and built into familiar routines, rather than as artificial or deliberate 'one-offs'.

B.   *Develop the school's capacity to 'listen to parents' – as both a philosophy and a way of working.* Find ways of consolidating and developing this and of responding to the material that is uncovered, which is likely to be rich and diverse. (For practical suggestions for this, see Atkin and Bastiani, 1988.)

C.   *Identify ways of making the school more responsive, through the development of appropriate mechanisms and activities.*

- Support a colleague's secondment (under the GRIST funding arrangements) for a term, to monitor the home/school programme as a whole. Use the report that is produced as the basis of staff discussion and policy-making.

- Set up a joint teacher–parent 'commission', with a brief to collect evidence rather than air exotic theories and unsupported prejudices.

- Pair off colleagues ('third eye' approach) to monitor each other's work in this area.

- Enlist the help of students in initial training and on teaching practice to undertake studies of parental attitudes and experience. It is surprising what a bit of extra manpower can achieve.

We have witnessed a spectacular example of this. Working with a primary school deputy head we arranged, by prior agreement with all concerned, to participate in a fourth year junior parents evening. Then we:

- interviewed parents as they arrived. We were particularly interested in the anxieties and concerns they hoped to raise during the interviews;
- recorded and transcribed the interviews themselves;
- re-interviewed parents on their way out, to see how far *their* agendas had been acknowledged and tackled.

Whilst an unusual and extremely intensive experience, the process acted as a catalyst in transforming home/school relations in that school, as well as generating valuable in-service material for use with teachers elsewhere.

D.   There is an established paraphernalia of *evaluative methods and techniques*, which is readily available for teachers in a growing number of clearly written handbooks for the teacher or researcher-evaluator. For, above all, evaluation can be an intensely *practical* activity, with plenty of scope for:

- the development of appropriate, tailor-made methods and techniques;

- for both informal and more systematic approaches, reflecting both the school's normal approach to its work and the need for more systematic, periodic review, or the concentration upon problematic areas;

- both individual and collaborative activity, within the school and involving parents and the wider community.

A general approach of this kind, suitably adapted to the philosophy and circumstances of individual schools and the communities they serve, offers the potential through which the evaluation of home/ school activity can, at one and the same time, contribute to the development of the school and its educational purposes, as well as shaping the development of an institution which is more responsive to the needs and experience of teachers, parents and pupils alike.

Part Five

Training and Teacher Development

Editorial Preview

As might be expected from a book of this kind, the final section attempts to bring a number of the recurring general themes of the collection to bear upon one another and to suggest, in outline, a number of strategies and priorities for future development. First, the collection as a whole provides a reminder of the distinctive, but overlapping, agendas of politicians, professionals and parents, and the working-out of their reciprocal rights, duties and responsibilities.

Secondly, the book provides a range of illustrations and examples of both organizational and professional development, together with strong indications of the appropriate mechanisms and forms, knowledge, attitudes and skills required for their continuing transformation. Special emphasis is given to the role of study and research and its contribution to the development of policy and practice, particularly to inquiry and action-based approaches.

Finally, the collection gives plenty of examples of the value of the dissemination of more effective thinking and practice, both informally and in a more systematic way, the critical review of existing experience and its thoughtful adaptation.

These general themes are bound together by the common importance they attach to the role of training and professional development. This is seen, not as a specialist activity for selected agencies and institutions, but as a complex task which calls for the collaborative efforts and the shared responsibility of the education service as a whole and at all levels.

Working from a picture that is grounded in the real world of teachers and parents, the National Consumer Council reviews the present pattern of relationships between consumers and providers. From within the strong frame provided by a consumerist ideology, the report charts the continuing gaps between parents' and teachers' (and LEAs') perceptions of what is happening. In that chapter, the report sets an agenda which involves, and requires consideration by, the education service as a whole.

Michael Marland's chapter is based upon a contribution to a conference. In it, he manages to combine, to an unusual degree, his extensive experience as a headteacher and the feel for particular practices and the institutional arrangements that these require, with a wider view of the education service as a whole. This puts him in an ideal position to reconcile the differing demands posed by the introduction of relevant legislation and broad policies with the identification of training and development needs, particularly at the school level.

In their chapter, Janet Atkin and John Bastiani draw upon different areas of their work in an attempt to make sense of the 'ad hoc provision and piecemeal development' that characterize training opportunities in the home/school field. From the picture that emerges, they move on to identify, in outline, a number of ideas for future development in two complementary areas – a role for the DES in providing a framework for the initial training of teachers and a very different role for LEAs in supporting development and change in their schools.

In the final chapter, Alistair Macbeth provides a wide-angled view of policy and provision, which raises a number of central concerns in a pertinent way. Drawing from his comparative study of home/school relations in EEC member states, he is able to locate such relations from a perspective which considers the provision of schooling against the background of law and formal obligation, as well as against custom and practice. By developing a conceptual map, he is able to identify a wide range of both values and practices, of priority and development, both within and between national systems. This enables him to draw from different traditions as well as offering the benefit of new perspectives. Finally, he outlines a hypothetical model for the *process* of institutional and professional development, which readers can use as a series of points of reference against which to evaluate both their present achievements and their future intentions. As with many of the contributions in this collection, it poses a number of questions about the relationships in this field between rhetoric and action, between thinking and practice.

The Missing Links Between Home and School: a consumer view

National Consumer Council

Some general issues

Our work during 1984–85 carried on where our previous surveys left off – trying to find out how the provision of information could be improved (particularly at the time when decisions need to be taken); what further information was needed; how parents could be encouraged to become more involved in their children's schools; whether young people themselves were satisfied with the information and help they were offered. Several general points are highlighted below from the survey undertaken for NCC by MORI.

Teachers' views of 'home–school links' do not always tally with what parents say

The different experiences of the parents and the teachers interviewed in our group discussions throw light on an issue which calls for further attention – that is, that what teachers say about 'home–school links' does not always tally with what the parents say.

Teachers seem content (apart from the occasional 'of course, the parents we don't see are the ones we really need to see') with the system devised by their individual schools to 'contact', 'involve' and 'consult' parents. In Shire, for example, teachers mentioned parents' evenings, year evenings (they had recently held two evenings for fifth form parents and were about to hold one for the next first form intake), open evenings (including evenings when parents are taught a subject lesson as a means of learning about new ideas or methods), careers' evenings, parent–teacher associations as well as varied social events and opportunities for visiting the schools as and when the parents saw necessary.

Parents in Shire, on the other hand, commented that they were not invited to many social events, that one school's PTA had been disbanded, that there was no opportunity for parents to attend some of the more practical lessons to help or take part, that many had had no opportunity of meeting other teachers apart from the headteacher, that their views on what went on in the schools were often ignored, that the 'open' invitation to visit the school was not, in practice, workable. There was no evidence to suggest that the City area parents felt significantly different.

Parents want to know what's going on in the school

Linked to the first point, parents want to know more about what's going on in the school. This includes being able to learn about the subjects that their child is being taught, being involved in discussions about changes at the school (including opportunities to query decisions) and being kept informed of the child's progress.

Pupils as decision makers

From talking to pupils, we have had to recognize the importance they place (and indeed the importance their parents place) on their own actions. More often than not, pupils said that they decided on their choice of subjects at the end of the third year and that the decision what to do at the end of the fifth year was almost entirely their own. From further discussions with pupils and parents, we can suggest that this emphasis on pupils' own decisions lies with the belief of many that school and home are entirely separate – either the pupils believing that their parents 'can't' help and therefore shunning their interest or the parents feeling that they don't know enough to be able to help and therefore foregoing any opportunities to become involved. Whichever is the case, further help and information to break down these barriers will serve to improve communications between the three 'sides' – school, parent and pupil – and improve the pupils' progress at school.

Existing channels of communication not working

It became clear that the 'formal' channels of communication – PTAs, governing bodies, schools councils – were not seen by the consumers as effective means of disseminating information or of consultation. The PTAs were seen as fund-raising associations only, which positively avoided any discussions about wider educational issues; governing bodies were seen to be too remote and in the pocket of the local education authority; schools councils were viewed as a sop to pupils when 'the school' had no intention of acting on or even listening to their views.

Through the survey, we have found parents who want to be involved in their children's education – some who have continued to play an important role in advising their child, others who have come up against barriers to such involvement. Few expressed no interest whatsoever although one in ten parents in our survey had had no personal contact with the school during the previous 12 months. Our survey concentrated on those times during a secondary school life when decisions have to be taken, examining whether the consumers felt able to make 'good' decisions – our view being that no decision can be good if it is not informed. At all stages, we found parents and pupils who would have appreciated further help and information – whether that came through written guidance or details, or through more meetings and contacts.

We are concerned, however, about the training given to teachers – both on initial and in-service courses – on communicating with parents. The work carried out by the Nottingham University School of Education (Atkin and Bastiani, 1984) concluded that about a half of secondary trained teachers receive little or no preparation to work with parents; and for those who train during a postgraduate year's course, the proportion who receive no training rises to 56 per cent. If the move is towards greater teacher–parent contact (as seems to be desired by the parents), much more thought needs to be given to what teachers are told and how the training in dealing with their school's consumers is given.

Information for decision making: the gaps

For parents about schools

At the time of moving to secondary school, over one in ten parents felt the school to have done a 'fairly poor' or 'very poor' job in providing help and information. The proportions were similar in both areas even though the procedures differed. Parents need greater access to the secondary schools in terms of visits and open days with opportunities to discuss ideas and raise queries with teachers. Such access should include details of open days and visits to all schools in the area if parents are to be helped to make informed decisions.

This is also true of brochures – many of which are currently being received too late to be of any practical help in deciding where to send their child. In City, where a linked high school system is operated, the decision is taken for the parents, unless they positively disagree and ask that their child be allowed to go to another. Little help is offered, therefore, until it is requested – which many parents find difficult to do. The diversity of school brochures in the same area allowed each school to highlight what it saw to be important – one, for example, giving a list of the staff and detailing the structure within the school, another, including a plan of the school and outlining potential contacts between parents and school during a school life, another specifying curriculum plans in detail. But without seeing these brochures and being able to decide their own priorities on the basis of such knowledge, parents start making decisions on the basis of hearsay or personal bias.

About options and careers

By the time decisions need to be taken on options or on what to do at the end of the fifth year, our survey showed clearly that a large proportion of parents and pupils were unhappy with the role of the school in providing them with the help and information they needed to make the decision. Parents do not understand 'why' or 'how' decisions on options have to be taken and do not understand the implications of these choices. They need much clearer guidance from the school, with more and earlier education on what subjects are being taught and what is on each syllabus.

Many parents said that a barrier to their involvement was raised by their own ignorance of 'what goes on at school'. Much of this is linked to the new subject areas and changing priorities but some is also linked to parents' dissatisfaction with the way children's progress is reported and recorded. Schools should be able to offer parents much more detail of what is being taught and how – indeed, improving parents' understanding can only help to lower the strict home/school divide that many perceive – and should examine their reporting procedures.

For pupils about options and careers

Pupils need help too. Some of the sixth-form pupils who attended our discussion groups complained about the way schools treated them, and this is borne out by the finding that young people feel that decisions they take at school are not the subjects of adequate or relevant discussion or information. Those young people who had left school at the age of 16 in particular found the school to have been a poor provider of help and information about what to do. And a third of all respondents said that, looking back at which subjects they had taken in their fourth and fifth years, the school had not given them enough information to help them make a decision.

Many of the concerns raised by our survey point to an important conclusion – that improved contact between teachers (school) and parents, between school and young people and between parent and pupil will result in better understanding and, hopefully, better decisions. When parents complain that their visit to the school or their letter to the headteacher has not been satisfactorily dealt with; when parents' evenings (one of the more popular visits to the school) give rise to grumbles; when parents feel that their views are not wanted; when pupils don't know where to go for help – the partnership envisaged by our 1977 code of practice or by the Department of Education and Science 1985 white paper has not been successful.

Recommendations

We are of the view that schools, parents, and local education authorities are trying harder to communicate with each other. Many are already assessing the effort in time and resources that schools currently give to such communications. But our research finds that there is still an enormous gap between parents' and teachers' (and LEAs') perceptions of what is happening. Very much more effort is needed to close that gap. We believe that communication between consumers and providers is an important part of the school function. This raises the question whether such communication should form a part of a teacher's contract. The participants in the discussions currently underway on the precise nature of the teachers' contract need to recognize that.

In particular, we suggest the following.

To the schools, for parents

Schools should develop a strategy for informing, involving and consulting parents which goes further than producing brochures or newsletters and arranging evenings and PTA meetings. We believe that parents are becoming more aware of the need for better communication and that such a strategy would benefit the schools themselves. Some of the suggestions mentioned during our work are put forward here. While these emphasize collective systems for contacting parents, they should not in any way be seen as substitutes for individual contacts, (which should be strengthened):

-   group discussions. These could involve teachers and parents or parents only and would provide the opportunity for parents to discuss common problems and to comment on what was going on in the school.

-   class parents' evenings. The parents' evening to discuss a child's progress are seen by parents and teachers as an important means of getting together, but our findings showed that parents are not content, often because of long queues and the difficulty of seeing the right teacher at the right time. Breaking such evenings into class events could be one way of easing the problems.

-   the timings of meetings. Many parents find it difficult to attend evening meetings; others find afternoon visits impossible. Schools need to review these arrangements in the light of discussions with parents.

-   location of meetings. Parents are ready to discuss their children's education – and indeed were readily recruited for our evening group meetings – but often feel 'out of control' in the school environment. Schools need to consider the possibility of arranging some meetings outside school.

- how queries or complaints are dealt with. Parents we spoke to complained about the way they felt the school treated their approach to the headteacher. Schools should re-examine their internal arrangements for dealing with complaints, queries, suggestions – which would in turn encourage parents to keep schools informed of home circumstances.

- early notification of problems. Parents, if they are to become more involved in their children's school life, feel that they need and want to be notified and involved earlier when problems occur.

To the schools, for pupils

Schools also need to develop a strategy for informing, involving and consulting pupils. Evidence suggests that young people now play a much greater role in deciding the course of their education but are often doing so without enough information and without any means of consultation. If schools are allowing them to make such decisions, they need to ensure that actions are being taken on the basis of appropriate knowledge.

To teacher training institutions

Teacher training institutions need to recognize the growing importance of the parent and the pupil as consumers of a service. Much more thought should be given to the content of the training courses (both the three or four-year or one-year courses and initial or in-service training) which should offer specific lectures and practical training in dealing with parents in person and in writing, and in exploring how best to involve pupils in the discussions and decisions.

To the Secretary of State

The Secretary of State for Education and Science should place a duty on the school inspectorate to examine schools' links with parents. This would be one means of producing a body of expertise on what constituted good (or bad) practice and would, through the inspectorate's published reports on schools, be a means of easily disseminating such knowledge. In carrying out such an investigation, inspectors would need to consider examining whether the schools had made any efforts to review their links with parents. Resources might need to be made available for inspectors themselves to seek the parents' views of these links (especially given the apparent mismatch between parents' and teachers' perception of what happens).

To the government, for school governors

Government should place a duty on governing bodies to assess their school's ability to, and success in, involving and consulting their parents. The green paper in May 1984 (GB. DES, 1984) suggested that governing bodies could 'exercise a general oversight over how well the school's working methods were fostering its aims and objectives; how successfully the school planned for and adjusted to changes in circumstances; how far the school held appropriate expectations of staff and pupils; how well the school capitalized on its strengths and identified and tackled its weaknesses; and how effectively it consulted parents and others on such issues as pupil behaviour, discipline and school uniform'. This is, obliquely, confirmed in the white paper which states that the governing body is to '[be] the guarantor of the school's identity...and exercise an important influence over the ethos of the school and on many other matters which affect the school's success' (para 231). In our original response to the green paper, the NCC suggested that governing bodies 'need access to funds to enable them to carry out small-scale survey work on pupil/parent/teacher attitudes to the school and its position in the community'. We reiterate this recommendation here.

To local education authorities, for school governors

Local education authorities should develop a series of induction and 'in-service' training courses for all members of their schools' governing bodies. In particular, such training should emphasize the importance of home/school communications and should be aimed at exposing governors to current thought and actions on 'good practice'.

Local education authorities and schools, in consultation with parents, should consider the production of checklists for parents which would help them ask the right questions of schools at the right time. Our research has shown that parents do want to know what is going on in their children's schools but find it difficult to ask. We believe that the discussions with parents have thrown light on some of these questions and ideas which we would be happy to follow up with interested LEAs or parents' organizations.

Parenting, Schooling and Mutual Learning

Michael Marland

Attitudes and reactions

Two complementary assumptions about schooling and parents linger in Britain: the first is that school is omnipotent, offering all the requirements for a full life, and the second is that parents do not care, and are incompetent to support their children's education. I have frequently met unwarranted criticism, resentment, patronizing condescension, and sheer blindness to the real attitudes of parents. In schools in 'difficult' inner-city areas the pressures of teaching can lead to a gross under-valuing of parents.

When I took my own first children to infant school 20 years ago, I found a total refusal by the Headteacher to meet my wife and me the term before, a tatty notice pinned to the door saying 'Please do not help your children to read' (!), and the key decoration in the Headteacher's study was an officially printed notice describing the legal penalties for parents who used offensive language or refused to leave the premises.

Occasionally I note that we teachers complain either that parents don't take enough interest, or that they 'fuss too much'. It is as if we have a clear generalized idea of the perfect parent, who has no role other than 'supporting' the school – and carries that out discretely and obediently: 'Their's not to question why'! It may be the case that the profession has not a great deal to be proud of in the thoroughness, intelligence, sensitivity, and sheer professionalism of its work with homes, though matters are improving.

Ethnic minority families

Communication with the homes of ethnic minority families deserves particular attention. I concur with the findings of a Birmingham study:

The immigrant parents' expectations of the schools and the definition of their children as a problem, both by educational policy-makers and by teachers, produce a situation of misunderstanding at best and direct conflict at worst. (Rex and Tomlinson, 1979)

An earlier study of *Organisation in Multi-Racial Schools* reported depressingly:

> In general, home–school relations appear to be one of the most unsatisfactory areas of life in multi-racial schools. (Townsend and Britton, 1972)

Teachers tend to blame the home, and interpret, for instance, lower attendance at parents' evenings (confirmed in Black People's Progressive Association, 1978; and Rex and Tomlinson, 1979) as signs of 'apathy' – a word I have heard too often in schools – and 'poor family circumstances'. Both need re-considering. The evidence does *not* support the charge of 'apathy':

> Contrary to widespread beliefs that some minority group parents do not take much interest in their children's education, our study indicated that not only do they take great interest, but both West Indian and Asian parents have made particular efforts to try to understand a complex and unfamiliar system, and they have high expectations of school. (Tomlinson, 1980)

My experience of parents' meetings at North Westminster confirms that of the Rex study in Handsworth (Rex and Tomlinson, 1979) that 'Asian' parents are likely to include a rather high proportion of non-visitors to school. Their reasons, however, were *not* those of the apathetic; rather they are largely the practical problems of shift hours, language difficulties, and the fact that school is often the only major 'white' institution with which an Asian in an English city has to relate – for many Asian workers who have lived in England for many years work, shop, and socialize almost wholly within their ethnic community. These factors combine with an attitude to schooling that leads them deliberately not to wish to 'interfere'. Rex and Tomlinson found, as I find weekly, *no* signs of apathy, indeed considerable evidence in most families of extreme concern.

Indeed, David Quinton's family studies and review of the research compellingly refute many aspects of the stereotype (Quinton, 1980). In the meantime, the split widens. As Maureen Stone says:

While schools try to compensate children by offering Black Studies and steel bands, black parents and community groups are organising Saturday schools – to supplement the second-rate education which the school system offers the parents. There is a mis-match between the system and the community. (Stone, 1981)

Those of us responsible in schools must look to ourselves; our image, language, practical arrangements, attitudes and knowledge. Each has to be improved if the links are to be improved.

Official leadership

Over the last twenty years there has been an unsteady but definite increase in official regard for the importance of home/school links from Local Education Authorities and at national level. In 1964 my inquiries to the then Ministry of Education gained the reply:

There is very little information in the Ministry concerning the relationship and communication between parents and school.

At the same time the London County Council (as it was then called) informed me in writing that it had no clear or firm policy in this field.

Since those days there has been a series of official advisory reports, giving increasingly frantic exhortations to get linking. The first was in connection with the pupils of 'average or less than average ability'.

There is urgent need to strengthen all existing links between home and school, and in difficult areas to create new ones, as, for example, in the appointment of members of staff with special liaison or home-visiting responsibilities. (Newsom Report, 1963.)

A few years later the Plowden Committee looking at primary education in England built much of its argument round better links: regular meetings with parents, open days, booklets, reports and contacts with parents who did not visit the school. (Plowden Report, 1967). When the Bullock Committee came to consider the teaching of reading and the uses of language, it too emphasized parental involvement in a number of ways (Committee of Inquiry, 1975, recommendations 40 and 52, pages 519 and 520). By the next decade, when the children of ethnic minorities were the subject of a worried inquiry, the Rampton Committee started again; but now in the wider context of the community. It called for senior staff to co-ordinate links, materials easily understood by parents from ethnic minority groups, home visiting by teachers and the involvement of PTA's in educational matters (Committee of Inquiry, 1981). The Schools Council English Committee was one of the first to start worrying about the professional skills required (Schools Council, 1979).

Despite this stream of exhortations, I have some doubts about the detailed knowledge and practice by education authorities and Her Majesty's Inspectors, just as I have considerable doubts about the advice available from many official advisors at local level on how to meet these exhortations.

After the Plowden Report, the Department of Education and Science published a handbook of good practice, but it might be fair to say that schools are not really very different now than twenty years ago. I do not consider that the teaching profession has been given sufficient leadership by central government or LEA Advisors. I should like not only clear Local Education Authority guidelines, but for this aspect of the work of a school to be specifically and methodically monitored by official Advisers and Her Majesty's Inspectors.

Can we manage it?

Our present problems would seem to be a result of three main different but interlocking factors:

(a) Attitudes
(b) Time
(c) Facilities

Teachers are no more 'typical' than parents, but it is probably fair to say that they almost all appreciate parental interest, and would in principle be happy to help increase it. Some, indeed, already go to considerable lengths. However, the constraints are great, and many are caught in limitations of tradition and practicalities.

Attitudes

I have already described some aspects of typical professional attitudes. We teachers easily tend to want all other adults to be like us. Those who don't share our assumptions we too readily call 'apathetic'. Few substantial attempts have been made to establish what parents actually feel and think. Perhaps the major English study is that of the 'Schools, Parents, and Social Services Project' funded by the DES between 1974 and 1977 (Johnson *et al.*, 1980). Its findings are a major adjustment of the received wisdom of schools: parents had seen primary school as a weaning from home, they did not then want to reverse this. They themselves did not necessarily consider it right to curtail their children's activities, and did not therefore see it proper to interfere too much in school. They found it strange that teachers admitting to difficulties in handling teenagers should expect parents to wield undiminished authority over them! To many parents, the encounters with teachers appear as demands by the school for accounting for their parenting, or for mere support of school.

Whereas teachers judged support only in terms of home/school links, parents saw home-based support as very important – and gave it far more often than teachers realized. Often schools knew virtually nothing of the range of ways in which ordinary homes encouraged, supported, taught, and transported to classes or sports. Teachers were especially blind about the help given by older siblings, who were often able to give advice and encouragement that was far more acceptable than that from other sources.

It is clear from such research studies that not only are the huge majority of parents *not* apathetic but very concerned, and also that the nature of their concerns and the modes of their support have a great deal to teach us teachers. How is it that most teachers' perceptions do not include this? Why are our attitudes so inappropriate? It must be the leadership task of the school as a whole and of the school system to help teachers see afresh.

Time

Schools are busy places, and the need for pupils to be supervised constantly uses a great deal of adult time, as do curricular commitments. In the 'practical' questions facing education authorities and schools which Alastair Macbeth isolates (Macbeth, 1981), he includes: 'Many teachers have become accustomed to an occupational routine which does *not* include regular contact'. This is certainly so, and can be changed only by a combination of approaches, including his 'implications for teachers' terms of service and pay'. A nation must not ask too much of its professional servants.

It is difficult to see how the flexible requirements of good liaison could be met by some of the proposals made to provide the capacity in the profession for it. For instance, Macbeth quotes 'liaison pay' (special payments for liaison overtime) and 'status opting' (whereby certain teachers with full professional status and higher pay take on the open-ended commitment, but others are contractually less flexible 'day teachers' (Macbeth, 1981). The former would give liaison a different status from any other of the profession's tasks, and would make its motives suspect. The latter would not fit the 'one profession' concept that UK teachers and their unions value so highly.

In the English and Welsh school at least, the prime leadership task for home links is that of the 'pastoral staff' (see Marland, 1974). However, I should argue strongly against 'specialist home–school liaison teachers' being the general rule (Macbeth, *op. cit.*), for a number of reasons, chiefly that on the one hand parents will not so fully accept this mode of communication, and on the other hand that the valuable learning about the families will not thus be generalized throughout the staff.

I can suggest only that a study is made of the precise time implications of all those exhortations in government-sponsored reports. Perhaps a pilot plan should be introduced in one area, and evaluated. Then the hours required could be roughly estimated. In my view these would best be met by an ear-marked addition to teaching staff resources with an obligation (however they are dispersed) to devote the agreed time to liaison.

Facilities

Good home/school links, it regrettably has to be pointed out, depend also on the mechanics of communication: reception facilities, telephones, typing. Most UK schools are lamentably under-provided, not only because no one appears to have troubled to have translated the concept of 'keeping in touch with homes' into practical outlines of the consequential facilities required. Dictating and audio-typing facilities for pastoral team leaders would do more good than continued rhetoric and exhortation!

The community school

The concept of the community school offers a new approach to home/school relationships. If the school is to be an educational centre for a range of provision through to adults, it could be that the position of parents would be one of a triangle of community, parents and school. Perhaps concentric circles would be a better visual pattern: the school is the centre circle, with parents around it, and non-parental members of the community as the outer ring. The important movement towards community schools (see Poster, 1982) offers a new hope for this link: in the true community school parents are partners in the whole educational enterprise and their rights are not dependent on having children in the school.

Teacher preparation

I have found no reason to challenge Macbeth's cautious conclusion: 'My impression was that relations between schools and families did not play a large part in either the training of new teachers or in the re-training of established teachers' (Macbeth, 1981.) Research in Sussex also confirmed this:

> Some teachers, especially the younger ones, felt very strongly that their training had not equipped them to deal with parents: they did not wish to escape from the responsibility of doing so, but they would like to have had the benefit of more advice as students. (Becher *et al.*, 1981.)

Despite the probably realistic note of caution by Mortimore and

Blackstone (1982) that 'Better preparation in their training may be insufficient to overcome the resistance felt by some teachers', I have no doubt that initial training must include a measure of knowledge, attitudinal and skill aspects, and that in-service education must then expand on this and include organizational considerations.

Macbeth asks what the nature of training should be in regard to home/school relations (Macbeth, 1981). I have argued in 'Preparing for Promotion in Pastoral Care' (Marland, 1983) that there are very definite skills and knowledge which are likely to be useful. These can be divided into the two categories, one of which is not effective without the other: knowledge and skills.

A. Knowledge

A teacher needs to know about the relationship between different social environments and the way of life. How *do* people make the pattern of their lives in these or those circumstances? What happens to the Bangladeshi family, culturally and socially, when a family is reunited in a British city? What do we know from studies of what family life is actually like? What lies behind the broad sociological generalizations of 'class'?

There is then knowledge of the concern that parents have for their children's education, how they express it, and often how they divert or suppress it. That is, I should want a specific focus on the way the parental desire for education fits into their lives. This would lead to a consideration of the home pressures on the child:

> The Sussex research revealed an extensive black market in education, with children at all social levels being coached, cajoled, and coerced at home by parents or by paid tutors. (Becher *et al.*, 1981).

And it would also involve considering home/school contacts *from the point of view of the parent.*

At the present general level there are psychological problems. As one commentary puts it:

> Many teachers find parents potentially threatening, both to their authority in what is often a relatively isolated situation, and to their professional prestige. (Mortimore and Blackstone, 1982.)

B. Skills

Although most of the skills involved could be regarded as part of the ordinary abilities of an adult professional to be able to communicate, there appears to be a need to focus on them in this context.

(i)   Report writing;

(ii) Drafting letters, both about individual cases and on general aspects of the curriculum;

(iii) Explaining in a way which is both open to question and comprehensible;

(iv) Listening to parents!

(v)   Joint planning.

Too much UK teacher education leaves out the institution of school, its planning requirements (curriculum and more general), and its dependence on working within a series of adult professional relationships. From one point of view, a teacher's life is a sequence of negotiations with other adults, professional and lay, about curriculum and courses of action. Teachers need as much help with these skills as, for instance, those in business.

I should add the view that schools *need* more political and community support to strengthen their power. They won't get it if they try to go it alone. Marten Shipman has put this point powerfully in connection with the inner-city school:

> A way forward would be to strike a bargain between parents and teachers. Parents would offer more support and receive more power to affect decisions about central issues such as the curriculum. Teachers would yield some of their professional autonomy in exchange for support. This would require a major effort of mass communication to spell out the benefits that could accrue. It would require a whole-hearted effort by central and local government, and probably the definition of new legal responsibilities for parents and a stronger role for the courts if these duties were not fulfilled. Such a bargain might promote a

more consistent and sustained context for the education of inner-city and other children. It would also give the poorer child more of the advantages of his more fortunate peer. (Shipman, 1980.)

Parents not only deserve power, but the schools need them to have that power for the strength it gives the school.

I should also want to challenge the most euphoric versions of the view that parental interest correlates with high pupil attainment: parental interest can be improved by the school, *and so* pupil attainment can be raised.

The received opinion amongst many teachers is that the working-class child is disadvantaged at school partially at least because of weak parental interest in schooling in general and the child's educational progress: Douglas in 1964 (Douglas, 1964) and the Plowden Committee three years later (Central Advisory Council, 1967) in its own research claimed a very strong association between educational achievement and parental attitudes to school. These findings have become educational commonplaces even amongst those who have read neither source. However, later commentators have seen the measures that these researchers used as indicators of parental interest rather as manifestations of class behaviour, and Acland (1980) worked through the Plowden data afresh. The essence of his findings is that the variables most closely identified with parental involvement did not correlate strongly with achievement. Mortimore and Blackstone discuss the arguments comprehensively, and conclude:

> The evidence on parental interest, or lack of it, needs to be treated with caution. Sometimes at least part of the evidence is based on indicators which may not be the most sensitive or even the most appropriate and which may be measuring something other than parental interest...It seems likely that there are several possible explanations for behaviour which is often interpreted as lack of interest. (Mortimore and Blackstone, 1982.)

However, none of this is to deny that the greater mutual support and understanding, the better. Indeed I should like to stress how early this should start. The relationship needs to be considered not only throughout the years of schooling, but also in nursery, pre-school playgroups, and child-minding.

Ironically the most dramatic step in England and Wales towards greater sensitivity in listening to parents is the rapid drop in births! 'Falling numbers of pupils' has transformed a sellers' market, in which teachers were (in Musgrove's phrase), 'the high priests of society' (Musgrove and Taylor, 1969) to a buyers' market, in which parents can exercise real power: they can choose another school and get in! This could, sadly in a way, therefore be a good time for re-appraisal.

Many teachers have gone beyond the current expectations and have devised ways of working with parents, often giving up time well beyond the usual. Most teachers in my experience come from parents' meetings with a glow of pleasure. The sad thing is that they are then usually plunged into the next day's work without adequate opportunity to follow up.

Some teachers see the extension of a school's relationship with parents as no more than an opportunity to impress on them the school's points of view on aspects of curriculum. Some parents wait until things go wrong before they act. The evidence of my experience supports the 20 years of research and publications in this country: parenting and schooling are a partnership, each properly with different perspectives, but each gaining from mutual learning and support. School and family cooperation is not the chimera that some dread; we must take it out of the fantasies where it has been allowed to live; we must create close links as an everyday practicality.

Training Teachers to Work with Parents

Janet Atkin and John Bastiani

Setting the scene

Home/school relations have been the subject of research, policy and practice in the educational world for many decades. It is only in the 1980s however that recognition of the place of parents in the life and work of the school became a central platform for politicians, professionals, and parents alike. Consideration of the relationships between schools and homes and the attitudes and practices generated by them, are now a professional obligation rather than an optional extra for committed schools. A series of Education Acts from 1980 onwards culminating in the 1986 Act has given parents rights to information, involvement, and decision making of a kind unimagined when most teachers in schools today were trained. Alongside the development of policy has grown the accumulating evidence of the benefits of active parental involvement in the education of their children and the value of their support to schools. All of these changes have profound influences upon the nature of the role of a teacher and necessitate changes in the training and inservice education of the teaching profession. However, despite the centrality of parents in the political and professional arena the question that needs to be asked is how much of the rhetoric has been translated into reality in the provision of systematic and extensive opportunities for such training?

Both through the setting up of the Council of Accreditation of Teacher Education (CATE) and through the Grant-Related In-Service Training Programme (GRIST), central government now exercises greater control over the nature of teacher education. Has a national policy emphasizing partnership with parents been accompanied by a recognition of the training needs of teachers? Both at initial and in-service level the picture is bleak. The only reference in the CATE criteria for initial training to working with parents is the somewhat vague phrase, 'Students should be made aware of the wide range of relationships – with parents and others – which teachers can expect to develop in a diverse society, and of the role of the school within a community.' Moreover the national priorities of the first two years of GRIST funding have been almost entirely concerned with curriculum matters and have made no mention of training for work with parents. We would argue that a genuine partnership with parents requires such a substantial change in teacher attitudes and practices that a coherent pattern of induction into the profession supported and extended by further opportunities for development when in post is essential for both serving and intending teachers. The ways in which such a programme might be translated into practice is considered in the second half of this article. That such changes are necessary we substantiate through an examination of the present picture in initial and in-service education.

Initial teacher education

Since the early 1970s teacher training institutions have undergone considerable upheaval, reorganization, contraction and expansion, and in some cases complete closure. Student members sharply declined from around 120,500 in 1974 to a low of 16,500 in 1984. During this decade the Certificate of Education ceased and entry into teaching became dependent on a graduate qualification. The proportion of students training via the one year Post Graduate Certificate of Education increased steadily and now represents about half of all new entrants to the profession. Another significant change has been a shift in the balance of teachers required for the primary and secondary phases so that many tutors who previously trained as secondary teachers have had to equip themselves for the primary sector. Since 1984 institutions have had to get their courses approved by CATE and this has required much rethinking and reorganization. All of these changes have placed considerable demands upon training institutions and it is as well to bear this background in mind when we seek to show the extent to which students are currently prepared for a role which now requires an active partnership with parents.

Our own interest in initial training in this area was prompted by our experience of many years of in-service education with teachers. We became accustomed to their claims that their initial training had left them ill-equipped and unprepared for the new kind of role they were being expected to undertake. The only memory many of them could dig up was of the lectures they had received on social class and educational attainment and their imputed support for working class apathy towards education. During the workshops we have run over the last decade on written communication, parent–teacher interviews, involving parents in the curriculum, and other aspects of home/school relationships, we have been both impressed by the willingness of teachers to tackle new ways of working with parents and depressed by their criticism of their initial training, or lack of it, in this area. Was it possible that the teachers we met were unrepresentative – might not their feelings of inadequacy have prompted their attendance at our courses? Moreover we personally knew many tutors in teacher-training who had a commitment to the development of home/school relations and could not imagine their students would feel the same as the teachers we met. However our own experiences were being supported by findings from surveys and inquiries such as Cyster *et al.*, (1980) 'Parental Involvement in the Primary School', the East Sussex/Sussex University Accountability project, the HMI (1982) document on 'The New Teacher in School' and others. The familiar comments about lack of training and inadequate preparation were being made by teachers from all over the country, not just our region, and from probationers as well as long-serving teachers. All this data, however, relied on teachers' memories and accounts of their experience as students and it is well known that many teachers have sceptical views about their training and not necessarily accurate recall about their courses. We therefore came to the conclusion that the only way to get a picture of what provision the training institutions themselves made and how they perceived the importance of this aspect of a teacher's role was to ask them.

Getting an accurate picture

Accordingly we sent a letter to all institutions running initial teacher training, with the exception of a few specialist courses such as Music or Business Studies. In it we invited them to describe their provision, discuss where they saw the major responsibility for preparation lay, and comment on any problems, such as resources, materials etc. The overall response rate was 84 per cent (ranging from 81 per cent from University departments to 90 per cent from Polytechnics) and there was no bias in the responses from any particular region, form of course or phase of schooling being trained for. A full report described the survey, points out its limitations and some caveats about the data, and stresses that we do not claim to have produced a definite picture of the situation (Atkin and Bastiani, 1984).

However, we do believe our survey provided sufficient evidence and an outline picture of provision that enabled us to make some claims about the preparation teachers received at the time of the survey in 1984 and to confirm us in our view that much remained to be done both in initial and in-service education.

Possibly the most disturbing finding was that one-third of primary and nearly half of secondary students got little or no preparation to work with parents, thus supporting our personal impressions, those of other researchers and the teachers themselves. This overall picture changed somewhat if the route to qualification is taken into account. If the student was following a BEd course, whether primary or secondary, the proportion dropped to 25 per cent. However, bearing in mind the growth of proportionately more students training by the PGCE route the figures here were much less encouraging. We estimated that 44 per cent of primary and 56 per cent of secondary students received a little or no preparation. Clearly the pressures that training a teacher in one year produces must be the major explanation for this finding, although it is interesting to note that, as some PGCE courses *did* give systematic attention to the issue, while some BEd courses did not, perceptions about the importance of it amongst teacher-trainers themselves, must also be seen as a significant factor.

Another finding that has considerable relevance to providers of in-service education and to LEA advisers responsible for new teachers, was that 37 per cent of the institutions believed that the major responsibility for preparation for work with parents, should be left to in-service or induction schemes. There were wide differences *between* institutions on this point, in that 24 per cent of University departments, 38 per cent of Colleges or Institutes of

Higher Education and 53 per cent of Polytechnics held this view, which perhaps points to different perceptions of the adequacy or otherwise of post-training provision. We believe this finding, together with others from the survey, highlights the need for teacher education to be seen as a coherent and integrated system where the foundations laid in initial training are developed and extended through in-service education. The present system undoubtedly leaves the student at the mercy of the particular institution, the schools where teaching practice takes place and the subsequent local authority employer.

The part that schools themselves play in preparing students also seemed to vary considerably and points to tensions in the relationship between them and training institutions. Some institutions consciously take the initiative in guiding students on their role vis à vis parents while they are on teaching practice, while others leave the decision entirely to the schools. Variation in practices between schools, and even resistance from schools which regard the issue as their province, means that many students' experiences are haphazard, unsystematic and rarely followed-up and discussed. Many institutions seemed to believe that the appropriate knowledge, attitudes and skill for working with parents grows naturally and inevitably out of the experience of working in schools and that being prepared to be a 'good' teacher is sufficient. We suspect that this view derives from an assumption that home/school relations are unproblematic and that the 'good' teacher is one who 'handles' the parent as part of a professional/lay relationship where professional knowledge and client ignorance are the key features.

One further finding we would draw attention to here is that it appeared that most institutions, though there were very interesting exceptions, treated the *academic* topic of home/school relations separately from the *professional* preparation of students. This division is amplified by the organization and structure of courses and by the division of teaching and tutorial responsibility. It means, for example, that while students may hear about the crucial effects of home background in one course, the implication for their work as teachers, and the possibilities of reform and change are dealt with elsewhere, if at all. The most striking exceptions to this general pattern seemed to be particular courses on nursery or infant education, children with special needs and education in urban areas. There were examples here where the artificial distinction between theory and practice were avoided and where there was extensive collaboration between training institutions, schools and indeed parents themselves.

What is clear as a result of our inquiry is the patchy and un-systematic nature of the training teachers receive in the home/school area. Although there were some indications that many institutions were rethinking and redesigning their courses and prac-tices to take account of recent developments, we suspect that the pressures upon training institutions have not lessened since our survey and that the picture it revealed is little changed. We acknowledge that this can only be speculation but what is clear is that given the large numbers of serving teachers who had no such preparation there remains a major task for in-service education if a partnership between home and school is to become a reality rather than empty rhetoric.

In-service education and training

The difficulties of putting together a reliable picture of provision in the initial training area pale into insignificance alongside the task of doing the same for current opportunities in the post-experience field, a task which several organizations have tried to carry out but none satisfactorily completed. For the world of in-service education and training (INSET) provides a series of powerful illustrations of the tradition of ad hoc and piecemeal development, so characteristic of much of our education service, with its diverse range of providers, locations, patterns of involvement and ways of working.

So, according to where they live, teachers have very varied opportunities to participate in in-service courses that can range from a single, half-day session to opportunities for more extended courses in higher education establishments and teachers' centres, on a day-release or other basis; they may, if they are lucky, live in one of the few areas where relevant courses are available as part of the award-bearing programme for teachers; they may even work in one of the handful of LEAs that takes special initiatives or make their own arrangements in this area. As big as a problem for teachers, however, as the inconsistent and widely-differing provi-sion of in-service opportunities in the home/school field, is the lack of co-ordinated information about what *is* available and accessible.

Training needs and opportunities: two major examples

We have learned that, in order to be effective, a training strategy which contributes to the improvement of home/school relations needs to be coherently planned and should draw upon the education service as a whole, with its wide-range of resources and experience.

In the space available we are not able to provide a comprehensive view, but have chosen instead to sketch, in outline, a training strategy in two major areas:

(1) a national DES-led strategy for initial training;

(2) the role of LEAs in the development of local initiatives, support for the work of schools, and the professional development of teachers.

(1) A national plan for initial training: 'Preparing Teachers to Work With Parents'

A number of contributions in this collection draw attention to the actual and potential role of national initiatives, through the interplay between central government and the Department of Education and Science. Our view is that, perhaps in spite of recent experience, there *is* an important role for the government and the DES to play in the passing of enabling legislation, the establishment of general guidelines and priorities, the formulation of general policies and the allocation of resources and, finally, in the sponsorship of important research and development work in key areas.

We also feel that, given the patchy and uneven development in institutions of higher education, a national training initiative would be both opportune and helpful. Here the DES, in consultation with relevant bodies and institutions, might:

- Establish a planning process and support the establishment of appropriate and effective mechanisms for this.
- Support the identification of a framework for an initial training programme, together with relevant materials and resources for its implementation.
- Allocate responsibility for its operation and support arrangements to monitor its effectiveness.

In addition to the development of an overall strategy, a national initiative might usefully attempt to identify a coherent and integrated view of home/school issues, together with a planned rationale for the development of appropriate knowledge, attitudes and skills. This would also need to relate to current developments in the discussion about teacher contracts.

In our view, the cornerstone of an effective plan would be a genuinely collaborative programme between

- departments/courses in the training institutions
- those institutions and the schools and other locations in which students undertake teaching practice or an attachment. (The IT/INSET model of training is particularly relevant here (Ashton, *et al.*, 1982). At present too many students appear to be at the mercy of individual schools' attitudes to parents and the degree of contact and cooperation that exists between them. In addition the role of students vis à vis parents is often left to the schools to determine.
- institutions, local authorities and schools responsible for the new teachers' probationary period so that help and advice is still available.

It would also need to recognize the need for in-service education as part of the teacher's normal career, where the foundations laid in initial training can be developed and extended. Given the proportion of teachers in post now who have received little or no preparation for work with parents this would also seem an urgent matter for local authorities and in-service providers to take up.

Elements of a systematic training programme

(i)   The exploration of home/school issues, through research and study, involving elements of a taught programme, discussion and course work. An important consideration here is that there is tutorial guidance which links these elements to the applied tasks and activities.

(ii) Maximizing opportunities to participate in home/school programmes during periods of school practice: this might involve the development of the present links between college and school-based tutors. Such experience should definitely include:

- participation in parents evenings, (and other forms of communication, contact and involvement between home and school) with school guidance and support.
- opportunities to monitor and evaluate elements of the home/ school programme, and more general aspects of the relationships between the school and the families of its pupils.

(iii) Additional opportunities to work directly with, and alongside, parents – in a variety of settings such as schools, family-centres and projects, family attachments etc. This will probably involve co-operation with a number of agencies concerned with the education, welfare and development of children and young people.

Apart from providing direct experience of working with parents, this experience should be planned in conjunction with the school practices, to complement their strengths and weaknesses. There should also be plenty of opportunity to discuss and reflect upon this experience.

(iv) College-based workshops to develop practical skills, using real and simulated materials in tackling the writing of reports, visiting homes, running group discussions, writing letters to parents etc.; and to develop understanding/problem-solving and decision-making skills – through the exploration of case-study and case-conference materials which illustrate problems involving teachers, parents and children.

The main feature of such a package is that the elements are planned together, as a coherent whole, even though teaching and tutorial responsibility is divided.

Such a programme needs to be able to draw from a growing range of available resources, in different forms. Where necessary, publicly available resources, such as audio and video-tape, case-study and role-play materials etc. can be supplemented by appropriate 'home-made' materials.

(2) The role of LEAs in the development of the educational services support for the work of schools and the professional development of teachers

The local education authority has, and will continue to have, a crucial impact upon the development of home/school thinking and practice in our schools. For it is LEAs who are, in the end, responsible for translating national initiatives and directions into effective action, by relating them to local needs and circumstances; it is LEAs who are empowered and motivated to take important initiatives of their own or to sponsor projects, under the aegis of Inner City, EEC or MSC funding. Above all, however, it is the LEA, through the collective experience of its advisory, inspection and support services, which is closer to the work of individual schools than national bodies can ever be. This can bring a sharpness to the formulation of policy and the distribution of resources and services and can allow for the widely differing experience and circumstances of individual schools, making their efforts much more likely to be effective.

Typical elements in an LEA INSET programme: 'Working with Parents'

The key elements of an effective programme at local authority level, we suggest, are:

(i)   the existence of a coherent policy for home/school relations, formulated through collaborative discussion with teachers, parents, officers and politicians

(ii)   the facilitative machinery to initiate local projects, support developments and monitor their effectiveness

(iii)   the provision of opportunities for INSET work and planned programmes of training, including arrangements for the release of teachers to examine their own work or develop particular ideas

(iv)   enabling schools to have access to high quality technology and design assistance, for the production of materials that support their work with parents

(v)   a mechanism for local dissemination of development work and examples of good practice

(vi)   a policy for the allocation of posts of responsibility that both firmly acknowledges the importance of the task but also recognizes that every teacher has a professional obligation to see work with parents as part of their role

(vii)   the creation of a mediating service for the use of both schools and parents. Its functions might include the provision of advice and information, conciliation services in disputes between parents and schools and the capacity to seek the views of parents on wider issues, such as reorganization

(viii) monitoring the needs of particular groups of parents (for example, ethnic minority parents and parents of special needs children) and facilitating an effective response to such needs.

Most of these suggestions are not particularly new or radical proposals – indeed some of them can already be found sporadically in different LEAs around the country. Like both initial training and the development of practice in schools, though, they tend to be both piecemeal and ad hoc. What is needed, at the present time, is a more systematic approach, at local authority level, to both the support of interesting new initiatives and to the spread of consolidated experience throughout their schools.

In this article, we have tried to assemble some of the key elements of a programme of training and support that would enable teachers to work more effectively with the parents of the children they teach. We have done so by highlighting two central aspects of a broad strategy – the importance of a national, (probably DES-led) plan for the relevant aspects of initial training, followed by a brief outline of the actual and potential role of LEAs in supporting the development of the work of schools locally.

In both cases, our suggestions are underpinned by the belief that the development of the new attitudes and the new ways of working that are required for the improvement of home/school practice cannot, and should not, be considered simply as the responsibility of individual schools and teachers. For such a major, complex and demanding task calls for the collaboration and support of the education service *as a whole*, together with the thoughtful use of its wider experience, its practical forms of support and the benefit of the additional resources that such a task requires.

The Future: proposals for a school and family concordat

Alistair Macbeth

Home/school liaison is a complex but important educational matter. It is not, as one headteacher suggested, 'just a matter of being courteous'. Questions of responsibility for a child's education, the effectiveness of the learning process, equality of educational opportunity, liberty of conscience, local democracy and other fundamental social and political problems are involved. Active partnership between schools and families is recognized as desirable. The problem is how to implement it. There are impediments to liaison, some practical and some attitudinal. Various schemes have been attempted to improve the quality of relations between schools and families as this report shows. Some of these schemes have been more successful than others. There are also examples of actions which have been successful in one place but less so in another.

Generally, however, educational *partnership* between home and school has not emerged. Enthusiasm and exhortation have achieved some impressive results locally, but the process has been uneven. What more could be done?

In this section I shall advance some suggestions for actions which arise from the evidence in this report. I wish to stress that these are my personal views. Also, the actions which I advocate should not be seen as being in isolation from each other. Rather they interrelate and depend one upon the other. They should be seen as a whole, not as a list from which selections are made. Since the elements are interdependent, I refer to a *School and Family Concordat*.

The word 'concordat' implies friendly understanding and mutual trust. These are essential ingredients of the relationship between parents and the teachers of the individual child. But the word concordat also implies a formalized contract. I am suggesting that there should be a framework of contractual obligations for both parents and teachers more specific than those which are expressed in general terms in laws at present.

One may see such a concordat as a logical development from the present situation. At present there is much local variation of practice within EEC countries, but it is possible to discern three broad stages of progression in the growth of home/school partnership. These might be labelled:

Stage 1 : the self-contained school stage
Stage 2 : the stage of professional uncertainty
Stage 3 : the stage of growing confidence

These are not absolute categories into which a school or a country can be placed. Rather they are descriptions of attitudinal tendencies and, being attitudinal, there are differences of approach between institutions and even within one institution. However, the evidence of this study indicates validity in such a breakdown and that certain actions and structures are associated with each stage. I shall describe these briefly and I shall then outline the School and and Family Concordat, which I see as a fourth practicable stage.

Stage 1 : the self-contained school stage

The basic attitude of this stage is that the school should be a closed institution where professionals carry out specialist functions neither influencing nor influenced by families or the world outside the school. This attitude may either stem from an assumption that schools provide all worthwhile education, or from an assumption that didactic, value-free education can be provided by schools whilst value-laden moral education is provided outside school, so that each can operate separately. The self-contained school stage tends to be characterized by:

Emphasis upon teacher autonomy.

Routine contacts with parents infrequent, formalized and impersonal.

Other contacts with parents discouraged except in crises.

Parental acceptance that families are irrelevant to what happens in school.

Pupils allocated to schools by administrators: little parental choice.

Absence of participatory councils.

School parent associations discouraged or confined to minor roles.

National parent organizations timid and treated with indifference by authorities.

Teacher training neglecting home/school liaison.

Parents denied access to records held in the school about their child.

Teachers making decisions about what courses a child shall follow, what public examinations he will take and the methods of teaching him.

Stage 2 : the stage of professional uncertainty

With the spread of participatory arguments and evidence about the value of home/school liaison, members of the teaching profession divide in their attitudes towards families, whilst parents often retain assumptions that the school should be self-contained. Features may be:

Growing recognition by teachers that home factors influence pupils' school performance.

Variation in teachers' practice in regard to liaison with families.

Increased preparedness to 'blame' homes for low pupil attainment.

School administrations tending to retain attitudes of stage 1.

Localized experiments in liaison techniques.

Traditional formal and limited routine contacts with parents continue.

Voluntary parent organizations more readily tolerated in schools, but functions remaining peripheral.

National parent organizations becoming more confident.

Teachers' organizations ambivalent.

School council established for each school, but with minor and non-educational functions.

Teacher training mentions home/school liaison as a side-issue.

Stage 3 : stage of growing confidence

As the logic of home/school liaison spreads and more experiments are attempted, so both parents and teachers find that mutual confidence gradually replaces mutual caution. It is bound to be a gradual process with over-high expectations sometimes disappointed and excellent schemes damaged by the hostile attitudes of determined groups. Features of this difficult stage may be:

Increased encouragement of liaison by school management.

More parent–teacher contacts without reference to senior school staff.

Parents entering school and classrooms informally.

Class meetings of parents developing.

The school council for each school dealing with educationally central issues.

Voluntary parent organizations accepted as part of the school community.

Home/school liaison teachers for exceptional problems.

Parents encouraged to teach their children at home as reinforcement of school teaching.

Emphasis on the value of home–school liaison by administrators and politicians.

National parent organizations get official recognition and finance.

National teacher organizations recognize value and status of parent organizations.

Increased parental choice between schools and choice of courses and examinations within schools.

Teachers' training includes home/school liaison as a main feature and runs special courses for both teachers and parents.

Parental access to records held in the school about their child.

Two-way reports in which parents express views to the school.

Consultations about the child's progress increasing in frequency, being genuinely private and based upon exchanges of views expressed in two-way reports.

Stage 4 : the school and family concordat

The temptation at this point is to be idealistic and to describe a situation in which all adults concerned with children's education act with dedicated zeal in harmony and mutual respect, unhindered by restraints. Such idealism would convince nobody. The main problem with the stage 3 approach is that it depends upon voluntary dedication. The result is unevenness of practice. Generally it has only been in regard to the establishment of participatory school councils that some degree of consistency has been established. As has been pointed out several times in this report, the establishment of representative councils may have little or nothing to do with educational partnership for the benefit of the individual child. The most important element of stage 4, therefore, must be a system by which personal parent–teacher partnership can be established in regard to each individual child according to the best of the experimental practices used in stage 3. In my view this means a shift away from regarding liaison as an optional right, and towards an emphasis upon duties.

By this scheme, parents would be reminded of their prime legal obligation to educate their child and in return for a place at a school, parents would sign a 'parents' contract' by which they would undertake to cooperate with the school in specific ways. Entry and retention of the child in school would be dependent upon parental cooperation. The school, in turn, would also have liaison obligations to parents as would teachers. With mutual commitments clearly understood from the start, parents and teachers would be able to develop a friendly professional partnership.

This contractual framework could be negotiated at national, provincial or education authority level, influenced by the appropriate interest groups, and school councils (one for each school) would provide the mechanism for checking that all those with obligations were indeed fulfilling their duties. In brief, I am suggesting that a system of duties should be negotiated at the political level to enhance professional partnership at the personal level, which would be monitored at the participatory level.

Such a formalized step must be accompanied by understanding. To obtain supportive attitudes requires publicity and instruction. A social system cannot work unless people believe in it. Therefore knowledge and persuasion are important. Structural changes in the school itself (especially in regard to timetables and working hours) will also be needed.

I am suggesting a combination of contractual commitment and motivational understanding. It may be noted that there is little self-interest which will motivate people in regard to liaison between parents and teachers. Home/school liaison is for the benefit of the child and is therefore altruistic. If we continue to rely on professional and parental consciences without any contractual commitment, liaison will be varied and unsure. But contractual commitment without understanding or conviction will be resented and ineffective. A School and Family Concordat would therefore be a combination of obligation and persuasion.

References

ACLAND, H. (1980). 'Research as Stage Management: The Case of the Plowden Committee'. In: BULMER, M.J.A. (Ed) *Social Research and Royal Commissions*. London: Allen and Unwin.

ARMSTRONG, G. and BROWN, F. (1979). *Five Years On: A follow-up study*. Oxford: Oxford University Press.

ASHTON, P. *et al.* (1982). *Teacher Education in the Classroom*. Beckenham: Croom Helm.

ATKIN, J. and BASTIANI, J. (1984). *Preparing Teachers to Work With Parents: A Survey of Initial Training*. Nottingham: University of Nottingham School of Education.

ATKIN, J. and BASTIANI, J., with GOODE, J. (1988). *Listening to Parents. An approach to the improvement of home/school relations*. Beckenham: Croom Helm.

BASTIANI, J. (1983). Listening to parents: philosophy, critique and method. Unpublished PhD thesis. University of Nottingham.

BECHER, T., ERAUT, M. and KNIGHT, J. (1981). *Policies For Educational Accountability*. London: Heinemann.

BECK, I.M. (1986). The response to the 1980 Education Act relating to parental preferences 1984/85. Unpublished MEd thesis. University of Liverpool.

BEVINGTON, P., GARDNER, J. and COCKS, R.P. (1981). 'An Approach to the Planning and Evaluation of a Parental Involvement Course', *Child Care, Health and Development*, 4, 271, 227.

BLACK PEOPLE'S PROGRESSIVE ASSOCIATION (1978). *Cause for Concern: West Indian Pupils in Redbridge*. London: Commission for Racial Equality.

BOUCHER, J. (1981). Parents as Partners. Talk to DES course. 'Applications of Warnock'. University of Manchester.

BULLOCK REPORT. GREAT BRITAIN. DEPARTMENT OF EDUCATION AND SCIENCE. (1975). *A Language for Life*. London: HMSO.

BUTLER, D. and CLAY, M. (1979). *Reading Begins at Home*. London: Heinemann.

CENTRAL POLICY REVIEW STAFF (1978). *Services for Young Children With Working Mothers*. London: HMSO.

COMMUNITY EDUCATION WORKING PARTY (1982). *Teacher/Parent Interviews: Some materials for teachers.* Nottingham: School of Education, University of Nottingham.

CONSERVATIVE PARTY (1984). *Putting Britain First.* London: Conservative and Unionist Central Office.

COONS, J. and SUGARMAN, S. (1978). *Education By Choice, The Case For Family Control.* California: University of California Press.

COMMUNITY RELATIONS COMMISSION (1975). *Who Minds?* London: Commission For Racial Equality.

CUNNINGHAM, C. and JEFFREE, D. (1971). *Working with Parents: Developing a Workshop Course for Parents of Young Mentally Handicapped Children.* London: Mencap Publications.

CUNNINGHAM, C. and JEFFREE, D. (1975). 'The organisation and structure of workshops for parents of mentally handicapped children', *Bulletin British Psychological Society,* 28.

CYSTER, R., CLIFT, P.S. and BATTLE, S. (1980). *Parental Involvement in Primary Schools.* Slough: NFER.

DOCKRELL, W.E. and HAMILTON, D. (Eds) (1980). *Rethinking Educational Research.* London: Hodder and Stoughton.

DOUGLAS, J.W.B. (1964). *The Home and the School.* London: MacGibbon and Kee.

EAST SUSSEX LEA/UNIVERSITY OF SUSSEX (1979). *'Accountability in the Middle Years of Schooling' Project. Final Report 1. An Analysis of Policy Options.* Educational Development Centre, Brighton: University of Sussex.

EVANS, K. (1985). *LEA Initiatives in Clwyd. Outlines 2.* Coventry: Community Education Development Centre.

FANTINI, M.D. and CARDENAS, R. (1980). *Parenting in a Multicultural Society.* Harlow: Longman.

FIELD, F. (Ed) (1977). *Education and the Urban Crisis.* London: Routledge and Kegan Paul.

FIRTH, G.C. (1977). *75 Years of Service to Education: The Story of Coventry's Education Committee.* Coventry: Education Dept., City of Coventry.

FOWLER, G. (1986). 'A Reply to Jack Tweedie'. In: STILLMAN, A.B. (Ed) *The Balancing Act of 1980.* Slough: NFER.

GARDNER, J. (1982). 'Partnership Between Parents and Teachers'. In: MITTLER, P. and McCONACHIE, H. (Eds) *Approaches to Parental Involvement.* Beckenham: Croom Helm.

GREAT BRITAIN. DEPARTMENT OF EDUCATION AND SCIENCE. (1977). *Admission of Children to Schools of Their Parents' Choice.* Consultation Paper. London: HMSO.

GREAT BRITAIN. DEPARTMENT OF EDUCATION AND SCIENCE. (1980). *Education Act.* London: HMSO.

GREAT BRITAIN: DEPARTMENT OF EDUCATION AND SCIENCE. (1981). *Education Act*. London: HMSO.

GREAT BRITAIN. DEPARTMENT OF EDUCATION AND SCIENCE. (1984). *Parental Influence At School*. A Green Paper. London: HMSO.

GREAT BRITAIN. DEPARTMENT OF EDUCATION AND SCIENCE. (1986). *Education Act (2)*. London: HMSO.

GREAT BRITAIN. DEPARTMENT OF EDUCATION AND SCIENCE. (1987). *Education Bill*. London: HMSO.

GREAT BRITAIN. DEPARTMENT OF EDUCATION AND SCIENCE. COMMITTEE OF INQUIRY (1975). *A Language for Life*. (The Bullock Report.) London: HMSO.

GREAT BRITAIN. DEPARTMENT OF EDUCATION AND SCIENCE. COMMITTEE OF INQUIRY (1981). *The Education of Children from Ethnic Minority Groups*. Interim Report. 'West Indian Children in our Schools'. (The Rampton Report.) London: HMSO.

GREAT BRITAIN. MINISTRY OF EDUCATION. (1944). *Education Act*. London: HMSO.

GREAT BRITAIN. MINISTRY OF EDUCATION (1946). *Choice of Schools: Circular 83*. London: HMSO.

GREAT BRITAIN. MINISTRY OF EDUCATION (1950). *Manual of Guidance, Schools No. 1; Choice of Schools*. (23rd August). London: HMSO.

GOBLE. N.M. (1977). *The Changing Role of the Teacher*. Slough: NFER/ UNESCO.

GORDON, I.J. (1969). 'Developing Parent Power'. In: GROTBERG, E. (Ed) *Critical Issues in Research in Relation to Disadvantaged Children*. Guildford: Princeton University Press.

HEWISON, J. (1981). 'Home is Where the Help is'. *Times Educational Supplement*. 16th January.

HER MAJESTY'S INSPECTORATE (1982). *The New Teacher in School*. London: HMSO.

JEFFREE, D. and McCONKEY, R. (1976). *PIP Developmental Charts (0–5)*. London: Hodder and Stoughton.

JEFFREE, D. and CHESELDINE, S. (1982). *Pathways to Independence: A Checklist of Self-Help Activities*. London: Hodder and Stoughton.

JOHNSON, D. (1982). 'Home–School Relations 1970–1980'. In: COHEN, L., MANION, L. and THOMAS, J. (Eds). *Educational Research in Britain*. Windsor: NFER-NELSON.

JOHNSON, D. *et al.* (1980). *Secondary Schools and the Welfare Network*. London: Allen and Unwin.

JOHNSON, S. (1977). Disadvantage in Education. *CED Journal Vol. 1, No. 2*.

LODGE, P. and BLACKSTONE, T. (1983). *Educational Policy and Educational Inequality*. Oxford: Martin Robertson.

MACBETH, A., MACKENZIE, M. and BRECKENRIDGE, J. (1980). *Scottish School Councils: Policymaking, Participation or Irrelevance.* Scottish Education Dept., London: HMSO.

MACBETH, A. (1981). *The Child Between: a report on school/family relations in the countries of the EEC.* European Commission, London: HMSO.

MARLAND, M. (1974). *Pastoral Care.* London: Heinemann.

MARLAND, M. (1983). Preparing for Promotion in Pastoral Care. *Pastoral Care. Vol. 1, No. 1.* Oxford: Basil Blackwell.

MEEK, M. (1900). *Learning to Read.* London: Bodley Head.

MEIKLE, J. (1987). 'Parent Power Promises to Open up Debate on Quality'. *Times Educational Supplement.* 8th May.

MITTLER, P. and McCONACHIE, H. (Eds) (1982). *Approaches to Parental Involvement.* Beckenham: Croom Helm.

MORGAN, A. (1983). T. Glyn Davies: A Welsh Pioneer. *Network Vol. 3, No. 7.* CEDC.

MORTIMORE, J. and BLACKSTONE, T. (1982). *Disadvantage and Education.* London: Heinemann.

MUSGROVE, F. and TAYLOR, P.H. (1969). *Society and the Teacher's Role.* London: Routledge and Kegan Paul.

N.A.M.E. (Undated) *Home/school Liaison: A multicultural perspective.* Manchester: National Association for Multicultural Education.

NATIONAL AUDIT OFFICE (1986). *Department of Education and Science: Falling School Rolls*; Report by the Comptroller and Auditor General. London: HMSO.

NATIONAL CONSUMER COUNCIL (1977). *Advise and Consent.* London: National Consumer Council.

NATIONAL CONSUMER COUNCIL (1986). *The Missing Links between Home and School: a consumer view.* London: National Consumer Council.

NEWSOM REPORT. GREAT BRITAIN. DEPARTMENT OF EDUCATION AND SCIENCE. CENTRAL ADVISORY COUNCIL FOR EDUCATION (ENGLAND) (1963). *Half our Future.* London: HMSO.

PLOWDEN REPORT. GREAT BRITAIN. DEPARTMENT OF EDUCATION AND SCIENCE. CENTRAL ADVISORY COUNCIL FOR EDUCATION (ENGLAND) (1967). *Children and their Primary Schools.* London: HMSO.

POSTER, C. (1982). *Community Education: It's Development and Management.* London: Heinemann.

QUINTON, D. (1980). 'Family Life in the Inner City: myth and reality'. In: MARLAND, M. (Ed) *Education for the Inner City.* London: Heinemann.

RAMPTON REPORT. GREAT BRITAIN. DEPARTMENT OF EDUCATION AND SCIENCE. (1981). *West Indian Children in Our Schools: An Interim Report.* London: HMSO.

RAVEN, J. (1980). *Parents, Teachers and Children*. London: Hodder and Stoughton.

REX, J. and TOMLINSON, S. (1979). *Colonial Immigrants in a British City*. London: Routledge and Kegan Paul.

RHEUBOTTOM, S. (1982). 'Handicapped Child Equals Taxi!' In: MITTLER, P. and McCONACHIE, H. (Eds) *Approaches to Parental Involvement*. Beckenham: Croom Helm.

SCHOOLS COUNCIL (1979). *English in the 1980's: a programme of support for teachers*. London: Evans/Methuen.

SHIPMAN, M. (1980). The Limits of Positive Discrimination. In: MARLAND, M. (Ed) *op.cit*.

SMITH, B. (1982). Collaboration Between Parents and Teachers of School Age Children. In: MITTLER, P. and McCONACHIE, H. (Eds) *op.cit*.

SMITH, T. (1980). *Parents and Pre-school*. Oxford: Grant-McIntyre.

SOUTH GLAMORGAN HIGH COURT, (May 10th 1984) Regina vs the South Glamorgan Appeals Committee, ex-parte Dafydd Evans. Transcript available from Marten Walsh Cherer Ltd, London.

STILLMAN, A.B. and MAYCHELL, K. (1986). *Choosing Schools: Parents, LEAs and the 1980 Education Act*. Windsor: NFER-NELSON.

STILLMAN, A.B. (1986) (Ed) *The Balancing Act of 1980: Parents Politics and Education*. Slough: NFER.

STONE, M. (1981). *The Education of the Black Child in Britain*. London: Fontana.

TAYLOR REPORT. GREAT BRITAIN. DEPARTMENT OF EDUCATION AND SCIENCE. (1977). *A New Partnership For Our Schools*. London: HMSO.

TIZARD, B. (1978). 'Carry on Communicating', *Times Educational Supplement*, 3rd February.

TIZARD, B., MORTIMORE, J. and BURCHELL, B. (1981a). *Involving Parents in the Nursery and Infant School*. Oxford: Grant McIntyre.

TIZARD, J., SCHOFIELD, W. and HEWISON, J. (1981b). 'Collaboration between teachers and parents in assisting children's reading', *Brit. Journ. Educ. Psychol.* 52.

TOMLINSON, S. (1980). 'Ethnic minority parents and education'. In: CRAFT, M. (*et al.*) (Eds) *Linking Home and School*. Third edition. London: Harper and Row.

TOWNSEND, H.E.R. and BRITTON, E.M. (1972). *Organization in Multi-Racial Schools*. Slough: NFER.

WIDLAKE, P. and MACLEOD, F. (1984). *Raising Standards*. CEDC.

WILLIAMS, S. (1985). Interview with Jack Tweedie and Andy Stillman. Unpublished.

WOLFENDALE, S. (1980). 'Learning difficulties: a reappraisal', *Remedial Education*, 1, 3.